Scarcity, Energy, and Economic Progress

Scarcity, Energy, and Economic Progress

Ferdinand E. Banks
University of Uppsala

Lexington Books
D.C. Heath and Company
Lexington, Massachusetts
Toronto

Library of Congress Cataloging in Publication Data

Banks, Ferdinand E.
    Scarcity, energy, and economic progress.

    Bibliography: p.
    Includes index.
    1. Natural resources. 2. Power resources. 3. Economic policy. I. Title.
HC55.B26   333.7   77-4630
ISBN 0-669-01781-7

Published simultaneously in Canada.

Printed in the United States of America.

International Standard Book Number: 0-669-01781-7

Library of Congress Catalog Card Number: 77-4630

For my students at Gifu, Lewis, S. Gmuend;
and Stockholm, Dakar, and Uppsala

Contents

List of Figures

List of Tables

Preface

The first seven chapters of this book are intended as an easy introduction to some of the more important aspects of energy, environment, depletable resources, and economic development. The last chapter contains an introduction to the econometrics of primary commodities, which should interest both students of economics and professional economists. Most of the material in this book is suitable for supplementary reading in various courses in economics; the book could be employed as a text.

As the reader will soon notice, I have not tried to avoid controversial issues. As President Carter made clear in his "energy" speech of April 20, 1977, the United States—along with the rest of the world—is facing a problem unprecedented in its history. What he did not say was that the time for solving this problem is now and that this time the solutions must make sense. Among other things, this means that the citizens of the major industrial countries must stifle their urge to tolerate or encourage incompetence in high places.

I also believe that the grandiosely labled "New International Economic Order" is an unadulterated fraud specifically intended to enhance the personal income and prerogatives of many aid officials, international bureaucrats, publicity-starved academics, and corrupt politicians and civil servants in the less-developed countries. Of course some people working to perpetuate this humbug are completely innocent of any ulterior motives; but when confronted with the consequences of their endeavors, I inevitably find myself thinking of Graham Green's classic observation: such innocence is a form of madness. Similarly, although some of the conclusions of "Limits to Growth" scenarios are unappetizing, no one can afford to dismiss them completely; this is true even though the so-called models generating these conclusions hardly deserve to be called trivial.

Except for the last chapter, technical material appears in the text infrequently, and then only briefly. Otherwise, mathematical presentations are confined to notes and appendixes where they can be ignored if the reader so desires. However, any one who has had an elementary course in economics or who occasionally reads *Fortune, Business Week*, or the *London Economist* should have no trouble at all with this book. Still, a few topics are quite abstruse by nature, and require a fairly high order of concentration. Anyone who would prefer not to expend any effort on these topics should simply continue reading, since these passages have been kept as short as possible.

At this point I should like to thank various economists for the invaluable assistance they have given me. In particular I must acknowledge the help I received from Doctors Jan Herin and Per Wijkman of the University of Stockholm, who permitted me to use material from their superb empirical investigation of international trade and inflation. I also received important advice on specific problems from my colleagues Yngve Andersson, Lennart Berg, Anders Burrell, Hans Danielsson, and of course my personal consultants on Swedish economic problems, Christian Nilsson and Villy Bergstrom—all of the University of Uppsala. In addition, I would like to take this opportunity to thank my colleague Barbro Gyllencreutz for present and past assistance.

Finally, I must acknowledge the work of the economists of the World Bank, the United Nations Conference on Trade and Development and the German Institute of Economic Research, Hamburg, whose important contributions I have never hesitated to consult on those numerous occasions when my own faculties proved inadequate. I would especially like to mention Kenji Takeuchi, John Cuddy, M.J. Colebrook, and H.J. Timm.

Ferdinand E. Banks

Acknowledgments

The following acknowledgments are in order. To Springer-Verlag Vienna, for permission to use material from my article, "An Econometric Note on the Demand for Refined Zinc"; to the *Ekonomiska Samfundets Ridskrift* for permission to use material from my article, "The Economics of Exhaustible Resources: A Note"; to the *Schweizerische Zeitschrift für Volkswirtschaft und Statistik* for permission to use material from my article, "A Diagramatic Presentation of Dynamic Supply Behavior"; to *Econometrica* for permission to use material from my article "An Econometric Model of the World Tin Economy: A Comment"; to the *Journal of Economic Theory* for permission to use material from my article "A Note on Some Theoretical Issues of Resource Depletion"; to the *Journal of World Trade Law* for permission to use material from my articles "Economics and Politics of Primary Commodities" and "Multinational Firms and African Economic Development"; and to *Resources Policy* for permission to reproduce material from my article "Natural Resource Availability: Some Economic Aspects." I have also employed considerable statistical material from United Nations documents that have been placed in the public domain; in accordance with the wishes expressed in some of these documents, I want to express my appreciation of the access that I had to material from the United Nations Industrial Development Organization, the United Nations Conference on Trade and Development, the International Bank for Reconstruction and Development, the United Nations Food and Agricultural Organization and the International Labor Office.

*War is ten percent fighting, ten percent
waiting, and eighty percent self-improvement*

Chairman Mao

*The superior man concerns himself with what
is right; the lesser man with what pays*

Confucius

1

Overview and Survey

This book will begin by considering several of the more interesting issues associated with the economics of natural resource availability—or unavailability, as the case may be. Although the influence of natural resources has been felt in the literature of economics since the eighteenth century, it was only promoted to a starring role because of such things as the Club of Rome reports and the recent 'energy' crisis. For better or worse (probably for better), these events reminded many of us that various resources which we take for granted are in fact embarrassingly finite; if we were to accelerate their depletion, our descendants might well find their standard of living falling drastically.

Economists seem to agree that there will be more than enough natural resources available at acceptable prices to maintain the present generation, and most likely its immediate successors, in at least the comfort to which they have become accustomed. What happens after that depends upon decisions that must be made soon, preferably very soon. As it happens, these decisions concern such things as mineral extraction rates at only second remove. First and foremost they have to do with increasing both the technical and economic efficiency with which natural resources are used in industry and consumption. If progress in this direction cannot be accelerated, and if it remains expedient to promote the fantasy that the entire world has the right to a North American standard of living, then we are on a collision course with disaster.

One of the major difficulties of dealing with resource availability is the popularity of the more extremist views on the subject. The "World Dynamics" and "Limits to Growth" models and their successors undoubtedly pose important problems; even if the conclusions they present are only partially correct, they still deserve to be brought to the attention of every person concerned with the future of our civilization. Even so, we should be clear about one thing. Viewed in the light of conventional scientific research, the numerous and glaring technical shortcomings of these constructions suggest that their results are strictly in line with the prejudices of their originators and sponsors. The "doomsday" models are not science but, in their pretensions, a travesty of science.

On the other hand, the optimists are hardly providing us with a better quality of research or information. Professor Wilfred Beckerman (1972) has observed that total stocks of metal in the earth's crust may amount to a million times known stocks, and he goes on to imply that at the present annual consumption level these can last another 100,000,000 years. Unfortunately,

1

however, at a growth rate of a mere 3 percent per year, even this impressive supply would be gone in 500 years. To take a more homely example, at the present level of consumption, stocks of coal in the upper kilometer of the earth's crust would last for over 5000 years; but if coal consumption keeps growing at the present long-term trend rate of slightly more than 4 percent, these stocks will be gone in about 130 years.

Furthermore, modern economic theory (as well as common sense) recognizes that the disutility of catastrophe outweighs the utility of *any* possible material gain; and so highly optimistic calculations and prognoses based on nonexistent or hypothetical mineral retrieval technologies have only limited scientific value. Put more dramatically, the trauma and social disorganization caused future generations by sudden resource exhaustion could be so overwhelming that our present actions should be based, at least to a certain extent, on a "worst possible" scenario. This means that although the Club of Rome epistles may not be paragons of analytical plausibility, it might be advisable to treat them with an overdose of respect—at least for the time being.

Primary Commodity Prices

Next we introduce a subject that is related, in one way or another, to many of the issues taken up in this book: nonfuel primary commodities. Various aspects of the supply and demand for these goods will be treated at considerable length in later chapters; at present we will concentrate on primary commodity prices and some of the factors influencing these prices.

The best place to begin our discussion is in the immediate past. In the early 1960s the story of the price of primary commodities in general, and industrial raw materials in particular was generally low, but as the war in Vietnam intensified and industrial production increased in Europe and the United States, raw materials prices began a rapid ascent. Later, as hostilities began to wane, the *rate* at which these prices were rising decreased. As a result, by the early 1970s the expectations of both producers and consumers pointed toward a gradual return to normality on the commodity markets, with most of the basic minerals once again available for prices that were relatively low in comparison to most of the other factors of production.

Unfortunately, the fulfillment of these expectations was upset by a new upswing in world business, which took place in 1972-73. This rise was unusual; it was synchronized across most of the major producing countries of the industrial world, inflating demand almost everywhere and providing new momentum for primary commodity prices. For the first time in many years the world experienced a significant hoarding of the most important nonprecious metals, and a growing militancy on the part of primary product producers in the less-developed countries (LDCs) led consumers to adjust their expectations in the direction of still higher prices.

The growing weakness of the dollar and of sterling—the two currencies in which most primary commodities are traded—also resulted in the purchase of sizable amounts of various metals as inflation hedges. Some of this buying went through the futures market, elevating prices on these rather sensitive exchanges and influencing prices and the psychological climate in all markets. In these circumstances, speculative and precautionary acquisitions soon reached a level completely unrelated to the demand for these commodities as inputs in current production processes.

At the time some claimed that the adjustments in exchange rates which were taking place in 1973 would eventually lead to repose on the commodity markets, but the October war in the Middle East and the ensuing oil crisis stifled such conjecture. Instead, users of the more important industrial raw materials, and many speculators, were stampeded into increasing their inventories by quantum amounts. The price of copper, for instance, was driven to a preposterous height; only large-scale unemployment in the industrial countries and a sharp decline in consumption and investment brought buyers to their senses.

In the scenario presented above, we have passed over at least one major acceleration of the world price level for all goods and services. The price of nonfuel primary commodities was influenced by this general price acceleration insofar as it involved an expansion in real production; but contrary to a great deal of ill-founded opinion, there was no appreciable feedback. Research performed at the Brookings Institution indicates that it would take an autonomous increase of 14.5 percent in the price of nonfood, nonfuel raw materials to increase the commodity price index in the United States by one percent; however, by using the effects of the rise in the price of oil as a datum, I estimate the maximum rise in the general price level to be somewhat lower. In fact, if copper were omitted from this group of commodities, the increase would be on the order of 0.25 percent.

We next go to price formation. This discussion focuses on the long run price, but the short run price deserves to be mentioned. The latter can often be explained by lack of information, unjustified euphoria, panic, mass irrationality, and so on.[1] For example, during some of the darkest days of the Great Depression, prices on the metal exchanges occasionally rose to the vicinity of their levels prior to the downturn. A similar situation prevailed on the markets for many of the primary metals in the period just after the October War: with industrial production stagnating or falling all over the world, and actual supply and demand indicating that prices would have to fall if the markets for current inputs were to be brought into equilibrium, speculation drove the price of copper so high that some of the more impressionable observers suggested that it be classified a precious metal.

As fascinating as short-run price movements are, they are more suitable for the ruminations of itinerant forecasters and newsletter authors than for a systematic analysis; and so we turn to our principal concern, which is the medium- or long-run price. Despite the bogus sophistication that salesmen of econometric devices regularly bring to this topic, the most reliable technique for estimating this price still involves relating trend supply to trend demand: when actual production capacity grows faster than estimated demand, for example, we should feel quite justified in predicting that there will eventually be a surplus of the commodity in question, and that its price will go down.

With trend demand, we are concerned first and foremost with the development of production in the major industrial countries, since the demand for minerals is, for the most part, a direct and uncomplicated function of this production. Just now indications are that during the next five or ten years at least, industrial output in North America and Europe will be lower than in the past decade. Many of the reasons for this will later become apparent, but the three most important can be listed immediately: (1) The rise in energy prices, (2) inflation and its effect on investment, and most important, (3) the continued breakdown of the link between productivity and compensation (including transfers), and the adverse effect of this breakdown on all economic activity.[2]

Before discussing trend supply, we must take note of the passage of industrial raw materials through the processing cycle. Generally we begin with mining, or extraction, from which we move to such things as smelting or refining, depending upon the product. Since we are not talking about fuels, the next to last stage is called semifabrication, which involves forming structural shapes that, in the ensuing fabrication or manufacturing stage, are turned into the particular finished item.

In mining or the production of ores, we should expect little alteration in either the direction or the rate of change of supply over the next decade, and perhaps longer. In the immediate future the situation will be determined by investment begun as long as ten years ago, when the incentive for mining investments was the high profit which could be realized from the early 1960s to about 1973. Moreover, the "stretching out" or lengthening of the gestation periods of investments, some of which began in 1974, was often terminated in early 1976 because of premature optimism about business conditions in the United States. The inelasticity of supply of producers in the less-developed countries (LDCs) is also important in the present context, but this can wait until later in the chapter. On the basis of a simple extrapolation of supply and demand, it seems likely that the industrial world will continue to have access to a satisfactory supply of the most important minerals (such as copper, bauxite, and iron ore) at acceptable prices for the foreseeable future.

If bottlenecks appear on the supply side, they will almost certainly be at the processing stage. The principal reason for this is that at the present level of world industrial activity there is plenty of smelting and refining capacity and little incentive to construct much more. Most processors are also afraid that energy prices might run amok again; the demand for refined products has been extremely uneven since the October War. Even more important, investment costs in these industries may be rising faster than the average level of world inflation, and sooner or later this will almost certainly put a damper on the expansion of capacity.

Although this brief catalogue of woes may appear impressive, optimism is still more realistic than pessimism where the supply of industrial raw materials is concerned. A dynamic, large-scale resurgence in world demand could conceivably lead to shortages and big increases in the price of refined or smelted products, but a protracted upturn of the type that heads of state hope for appears unlikely before the energy crisis is settled. For items such as copper and steel, moderation in demand and continued investment in these industries throughout most of the world seem to have removed all doubts about the adequacy of processing capacity for the time being. Still, the rate of increase of processing capacity is almost certainly declining, at least if the figures given in table 1-1 for the United States can be judged typical; if this tendency continues, the early 1980s could reveal a drastic change in the availability of these facilities.

In table 1-1 it is the "new capital" and "modernization" that are directly creating capacity, and given the downturn in the world economy since late 1973, the decline in these categories of investment has almost certainly continued. This does not mean that production capacity is no longer expanding, but that it is expanding at a slower pace. By the same token, investments in safety and pollution suppression are increasing, and while these are of course essential, they cannot be expected to add a great deal to productive capacity. On the other hand, the inflation component is strictly a loss, representing as it does merely an increase in prices. Moreover, as shown in the last line of table 1-1, the inflation component seems to be increasing relative to total spending.

Before closing this section, I will address commodity prices on a more fundamental level—that is, in relation to costs. Although it may not remain true

Table 1-1
Investment in the United States Nonferrous Metals Industries, Broken Down by Category
(1972 = 100)

	1969	1970	1971	1972	1973
New Capital	147	114	118	100	100
Modernization	114	129	96	100	94
Safety				100	150
Pollution	37	97	120	100	125
Inflation	34	70	81	100	108
Total	69	81	107	100	107
Inflation/Total[a]	0.093	0.163	0.143	0.190	0.190

[a]Calculated from monetary values

for the next decade or so, the money cost of most minerals has steadily increased over the past century, while their real cost, as measured by the goods and services that must be given up to obtain them, has generally been declining. For example, the real cost of copper is no higher today than it was a century ago, even though the amount of copper in a unit of extracted ore has fallen considerably; and as figure 1-1 indicates, this situation is even more pronounced with some other minerals.

In considering figure 1-1 it should be appreciated that these decreases in real cost are largely due to an acceleration in technical progress, particularly the substitution of comparatively low-cost energy for factors of production whose cost has been rising very rapidly. However, at least in the near future, we are almost certain to experience higher energy costs, and as a result we should expect to see a slowing down in the decline of these real costs. This does not, by

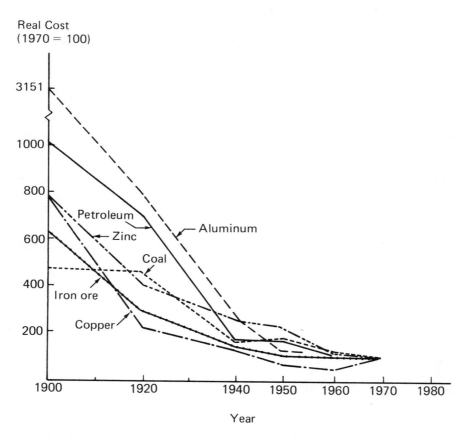

Figure 1-1. The Real Cost of Some Industrial Raw Materials.

itself, assure that the industrial world's social and economic progress of the last ten or fifteen years will begin grinding to a halt, but it does mean that the revolution of unlimited expectations that swept over much of North America, Japan, and Western Europe during the 1960s no longer has a basis in fact. Whether we like it or not, the days of explosive economic growth are over for awhile.

Pollution and Recycling

By projecting trends from a computer model into the twenty-first century, the Club of Rome "experts" predict that population and pollution will increase beyond the carrying capacity of the world's ecosystem. The outcome of this, they say, will be an explosion of the death rate in the poor countries, as well as a rain of discomforts and catastrophes in such cities as Amsterdam, and Paris.

Critics of the Club of Rome are quick to point out that had the seventeenth or eighteenth century been used as the basis for these projections, humanity would already have experienced doomsday several times over. Whether they are right or not is largely irrelevant, as we realize when we consider the population problem. The question here is not whether the rate of population growth will come to a halt, but what the conditions of life on earth be when it does. Clearly, a world population stabilized at 6 or 7 billion is a completely different proposition from one of 20 billion or more, with a substantial fraction of the latter ruled by neurotic and tyranical bunglers. The difference, to be precise, is that with a modest population, material changes for the better are possible for all through their own efforts; while with 20 billion people, nature alone is the arbiter of man's fate, and unfortunately nobody can guess just what sentence she will be inclined to pass—except that it will be severe.

Pollution is often described as a bedfellow of economic growth, and a great deal of valuable time and even more valuable ink has been spilled by various investigators making a case for abolishing, or at least limiting, what they would like the rest of us to think of as a pest. But as Paul Wonnacott (1974) has observed, while steel mills mean pollution, they also mean more pollution control equipment. Everything considered, pollution is a function of the type of production rather than the amount. Certainly everyone who has given any thought to the matter must realize by now that it is theoretically possible to have a material standard as high or even higher than that being enjoyed today, without tolerating a further deterioration of the environment. In environmental questions, however, it is a long way from an understanding of the options to the political and economic innovations that will translate them into reality.

To get some idea of how complex some of these issues are, we can look at the problem of pollution control for the mineral processing industries. As table 1-1 shows, controlling pollution has increased capital costs for installations under construction; and the enforcement of pollution control legislation has occasionally meant closing processing facilities. It is now estimated in the United States that antipollution legislation will add about 5 cents per pound to investment costs in the copper industry, while in Japan pollution control may cost as much as 100 dollars/ton for some processes. The trouble here is that many politicians and their constituents do not understand that much pollution is inherited from earlier economic activity, and as such is a community rather than a firm or industry problem. Thus, in one sense or another, at least a part of the financing of pollution suppression and environmental restoration should fall on the community as a whole—particularly because it would now be unnecessarily obtuse to pass and enforce legislation that will increase unemployment and decrease investment. This problem in particular must be made clear to the crank fringe of the environmental crusaders, many of whom still believe that it will be possible to take pollution control expenses out of the salaries, or the hides, of the directors of offending firms.

Earlier in the chapter we discussed the transformation of primary ores, but another important source of industrial feedstocks is scrap or secondary materials, which come either from the reduction and recycling of finished goods containing copper, aluminum, etc., or from some of the stages of processing in the form of shavings, etc.

In a well-known article Professor Solow (1974) pointed out that a certain amount of material is lost each time the metal is reprocessed; he likens this arrangement to the well-known multiplier of macroeconomic theory. The same has been noted by Banks (1976), who has written out this multiplier. In his latest book, however, Professor Pearce (1976) has cast doubt on the suitability of the multiplier analogy, primarily because of durability.

In attacking this problem we should recognize the input-output relationship between the annual use of an output and the flow of industrial activity. In other words, the amount of input used is directly proportional to output during a given period. As a result, if output is increasing yearly, so is the demand for inputs; on the other hand, the amount available for recycling comes from the lower input consumption of previous years. For example, if we assume for simplification that only automobiles are suitable for scrapping, that the "life" of an automobile is ten years, and that planned automobile sales for the present year are 5 million, while ten years ago they were only 1 million, we see that even if we could scrap and recover every nut and bolt in those ten-year-old vehicles and recycle them as inputs into today's production, we could still not account for more than a fifth of this period's production from scrap. In addition if, as is usually the case, only a fraction of the potentially recyclable material can be recovered, we would not even be able to construct 1 million automobiles from recycled materials.[3] If we take the average durability of items containing copper as 20 years—that is, after 20 years these items are scrapped, and as much copper as possible recovered and recycled into new production—and if the growth rate of copper usage is 3 percent, and if an average of 80 percent of the copper in various goods can be recovered, then recycled copper is capable of supplying 50 percent of current copper inputs.

Table 1-2 gives some idea of recycling percentages for the United States. These figures are only approximate, but they give some idea of the fairly large differences between current and possible recycling percentages in the United States for some metals. In addition, as we move across countries we observe important differences in recycling percentages. Britain's recycled lead consumption is about 61 percent, compared to 48 percent in the United States and 22 percent in Japan; substantial differences also show up for some other materials. Then too, the amount of potentially recyclable material available in most industrial countries would permit their economies to run for several years with secondary inputs exclusively. The only potential bottleneck is in secondary refining capacity. Grillo (1965) estimated that the stock of potentially recyclable copper in the world was about 60 million tons, and this has certainly increased by another 15 or 20 million tons in the last ten years.

Finally, in a no-growth society we might be able to achieve the ideal state envisaged by Professor Glenn Seaborg (1974) and others, in which secondary materials become the chief source of industrial feedstocks—particularly if a high percentage of "recoverability" were built into durable goods. However given that we now desire or need further growth, it is even more crucial that governments take initiative formulating viable recycling programs. It takes only 5 percent as much energy to melt down old aluminum as it does to produce virgin metal from ore, and remelt furnaces are comparatively inexpensive to construct.

A particularly impressive example of a high efficiency recycling system still in the development stage can be found in the German Democratic Republic (GDR). During 1975, about 517,000 tons of used paper was collected, which is equivalent to paper from almost 4 million trees. They also aim to collect 345 million bottles and 190 million tin cans which, among other things, will save 90 million kilowatt hours of energy. It seems likely that when savings can be made on this scale, they can support an entire recycling industry with perhaps thousands of employees, many of whom might otherwise be unemployed.

Table 1-2
Possible and Current Recycle Percentages for Important Metals in Various Years
(United States)

	Iron	Aluminum		Zinc	Copper			
	(1971)	(1956)	(1971)	(1971)	(1970)	(1971)	(1972)	(1973)
Current	47.3	15.5	17.3	16.5	45.7	45.0	43.5	42.5
Possible	49.0		42.6	34.5				50.0

Commodity Cartels

Until about 1973 the international economic system generally functioned so as
to provide the main industrial countries with all the minerals they required at
relatively low prices. The first hint that this arrangement might be breaking
down came in the months immediately following the October War of 1973,
when the price of oil from the Organization of Petroleum Exporting Countries
(OPEC) rose by almost 400 percent.

Along with this unexpected and unpleasant surprise for the big oil
consumers, rumors began to emanate from organizations like the United Nations
Conference on Trade and Development (UNCTAD) about a number of commodity cartels like OPEC that were forming or which could form. This talk was
immediately picked up and amplified by large sections of the press, as well as
various academics and bureaucrats specializing in the economics of the Third
World, even though the oil entering into world trade is about twelve times as
valuable as the nine most important nonfuel minerals, and as shown in an
important article by Varon and Takeuchi (1974), this ratio will increase.

What this means, quite simply, is that only if the producers of literally all
the primary products—including the "soft" commodities—were to get together
and simultaneously elevate all prices would the industrial world find itself in a
predicament even remotely similar to the 1973-74 oil crisis. The key word here,
however, is "similar," since substitution possibilities exist for many of the key
industrial raw materials even in the short run, and as was shown in World War II,
a number of soft commodities can be dispensed with entirely for long periods.
Also, as mentioned above, a very high level of recycling can be practiced in the
short run, and to take up the initial shock of an excessive price rise or blockade,
fairly large stocks can be held. The United States, to name one country, has at
times held inventories of tin and manganese that were larger than the entire
consumption of the rest of the world, as well as a stock of copper that exceeded
a million metric tons. We can continue this discussion by examining table 1-3.

A useful condition for the operation of a successful cartel is that production
is concentrated in a few countries. As table 1-3 indicates, this does not seem to
be true for some of the most important metals. To some people this situation
has suggested a strategy whereby LDCs producing certain products passively
accept low prices for a long period of time, while progressively increasing their
production. This could drive high-cost producers in the developed countries out
of the market. A sufficient share of production capacity might then be located
in the Third World to make giant price rises feasible. However, this condition,
while important, is neither necessary nor sufficient in many cases—it is only a
condition which, combined with some other advantages, might allow a group of
countries or producers to dominate a market. (Or, from another point of view, it
might not be required at all. There are enough potential energy supplies outside
OPEC to hold the oil price near its present level, or even to roll it back

Table 1-3
Some Qualities of Nonfuel Minerals Important for Cartel Forming

| | Price Elasticities[a] | | | Good Substitut-ability | Good Recycla-bility | LDC's Share of | |
	Low	Price Range	High			Exports	Production
Copper[c]	−0.20		−0.60	Yes	Yes	56.5	37
Tin	−0.07		−0.10	Yes	Yes	80.7	92
Bauxite	−0.275	27-37	−0.60	Yes[b]	Yes	79.0	
Zinc	−0.10	16-25	−0.25	Yes	Yes		19
Silver	−0.10		−0.20				35.5
Lead	−0.10	14-20	−0.30	Yes	Yes		20.2
Manganese Ore			−0.1		No	60.0	37.6
Phosphate (Rock)			−0.10			60.1	39.7
Iron Ore	−0.10						

Source: Various documents
Note: Some supply elasticities are given in chapter 8.
[a]All price elasticities approximate; price range (in cents/pound)
[b]In the long run
[c]Refined copper

somewhat; but for diverse reasons associated with the ineptitude of its major clients, OPEC can count on being in the driver's seat for some time in the future.)

Then, too, nobody knows just what production techniques are possible in the long run. An extended period of low prices might cause mines in the developed countries to become more efficient, especially in replacing labor with capital and energy; and in the case of a commodity such as bauxite, the passing of time simply brings closer the day when large-scale aluminum production is possible with nonbauxite clays. Even so, a high level of producer concentration involving a commodity whose total production value is relatively modest provides circumstances favorable to unilateral price increases. Phosphates may fall in this category. In addition, there is no intrinsic reason for placing Third World producers and producers in the private sector of the market economies at opposite poles in these matters. When a chance at the top dollar comes along, either group is quite capable of a long and passionate cooperation.

It is also argued that a necessary condition for a producer cartel to be able to increase its earnings by restricting supply and raising prices is that the absolute value of the price elasticity of demand is less than unity: the smaller the absolute value, the more favorable the outlook for a successful cartel. Although econometric investigations of most commodity markets are generally not highly reliable, enough research has been done on price elasticities of demand to indicate that elasticities probably fall within a range favorable to cartels. But if we look at the ninety-year history of cartel-forming attempts in the copper industry, we see one failure after another. The point is that elasticities are static concepts, which exclude many of the dynamic phenomena of the real world—such as the marked inability of the directors of individual producing companies to remember their commitments to the cartel when things start going wrong and their jobs are at stake.[4]

Again, very few if any nonfuel industries enjoy the leverage of oil. Recycling oil is not possible at the present level of technology; very large stockpiles are economically infeasible; short-run substitution is very complicated, and made even more complicated by the political heterogenity and shortsightedness of consumers. Moreover, OPEC has apparently found a suitable answer to the various pressures put upon them by their clients: unity.

One of the most important factors working to prevent the effective functioning of nonfuel commodity cartels is the extensive nationalization that has taken place in many of the less-developed raw-material-producing countries. These transfers of ownership have come to mean that—for political reasons—production must be maintained at as high a level as possible, regardless of profitability and irrespective of the global level of investment in the particular industry. Just as important, the viability of investments outside the primary product sectors in many of these countries is so low that it almost precludes using scarce capital and foreign exchange for other than traditional activities. In many respects, this is what underdevelopment is all about.

A final point can now be made on the above theme. Although I am generally unsympathetic to the confrontation games originating in the various international talk shops, particularly those pretentious and logically perverse schemes concocted by well-meaning but unimaginative individuals suffering from acute jet lag, it can hardly be denied that the LDCs producing raw materials have little cause to be pleased with the rewards for their work. A 1972 report by UNCTAD makes the situation perfectly clear.

The terms of trade of these countries had deteriorated by about 15 percent compared with the mid-1960s, equivalent to a loss, in 1972, of about 10,000 million dollars. This is more than 20 percent of these countries' aggregate exports, and exceeds the total of official development assistance from developed market economy countries to developing countries in Africa, Asia and Latin America (some 8,400 million dollars in 1972). In other words, there was a net transfer of real resources over this period, from less developed to developed countries, with the flow of aid being more than offset by the adverse trend in the terms of trade of the developing countries.

Needless to say, with the rise in energy prices and the drastic collapse in the price of many primary products since 1973, it is unlikely that things have improved.

This does not mean that a campaign will be launched here to save poor countries from bankruptcy, since many of these nations are—because of certain easily recognized shortcomings—quite beyond rescue, and it is only fitting that choirs of creditors sing them to their fate. But that should not keep us from recognizing that the workers, administrators, technicians, and directors of the raw materials industries in the LDCs are making an invaluable contribution to the affluence of the rest of the world, and have every right to be rewarded accordingly.

The "Energy" Crisis

As noted above, the value of the oil exported from OPEC is more than twelve times the value of the nine most important nonfuel minerals exported from the LDCs. Prior to 1973-74 it accounted for 5 percent of the value of world exports, and jumped to about 12 percent in a relatively short period after the October War. Given the sheer physical amount of oil required annually by world industry, the ease with which oil production can be decreased, and the imagination—if not brilliance—of OPEC administrators in understanding and utilizing the situation, this means that the oil-importing nations of the industrial world are facing a monumental challenge.

Moreover, this challenge increases daily, not only because OPEC's financial position grows stronger with every barrel of oil shipped, but because the countermeasures of the major oil consumers are being systematically undermined by two myths. The first is that the oil crisis is largely monetary, and can be put right once exchange rate adjustments are completed and capital markets widened sufficiently to facilitate the "recycling" of OPEC funds (or "petro-dollars") into something other than blue chip securities and real properties in the better residential districts of London. The originators of this pipedream are, among others, the incompetent and overpaid bureaucrats of the International Monetary Fund (IMF), as well as the public relations experts of the large banks and financial institutions acting as intermediaries in this recycling. It is still going strong despite the already high rate of recycling and its almost imperceptible effect on the declining economic health of several of the major industrial countries.[5]

The second myth is that the industrial countries should be thankful for the opportunity to export to OPEC countries billions of dollars of capital goods and technical expertise in return for oil that is four times as expensive as it was only a few years ago. Among the chief mythmakers here we find scholars like Professor Maurice Adelman who, until a few months ago, was a prolific and influential supplier of assurances that OPEC was a delicate reed, and it was only a matter of time until the free market prevailed and this wretched cartel crumbled. Subscribing to this scenario we also find, among others, the distinguished Nobel Laureate in economics for 1976, Professor Milton Friedman.

Of late, however, Professor Adelman (1976) has discerned that the "elements of strength in the OPEC position are much more impressive than the elements of weakness," and that the cartel regrettably shows no sign of fading away. He also informs the faithful that OPEC is building up a powerful vested interest in the consuming countries. Using Morgan Guaranty as his source, Adelman states that OPEC imports went from 20 billion dollars in 1972 to 100 billion in 1976, and he explicitly reports that because of this trade ". . . thousands of people have jobs, and some are getting rich." This is an important statement in the light of what has happened to the economies of Western Europe and North America since the rise in oil prices; the thinking reader will do well to give its quantitative content his deepest consideration.

As a direct result of the cost push effects of the oil price rise, not thousands, but hundreds of thousands of people in the major oil-consuming countries lost their jobs, while millions were forced or will be forced to take or stay in positions incommensurate with their training or preferences. It also appears to be true that in Britain, Italy, France, and Denmark, for example, government attempts to restore, by monetary means, at least a part of the real purchasing power represented by transfers to OPEC seems to have been a major part of the impulse to the inflation that still prevails in these countries. Finally, it must be emphasized—for the sake of those economists and politicians who insist upon a rigid policy of noncomprehension in these matters—that it is when the *real* expenditure of oil consumers is decreased to make room for the expenditures of oil producers—by exporting goods they could have used themselves—that the aggregate standard of living of these consumers is lowered, and not simply when financial assets are being shipped abroad.

The oil-producing countries can import every year an amount of equipment and technical services approaching the value of the gross physical investment in the nonfinancial corporate sector in the United States in 1975, which is approximately one-quarter of the total world import of goods and services in the same year. Paradoxical as it may seem, the industrial countries as a group may not be able to afford to export this amount merely to pay for an input they were getting at a fourth of the price in 1973. The plain truth is that they need this exported equipment and expertise or its equivalent in real resources to offset the decelerating rate of productivity growth that characterizes much of the industrial world and which, if it becomes more pronounced, will almost certainly lead to new recessions—or worse.

Some comments are now in order about the macroeconomic side of the above theme, but first we should understand that the oil price rise meant an instantaneous fall in the "utility" that individuals were gaining from their holdings of durable goods, and also a decline in the yield of investments. To see the first of these we have only to realize that many people purchased automobiles, boats, and houses under the assumption that fuel prices would increase only gradually over time. The 300 or 400 percent basic increase in the price of oil meant an increase in the operating costs of these durables—and, everything else remaining the same, a higher price for each unit of satisfaction being gained from them. Of course it could be argued that this satisfaction could be regained via a more rapid expansion of personal incomes, and employees in countries like Sweden orchestrated this misunderstanding by demanding—and receiving—enormous increases in wages and salaries. But once the world economy began to adjust to the shift in real purchasing power, the standard of living of all the large oil importers came under a downward pressure. In many countries, including Sweden, the shock is being taken up primarily by those least able to defend themselves: the elderly, the sick, the socially and physically disadvantaged, and the unemployed—particularly young people just arriving on the job market. Most of the strong, including those holding well-paid sinecures, are managing to keep an upward trajectory.

A similar phenomenon exists on the investment side. As Dale Jorgenson and Edward Hudson (1976) have argued, capital and energy are complementary, and together substitute for labor. As a result, the higher energy cost eventually leads to a decrease in investment. On the whole new jobs may show a tendency to become less capital-intensive, and since the holders of these jobs have less capital to work with, they are less productive. Moreover, the fall in the capital intensity of new facilities lowers the overall average capital intensity, which switches the economy onto a lower growth track. (But even if the capital intensity of the average job remains the same, which is probably the case in the short run, we seem to be moving into a situation in which there is a decline in the rate of increase in employment. Thus we still get a decrease in the aggregate average capital intensity, and a lower growth rate.) A byproduct of this process can be an undesired change in the structure of production, causing certain skills to become obsolete, and depriving the people possessing them of current and future income, as well as the investment (in time and money) required to obtain them.[6] We can now list the additional cost of oil imports caused by price increases through 1974 for some of the main oil-importing countries as shown in table 1-4.

The question table 1-4 raises is how did the governments of these countries manage to maintain their composure in the face of the magnitude of these figures. (In some countries the loss of an export market for a hundred million dollars is regarded as a calamity, while an extra import bill of several billion was passed off as a bagatelle.) The answer is a profound lack of awareness or, to be less diplomatic, simple ignorance. Even when the escalation in oil prices was costing the United States 2 million jobs per year, $60 billion in real gross national product, and at least $60 billion in real personal income, some of the leading economists in the country continued to pontificate about petrodollars and recycling as if somewhere in the entrails of these nontopics there was a magic formula for the restoration of prosperity.

The matter of macroeconomic policies is also relevant, since it gives us some

Table 1-4

Supplementary Costs of Oil Imports Due to Oil Price Increases through 1974 and Percentage Export Increases to OPEC countries, 1973-76

Country	Additional Costs for 1974[a]	1973-76 Export Increase (%)
1. United States	15.00	247
2. Japan	11.20	230
3. Germany	5.00	257
4. France	4.70	175
5. United Kingdom	4.50	178
6. Italy	4.10	240
7. Spain	1.50	—
8. Belgium	1.50	174
9. Netherlands	1.40	183
10. Sweden	1.20	352
11. Denmark	0.70	228
12. Austria	0.38	379

Source: Estimated from consumption data given in various issues of *The Petroleum Economist*, and from price estimates in Banks (1976).

[a]In billions of dollars.

idea of the intellectual nimbleness of what is sometimes referred to as economic expertise, as well as an inkling of what we can expect when the next crisis comes along. Some governments, like the United States, responded to the oil price rises with a round of contradictory fiscal and monetary policies, while others attempted to restore purchasing power with expansionary monetary and fiscal activities. As it happens, both of these strategies were wrong, and both led to inflation, unemployment, and decreased output. Almost all governments failed to comprehend that there was virtually no way to escape a fall in real income given very large price rises for an irreplaceable input such as oil; they should have been making sure that this decrease fell as evenly as possible across all groups in the community, and particularly that those individuals who were prepared to make a genuine contribution to the economy did not become unemployed and disillusioned with the future of productive work. For instance, Sweden passed over the depression of 1974-75 with record low unemployment because they ignored the fiscal and monetary policy syndrome, and instead resorted to specific policy measures in direct support of employment and production. (Although, unfortunately, the Swedes maintained employment via increased consumption, instead of increased investment. This was a drastic mistake.)

Since a later chapter in this book will treat energy problems in some detail, this section will close with the opinion that, in the long run, the energy problem should be considerably simpler to solve than the problem of obtaining adequate supplies of depletable resources should the rate of world population growth press against its biological upper limit. We are now probably in transition from having limited supplies of fairly inexpensive energy resources, to having very large supplies at a much higher cost—in particular a capital cost. But once the new energy technology is constructed and ready for operation, costs could be as low, if not lower, than those being accepted now.

The important thing now is to choose the correct future technology. It goes without saying that dangerous or uneconomic technologies must be stopped or discarded at all costs, but first we must know just what is dangerous and what is not, and under what conditions. There has been more than twenty years of civilian experience with nuclear reactors in the United States without a serious accident, but the supply of reactors has yet not outrun the supply of capable technicians and service personnel needed to ensure their correct functioning. Whether this would be true if the number of reactors doubled or tripled remains to be seen but, everything considered, many observers see no reason to be optimistic on this point.

On the other hand, the destruction of the lakes in Central Sweden and the walls of the Acropolis is the work of fossil fuels, and who knows just what harm these fuels are capable of causing the human body, especially when their atmospheric concentration is increased. It might just be possible that nuclear energy is both cleaner and safer than fossil fuels, and if the problem of waste disposal or security could be solved—and this is largely a political problem—then a large increase in the supply of nuclear energy is justified. Of course the most important energy resource right now is the conservation of energy which, if practiced on a sufficient scale, could buy the time needed to choose and implement the correct energy strategy.

Just what will eventually happen on the energy front cannot be taken up here, but I suggest that much of the opposition to nuclear power has nothing to do with safety, but rather with the rejection of a technological society in which many of the antinuclear partisans, for various psychological reasons, feel that they have no place. In fact, behind an appreciable slice of the opposition to nuclear energy is a widespread and scarcely concealed hostility to all economic growth and the benefits that have resulted therefrom—except, of course, those which have devolved upon the antinuclearites' own persons and property. Just how far these disenchanted elements will be allowed to go in influencing the future is difficult to say, but one thing is clear. Without a massive augmentation of energy or conservation the present civilization will begin its long stroll to the exit.

Notes

1. This should not be interpreted to mean that a scientific discussion can be carried on in these terms—at least not yet. Some algebraic pricing rules that might interest us here involve changes in stocks. For instance, if stocks fall in

period $t-1$, the amount of the increase in price is proportional to the fall in stocks, or $p_t = p_{t-1} - \lambda \Delta I$. Similarly, the price in period t could increase if stocks in period $t-1$ fall below a given amount, or $p_t = p_{t-1} - \lambda(I_{t-1} - I)$. Where the econometrics of this topic is concerned, Ertek (1967) has worked with a relation of the type $\Delta p_t = \lambda \Delta I$. Other possibilities that have given good results are:

$$Ln\ p_t = \alpha_0 + \alpha_1\ Ln\frac{I_{t-1}}{c_t} + \alpha_2\ Ln\ p_{t-1}$$

and

$$p_t = \alpha_0 + \alpha_1\left[\frac{I_t}{c_t} - \frac{I_{t-1}}{c_{t-1}}\right] + \alpha_2 p_{t-1}$$

In these expressions I represents inventories and c consumption. For a summary of the econometrics of commodity models (see chapter 8).

2. As Nicholas Valéry (1977) points out, Britain has millions of people in "pretend" jobs, contributing next to nothing to the national well being. As I see it, if the pay of these people could be brought into line with their productivity, it might be possible to finance investments in productive employment that would eventually benefit everyone.

3. Let us represent industrial activity in the year t by the variable Y_t, where this might be an index of industrial production or even gross national product. We then take $C_t = \theta Y_t$, where C_t is the consumption of the input, and θ is a factor of proportionality which can be thought of as an input-output coefficient. We can also take n as the growth rate of Y, L as the average durability of goods containing the particular input, and λ the fraction of the input that can be recovered from final goods. We thus have:

$$C_t = \theta Y_t = \theta Y_0 e^{nt}$$

This is the amount of the input used in year t. With durability L, the amount available for recycling is that used L years earlier, or:

$$C_{t-L} = \theta Y_t e^{n(t-L)}$$

With a fraction λ of this recoverable, we have as the amount recovered:

$$R_t = \lambda \theta Y_0 e^{n(t-L)}$$

Thus the ratio of the amount recovered to the total consumption of the input is:

$$F = \frac{R_t}{C_t} = \frac{\lambda\theta Y_0 e^{n(t-L)}}{\theta Y_0 e^{nt}} = \frac{\lambda}{e^{nL}}$$

For copper in the United States, if we take $L = 20$, $n = 0.03$ (3%), and $\lambda = 0.80$, we get from the last equation an F equal to about 0.5 (50%).

4. The expression for the price elasticity that interests us here is:

$$E_{dc} = \frac{1}{m}E_{dw} - \frac{1}{m}(1-m)E_{dr}$$

where E_{dc} is the price elasticity of demand for the cartel's output; E_{dw} the price elasticity of world demand for the product; E_{sr}, the price elasticity of supply of outside producers; and m the colluding groups share in world output. On the importance of elasticities the reader should refer to Takeuchi (1972), while a brief survey of copper cartel forming can be found in Banks (1974, 1976) and Radetski (1975).

5. French banking houses, ostensibly with the blessing of their government, aggressively bid for petrodollars, which they lend to banks in Spain, Portugal, Greece, Italy, and a few other countries. For these services they collect a "spread" of about 2.5 percent on the going rate of interest.

6. The situation with a falling yield of capital was alluded to by William Nordhaus (1973) in a basic paper. In speaking of the rise of energy prices due to the increasing scarcity of energy resources, Nordhaus noted that if energy prices increased exponentially, they played havoc with the owners of capital goods who had thought they would rise more gradually—for instance, those who had "extrapolative expectations." Some reports of the Hudson Institute Europe for 1974-75 also took up this matter, and superb summaries of the macroeconomic issues are to be found in Brookes (1975) and Perry (1976).

Appendix 1A

This appendix treats briefly the effect of the rate of growth of consumption of a resource on the time to resource exhaustion. We can define g as the growth rate, and X_t as resource use during the year t. Thus we have:

$$X_t = X_0 e^{gt}$$

where X_0 *is consumption in the initial year. Cumulative resource use is then:*

$$X = \int_0^T X_t dt = \int_0^T X_0 e^{gt} dt$$

or

$$X = \frac{X_0}{g}(e^{gt} - 1)$$

From this we get years to exhaustion, or T_e, as:

$$T_e = \frac{1}{g} \ln \left(\frac{g\overline{X}}{X_0} + 1 \right)$$

In this expression $\overline{X}$ is the total amount of the resource available. We can now construct table 1A-1, where the number of years needed to exhaust the particular category of reserve is shown in parentheses next to the relevant item. In the case of uneconomical + hypothetical reserves, the figure in parentheses gives the additional number of years over that shown next to economic reserves.

In the case of a mineral such as lead, increasing the amount of reserves from 144 million metric tons to 1998 (144 + 1854), which is a factor of about 14, increases the time to exhaustion from 35.5 years to 131 (35.8 + 96), or by a factor of only 3.7. Although the "force of interest" argument on which this sad state of affairs is based is often regarded as trivial, it is one of those trivialities which the reader should not make the mistake of ignoring.

Table 1A-1

Reserves (in millions of metric tons) and Time to Exhaustion (T_e)

	Economic Reserves		Identified but Uneconomical	Hypothetical or Speculative	(1) + (2)	
Aluminum (Bauxite)[a]	3,600					
Copper	370	(30.6)	750	720	1,470	(32.7)
Lead	144	(35.5)	1,644	210	1,854	(96)
Tin	4.7	(19.3)	22.4	18.8	41.2	(68.4)
Zinc	131	(20.3)	1,665	3,941	5,605	(103)
Iron Ore[a]	97	(56)				
Chromium	466	(85)	1214	1,008	2,223	(140)
Cobalt	2.7	(62)	4.5			
Manganese[b]	2,437	(77)	5,325	3,750	9.075	
Nickel	46	(35)	70			

Source: United Nations Documents (1974)

[a]Potential resources huge

[b]Takes into consideration resources from underseas mining

2 Energy and its Torments

The energy crisis has taken its time arriving, but now that it is here it will not be leaving soon. In the United States, C. Sharp Cook (1976) claims that the first authoritative warning of trouble came in 1907 during a conference of state governors. According to Cook, on the first day of discussion President Theodore Roosevelt told the conference that such things as coal, oil, gas, iron ore, and so on were certain to be exhausted some day. As a result it was necessary to see that they were wisely used.

Of course, the depletion of natural resources is not necessarily a bad thing. The reader must never forget that through the transformation of mineral assets into various forms of capital and other assets, the superb technical and organizational skill of North America and Europe was created. Moreover, at least up to now, technical skill is certainly the most important resource, as can be easily seen by examining the situation in those countries unlucky enough to be without it. Even so, it is important to understand that the feast is over—at least for the present. There is no longer any room in the scheme of things for the throw-away society envisaged in Alvin Toffler's *Future Shock*; and although almost everyone clearly senses this, we are still not at the point where it can be said openly, before all types of audiences.[1]

To treat all the topics relevant to the energy crisis and the future of the world energy economy, a book several times the size of this one would be necessary. However the crux of the issue can be handled in a chapter or two, or even less. A brilliant article by Corden (1976) provides a thorough survey of the macroeconomic issues. This paper, first delivered as a lecture in December 1973, is a superb example of the power of elementary economic theory. On the microeconomic front the key question is whether alternative energy technologies or conservation can lessen dependence on oil. This matter will be taken up later, but it can be stated immediately that there are any number of technical solutions to this problem. What seems to be lacking is the political will to do the things that can be done, and which in the long run a majority of people undoubtedly want done.

The Macroeconomics of the World Oil Crisis (1)

Between 1950 and 1970 the real price of petroleum declined by a factor of almost two, while its monetary price was nearly constant. This sharply increased

23

the energy intensiveness of manufacturing in all the industrial countries, with sectors such as aluminum and plastics expanding at a very high rate, and caused remarkable growth in the demand for and supply of private transportation. A more noticeable climate of anticipation centered on a continuing fall in the real price of petroleum products for the remainder of this century, and only minor upward adjustments in the money price.

Thus the abrupt rise in the oil price—taking place as it did under conditions that could have been borrowed from the Airport-Skyscraper-Earthquake type of epic that was Hollywood's reaction to the episode—sent a vivid and lasting wave of anxiety through the oil-importing world. It would be hard to deny, though, that given the market power of OPEC and their basic willingness to use it, a major price rise was long overdue. In fact, the villains of this particular drama are not the OPEC countries and their officials, but certain academic economists whose misfounded and naive faith in the fragility of cartels provided theoretical justification for the do-nothing stance of the governments of oil-consuming countries in the decade preceding the day of reckoning.

Is money power? Some people enjoy saying that it is, and if they are correct then OPEC is on the way to acquiring its share, and perhaps a little more. The value of oil exports from OPEC should range up to $120 billion in U.S. dollars annually for at least the next three years. After that, if there is prosperity in the world, the amount will increase. As for their accumulated financial balances, table 2-1 provides estimates from various sources.

One of the things table 2-1 shows is how OPEC's financial assets have depreciated in response to the expected rise in the world price level. Under the circumstances it might have been better for all parties had the price of oil began to appreciate ten years ago, or earlier, and gradually worked its way up to the

Table 2-1
Accumulated Assets of OPEC, Estimated for 1974-1980

Source	1974	1975	1976	1977	1978	1979	1980
Morgan Guaranty Trust	100.0	148.6	189.5	217.6	225.6	211.7	171.1
Morgan Guaranty Trust (Real Value)	100.0	132.7	158.2	169.7	164.4	144.2	108.9
OECD	100.0	152.5	196.0	238.0	276.5	311.1	341.5
OECD (Real Value)	100.0	139.2	163.6	183.6	197.5	207.9	207.4
First National City Bank	100.0	144.0	174.0	195.9	209.7	214.3	208.8

Source: World Financial Markets, Morgan Guaranty Trust, January 1975; First National City Bank Monthly Economic Letter, June 1975; and various issues of the OECD *Economic Outlook*.

Note: Real values are the money values given in the previous row deflated to 1974 prices.

present level. Similarly, the record inflation we have been experiencing means that purchases of real property in Europe and North America by OPEC nationals and governments is probably good business, rather than just a parvenue itch. Although most of us have no choice, it hardly makes sense to accumulate liquid assets carrying a 7 or 8 percent rate of interest when the inflation rate, adjusted for uncertainty, is several percentage points higher.

Later in this section the revenues of oil exporting countries (OEC) will be considered in the course of a macroeconomic analysis of the effect of an oil price rise. At that time it will be postulated that all these revenues could be spent, all saved, or a portion spent and the rest saved. The last alternative corresponds to reality, but for pedagogical reasons the first two are also interesting.[3] The savings of the oil exporting countries (OEC), could take several forms. They could be in gold or foreign currencies held in the banks of OEC, or for that matter simply buried in the sand or concealed in mattresses in these countries. They could be held as deposits in the banks of the oil importing countries (OIC); or the OEC could buy bonds and stocks from sellers in the OIC and from organizations like the World Bank, or in the same vein they could loan money on the Euromarket or to other Third World countries, and so on.

Furthermore, money placed in financial assets can be invested on a long or short term basis. It would appear that up to now OPEC has favored short term or highly liquid loans in countries such as the United States, West Germany, and Switzerland; and on the London Eurodollar market. Turning this short-term money into the long-term loans required by the business sector of industrial countries entails a number of costs, and it appears that most of these costs are being absorbed by borrowers in the OIC. What is happening is that the shuffling of various financial instruments between individuals and institutions as their maturity is lengthened tends to reduce the efficiency of the capital market. See table 2-2 to get some idea of the distribution of OPEC savings.

We can now begin our analysis. To keep things simple, we shall specify in this section that the demand for petroleum products is strictly *inelastic*. This means that with an increase or a decrease in price, the same physical quantity of oil is demanded. Also, for expository reasons, we assume only one oil exporting country (OEC) or, alternatively, a politically homogeneous bloc of oil exporting countries. Similarly, only one oil importing country (OIC) is assumed, or a bloc of oil importing countries having a common currency. Despite these simplifications, the following exposition is applicable to the real world in all except certain comparatively unimportant details, and anyone following most of the argument in this section has almost all the insight into the macroeconomic aspects of the oil crisis that he or she will ever need.

Let us begin by supposing that trade was initially balanced, and then the oil price increases. With everything else the same, this immediately creates a payments deficit for the oil importer, who must buy the same amount of oil at a higher price. If we assume no change in the money value of output in the OIC,

Table 2-2
Placement Forms for OPEC's Financial Surplus, 1974

Country	Sum	Liquid Assets Bank and Private Debt	Government Debt	Direct Involvement	Direct Loan	Transfer
United States	11.0	4.5	6.0	0.5		
Europe (excluding U.K.)	5.0				5.0	
United Kingdom	8.0	2.5	3.5	- - - 1.5 - - -		
Japan, Canada	1.5				1.5	
Euromarket	20.5	20.5				
LDCs					- - - - - 2.5 - - - - -	
IMF's Oil Facility	2.0	2.0				
World Bank	2.25				2.25	
Unidentified	4.75		- - - - - - 4.75 - - - - - -			
	57.5	27.5				

Source: Herin and Wijkman (Den Internationaella Bakgrunden, Långtidsutredningen, 1975)

then having to pay more for the same physical quantity of oil reduces disposable money income. What about *real* consumption? If the OIC were to bury the increase in his receipts in the sand, and thus not buy a larger share of the physical output of the OIC, then the real consumption of the oil importer need not decrease, at least not in the short run. If residents of the OIC take money from their savings or can borrow money, then they can buy the same things they bought before the price rise. Similarly, their government could maintain disposable money income by arranging tax rebates, or simply by printing new money and having people stand on street corners and distribute this purchasing power more or less at random to passers by. This would make it possible for residents of the OIC to purchase the physical output of the OIC, and thus for aggregate real consumption to remain unchanged.[4]

Next we must remind the reader that in a *closed economy*, or an economy without trade, real income is equal to physical output. (We cannot do a great deal with this concept, however, because when we change the composition of output we change real income.[5] But note carefully the continued distinction between real output and the money value of that output). We must also note especially that in an *open economy*, which is an economy with trade, real income and real consumption can be more than real output because domestic residents can borrow from foreigners. By the same token it can be less, because a part of the real output can be loaned to foreigners. Finally, we should remember that the physical output of a country is usually divided into two categories. The first is consumption goods and services; and the second is investment goods, which for the purpose of this discussion will be taken as additions to the stock of real capital in the form of machines and structures.

We can now continue with the case where the OEC does not spend its additional receipts, but buries them in the sand; and purchasing power does not fall in the OIC because people save less, spend a part of their stock of savings, or the government pursues an expansionary economic policy. In this case the mix of goods being purchased could remain the same, and thus real consumption would be unchanged. It seems clear, however, that the combination of goods being purchased could easily change. When consumers borrow money or spend their bank accounts, they tend to be more conservative than when they spend from income.

We might now ask ourselves whether the government of the OIC would be doing the right thing if it accepted the same output mix after the price rise as before. Remember that some day the OEC is going to dig up those financial assets and go to the OIC to demand real goods in return for them. If this were to happen about the same time that they were raising the price of oil once again, and also spending these new receipts, it could cause a great deal of unpleasantness for the OIC. Thus it might make good sense for the government of the OIC to encourage a change in the composition of production, maintaining full employment but putting more emphasis on investment—for instance, investment in activities that would lessen the dependence on imported oil. In our model economy this means that real consumption in the OIC would fall; however the government could justify this sacrifice by pointing out that if it did not take place, consumers would have to accept a much greater inconvenience in the future.

The next question is what will happen if the OEC does not bury all its increased revenues in the sand but recycles them back to the OIC so that they can be borrowed by consumers and investors in that country. The answer is that basically this case is the same as the one taken up above, although it could be argued that it makes an important difference to the individual and the firm whether consumption and investment are financed out of real balances or via loans; and for the government whether these items are financed through foreign loans or by such things as newly created money, decreases in taxes, etc. But in this exposition we content ourselves with observing that with the help of these "petrodollars" (which signify the abstention of the OEC from claiming a part of the real output of the OIC) real consumption in the OIC could be kept up or, if desired, real consumption decreased and real investment increased.

Next we examine what happens when the OEC spends all of its new income on exactly the same things that were being purchased earlier by the residents of the OIC, and the residents of the OIC do not alter their savings habits to maintain their real consumption. In this situation disposable money income in the OIC need not fall, but real consumption falls because the products being shipped to the OEC cannot be consumed by the residents of the OIC, the machines being exported cannot be used to make other machines that will produce consumer goods next year, and the technicians that go out to work in the OEC cannot help to build expressways through the blighted sections of OIC cities.

But note that the citizens of the OIC may not voluntarily abstain from their former real consumption. They have access to bank accounts, credit, and so on, and so may not restrain their consumption, but attempt to compete with the OEC for that portion of the physical output of the OIC which the OEC wishes to purchase. In this situation we would expect the price level in the OIC to rise, because the amount of money bid for the output of the OIC would be larger than its money value. In the real world we see that the direct impact of OPEC spending has just started to reach the industrial countries, and since for the most part money wages in these countries still show a certain buoyancy, it seems unlikely that larger-than-normal price rises can be avoided. One of the problems that can arise here is that OPEC may someday link its pricing policy to the level of prosperity and the rate of inflation in the oil-importing countries. Thus if there is a general economic recovery in the industrial countries, but a high rate of inflation, the oil price will be adjusted upward to increase the transfer of real goods to OPEC and to compensate for the depreciation in purchasing power of OPEC financial balances.

We continue by examining a situation where once again the OEC spends all its proceeds, but on a mix of goods that is fundamentally different from that being produced before the oil price rise; and the residents of the OIC do not attempt to maintain their real consumption. This might lead to both inflation and unemployment, depending upon the ease or difficulty with which factors of production can be shifted from one industry to another. Suppose that the residents of the OIC normally prefer the goods produced in industry A, but the OEC prefers goods from industry B. Then an oil price rise could lead to a lowered demand in industry A and an increased demand in B; but prices in the real world go up more easily than they come down, and so we would expect price increases in B but hardly any movement in A. Accordingly, the net result would be a rise in the general price level. (This effect could be reinforced or weakened by a change in the spending pattern of residents of the OIC due to the price rise). Moreover, there could be some problem in reallocating factors of production from one industry to the other. Some employees and fixed production factors located in industry A might no longer be needed in A or useful to B. And even if these employees were needed in B and theoretically could be transferred immediately, rigidities in the wage structure might not provide any incentive for them to move, particularly if the work in B were considered less pleasant than work in A, or involved changing localities. Involuntary or voluntary unemployment might thus result.

Before closing this section, a question must be asked that undoubtedly has found its way into the readers' mind: if the macroeconomic issues associated with the oil crisis are actually so elementary, then why have the economies of the industrial countries been in chaos the last few years? The answer is that in the crucial months following the initial rises in the oil prices, politicians and their economic advisers could not be bothered with thinking through long-run options for the structure of production, but fastened on monetary issues and were duped—or duped themselves—into believing they could borrow their way out of their difficulties. To be sure, this could have succeeded had the borrowed money been used for productive investments with a rate of return at least as high as the effective rate of interest; but even though there are a large number of potential investments fulfilling this criterion in almost every country in the world, most of these loans appear to have been used to prop up consumption.

And what should be done? To begin, it is necessary to recognize the temporary bankruptcy of the old remote control economic strategies built around Keynesian fiscal policies, or the new "monetarism." Next, unemployment must be attacked directly. This can be done through subsidies to firms in the industrial sector for investment in equipment and inventories; through expanding the capacity for retraining employees made redundant by change in technology and demand; and if necessary through comprehensive programs of public employment at a remuneration that provides an incentive for the employee to move to other sectors of the economy when the opportunity presents itself.[6] Finally, as the principal long-run objective, the link must be reestablished—or established, as the case may be—between compensation and productivity.

Energy and Development

Economic development can be expressed in an extremely simple equation: development = technology + energy. To see the truth in this we have only to regard the access to technology and the per capita energy consumption of the haves and have-nots of this world, and what it means in terms of consumption. The 30 percent of the world's population living in the industrial regions of Europe, North America, Australia, and Japan has a per capita consumption that averages at least 7 times that of the 70 percent of the world's population living in the underdeveloped or semideveloped regions.

The United States, Sweden, and West Germany have almost equal per capita incomes, but per capita energy consumption in the United States is about twice that of Sweden and almost four times that of Germany. Differences such as this can be explained by a number of things, such as the pattern of ownership of durables and the intensity of their use, differences in lifestyles, and so on; but Sweden was relatively rich in energy as well as those products that require a great deal of energy in their processing, such as iron ore and timber, and thus it is only natural that the Swedish export industry would show a greater energy intensiveness than that of Germany.

In examining the rate of growth of per capita energy consumption it is sometimes convenient to distinguish two components. The first might be called an "energy-widening" component; it involves providing each new addition to the population with the same amount of energy as present members. The other component can be called "energy deepening," and has to do with increasing per capita energy consumption for new and old members alike. In the United States from 1960 to 1968, residential basic energy consumption increased by an average of 4.1 percent per year, compared to a population growth of 1.3 percent per year. Thus, energy was deepened 2.8 percent annually.

Fisher (1974) calls this energy increase "affluence related," which it is of course; but this expression does not tell the entire story. Materials such as copper, aluminum, and lead seem to be growing more productive in their various uses, with the rate of growth of gross national product increasing faster than the rate of growth of consumption of these metals. Something like this may be happening with energy, but compared to these other items it is becoming so productive and so adaptable in both consumption and production activities that we end up with more rather than less of it in a typical unit of output.

In line with this explanation we can refer to demographic and occupational changes in the structure of populations. More energy is used in cities than in rural districts, and with the intensified urbanization that has taken place in the United States and other industrial countries, energy intensities were bound to increase. The same logic can be applied to increases in the working force caused by larger female participation. More energy is used in factories and offices than in the home, and thus as women spend fewer hours in the home and more in outside employment, energy consumption rises accordingly.

Does this mean that we can expect energy consumption to continue to rise explosively? The answer is probably no, and in most industrial countries energy consumption should take on the appearance of a logistic curve,[7] which implies saturation at some finite level. This should happen when urbanization and increased female participation in the labor force have gone about as far as they can go. Then, too, the composition of output in advanced industrial societies may move away from increased energy intensiveness because cultural and work habits may change. If incomes were high enough and sufficient outdoor recreation facilities were available (such as tennis courts, swimming pools, and basketball courts), energy-intensive working places could operate shorter periods each day, and many people would be inclined to spend more time with these non-energy-intensive diversions.

In countries such as Sweden, Switzerland, and Germany, wealth per capita has increased even faster than energy use per capita. And in the United States, per capita energy use in 1950 was almost one half what it is today, even though per capita money income in the United States has increased by a factor of about four. Thus it is quite likely that for these high income countries energy use has already started to flatten out.

Next we can begin to examine how various countries are managing, or mismanaging, their energy policy. Excluding the centrally planned countries, we have witnessed two full-scale economic and psychological miracles since World

War II: the industrial recoveries of Germany and Japan. These can be attributed not only to those lovable qualities of self-confidence and discipline that other people are so fond of praising (though not of emulating), but to a new-found capacity to keep their delusions under control. This is something that other nations should begin to practice. For instance, just as a millionaire who has come down in the world must learn to curb his taste for yachts and caviar, the United States must learn that for both economic and political reasons it can no longer afford to import petroleum products costing $37 billion per year.

By way of contrast the real GNP of West Germany in 1976 increased 2.3 percent over 1975, but total energy consumption was down by 2.2 percent. As a result the German government altered its prognoses and directives for the growth in energy supply. Two years ago it was predicted that energy consumption in 1985 would be equivalent to 555 million tons of coal, but this has now been cut by about 10 percent, with the reduction falling mostly on nuclear energy. On this point Chancellor Helmut Schmidt has adopted the position that in the future the price of nuclear energy must cover all aspects of the fuel cycle, including disposal, which means that certain people have begun to have second thoughts about its introduction. He also made it clear that nuclear safety must have precedence over all economic considerations, as well he might, since the correct nuclear strategy for a country that now has direct control over only a small amount of nuclear fuel is to build as little nuclear capacity as possible.

The same tendency has been noted in Japan, which has steadily been reducing its import of oil. More important, that country has been scaling down its nuclear buildup. A few years ago the projected figure for 1985 was 60 million kilowatts. A short time later this was reduced to 49 million kilowatts, then to 35, and at the present time plans are for 27 million kilowatts; but even so Japan is once again planning for real rates of economic growth that will be among the highest in the world. How can they be so presumptuous? The answer is that if the Japanese tolerate a greatly increased import of oil or an accelerated expansion of nuclear capacity, they would have to start looking forward to a day when they surrender their competitive advantages instead of reinforcing them. Their best strategy is simply to drive conservation as far as it will go, and to accelerate the introduction of best practical technologies into their economy while awaiting the inevitable breakthroughs in solar or even nuclear technology. Even more important, their superb research establishment must attempt to take a more active part in perfecting the technology that will be used to exploit the huge deposits of coal and shale in various places in the world.

Our next concern has to do with increasing the labor intensity of industrial operations. In Sweden, for instance, people have started listening to schemes for altering the composition of inputs in the production process by raising the tax on the use of energy, which would tend to reduce the demand for this input, and using the proceeds of the tax to subsidize the employment of labor.

The problem here is that energy and labor may not be simple substitutes:

since energy and capital are apparently complements rather than substitutes, energy may also be complementary to labor in some ways. Portuguese workers are badly paid in Portugal and comparatively well paid in Germany because, among other things, in Germany the quantity of energy cooperating with each worker is large, while in Portugal it is small. If a tax is put on energy and the proceeds given to firms to pay workers—and we specify that the wage is to remain the same—total employment falls, because the technical possibility of substituting labor for energy is limited. Put another way, if we replace X dollars worth of energy with X dollars worth of labor, we expect total production to fall. But does this mean that employment must fall? The answer is yes in most cases because, with a given amount of capital and other production factors, including energy, if we reduce one production factor (other than labor) and specify a fixed wage, then the productivity per worker must rise to a level that will justify this wage. This, in turn, requires a fall in employment.[8]

We can now ask what happens if we take away the constant wage restraint and dictate that employment must not decrease. In this case the falling productivity per worker would eventually lead to a falling wage. In the long run there is no escaping this fact. In the example used in the previous paragraph, if the tax-subsidy arrangement were applied in Germany, the visiting Portuguese worker would probably have to content himself with a Portuguese wage or lower.

What happens as we move in the other direction? Economic progress can often be boiled down to energy-intensive rationalizations that eliminate less productive jobs or production factors or both, raising the wage or rental of other factors—including various categories of labor—which raises the demand for all sorts of goods and services, which in turn results in investment that leads to the reemploying, at higher wages, of individuals freed from less productive work. Admittedly, increases in energy consumption have not always led to proportional increases in human contentment, but I don't think most of the individuals singing the praises of a low energy community take their vacations in Cayenne or on the Mauretanian Riviera.

We can conclude this section by referring to some remarks of T. Bradshaw (1977), a not-so-typical president of one of the major American oil companies. In a surprising burst of candor, Bradshaw acknowledges that the duties of good government rise above self-inflicted impotence and include some contingency planning for the distant future. In terms of the present discussion this means that they must be prepared to take direct action when, in their opinion, market incentives are likely to prove insufficient to give the future the desired content. As Bradshaw makes clear, no individual firm or conceivable combination of firms, would be prepared to finance the research needed to make the United States or any other OIC independent of foreign oil. For this type of commitment, with its high risk and low return, governments must move ahead on the basis of criteria that have no place on a private company's profit-loss statement.

Bradshaw's agenda for increasing energy supplies includes a large increase in the production of synthetic oil (with the help of government subsidies), and he apparently wants a high-pressure research program aimed at forcing a break-through in fusion or solar energy. He is also in favor of taxes designed to reduce the size of automobiles, and for subsidies to homeowners for insulating their houses. Unfortunately he makes no substantial comment on nuclear energy, and so that will be supplied here. Nuclear energy must be kept to a minimum: enough to prevent a slide in living standards and to provide a part of the margin of safety that would be needed in the event of a prolonged oil boycott. As things stand, without resorting to the still unreliable breeder reactor, a nuclear strategy based on a massive introduction of existing nuclear equipment would run up against a shortage of fuel in a few decades or so—although it may be possible that new deposits of low grade, high cost uranium ores can be exploited in the United States in the near future. Intensive research on the breeder must continue, but certain absolute guarantees concerning safety must be forthcoming before it is introduced. Since most governments and their senior civil servants lack even the minimum intelligence required to keep hard drugs from being sold openly in the center of their large cities, it seems perfectly clear that they should be spared responsibility for the fairly complex security problems that would accompany a plutonium economy.

The Macroeconomics of the World Oil Crisis (2)

A few remaining macroeconomic issues that are important to our exposition will be treated in this brief section. Although balance-of-payments effects were straightforward when we assumed just one importing country, they become more difficult when we have several countries importing oil. If the oil exporter wants payment in certain currencies, then the demand for these currencies tends to go up relative to the demand for other currencies. If lira are not desired by OPEC but dollars are, then lira are offered in exchange for dollars on the various foreign exchanges, driving the price of lira down relative to dollars. Among other things this makes oil more expensive for the Italians, since the price of oil is quoted in dollars. Similarly, the fairly modest price inflation in Germany has helped make German products attractive in comparison to those of other countries, which in turn increases the demand for German currency relative to other countries, which appreciates its value. The effective price of oil has therefore risen less for Germany than for countries like Sweden and Britain.

A multicountry importing world also means that governments must be extremely careful about the mix of commodities being produced, since the problem has been expanded to one of maintaining competitiveness vis-à-vis other countries. Before the oil price rises there was a great deal of speculation about the service economy, which deemphasizes the manufacturing sector or sectors.

Now it appears that welcoming ceremonies for the service economy will have to be postponed, because the manufacturing sectors in almost all industrial countries will have to be strengthened either quantitatively or qualitatively in order to maintain economic and social progress in the face of higher energy costs. In broaching this point we can also observe the difference between the present transfer of resources to OPEC and the capital transfers from the United States to Europe during the Marshall Plan—something that certain executives of the World Bank fail to comprehend. The purpose of the Marshall Plan was to resuscitate some of the most productive economies in the world; and since this eventually meant an increased flow of manufactured goods from these countries and an expanded world trade, the net result was clearly an increase in global welfare. No such implication can possibly be attached to the present situation—at least not now.

In sorting out winners and losers in the present situation we see that countries exporting products that are not heavy users of energy can often gain at the expense of those exporting such things as automobiles. Severe strains on the international monetary system can also result if the oil exporters choose to hold gold, or for that matter if the general change in the international economic situation causes drastic gold movements throughout the oil-importing world, leaving some countries with depleted gold reserves. Corden (1976) suggests that this type of ailment should be treated by an injection of special drawing rights (which are an international monetary asset issued by the IMF, and sometimes called paper gold). The dilemma here is the growing politicization of the IMF, which is probably inevitable in an international organization whose officials are appointed without the slightest regard for technical competence; however, because the problem of stabilizing the international economy primarily concerns the major industrial countries, a better idea is to disregard the IMF and handle this problem with borrowing and bookkeeping adjustments under the auspices of the Bank for International Settlements or the OECD.

There has also been a great deal of talk in the past few years about the possibility of OPEC breaking up. On this issue everyone seems to be hedging his or her bet, with economists who once swore that cartels were a transgression of the law of nature now beginning to see signs of strength in these unholy alliances. On the other hand, individuals who privately express faith in OPEC's longevity often find it necessary to quote reaons why it could crumble when confronted by influential people who don't want to hear that OPEC is a permanent fixture.

This issue can be settled quite easily. Whether OPEC continues under the same name, or abandons its headquarters on the fashionable "Ring" in Vienna and splits into many little OPECs with offices in places like "Monte," "Kitz," or "Vegas," or if some member of the cartel occasionally sells an odd barrel of oil at a lower price, the simple truth is that the only gesture that will assist the oil-consuming countries in their present plight is a complete turnaround in the price policies of Venezuela and the Middle Eastern countries—and nobody really believes this is going to take place. Under the circumstances, the contention of Basevi and Steinherr (1976) that "it is a mistake to promote or even assume the stability [of OPEC]" is a distinguished piece of nonadvice. The stability of OPEC is based on that most tenacious of all adhesives: proven self-interest. In choosing between assuming the stability or instability of OPEC, we can only hope that no people in responsible government positions in the oil-importing countries are tempted to assume the latter.

Finally, it should be pointed out that there are industrial countries that could, in the long run, be helped by very large increases in the oil price. This might happen because their relative position was improved. For instance, the price rises that have already taken place have favored Japan more than Britain because of the greater efficiency of Japanese industry. But had the price of oil increased by 4000 instead of 400 percent, for example, it would not make any difference how long, hard, or effective the Japanese were willing to work, they still could not compensate for Britain's large domestic supplies of oil and coal. As a result, they would be outcompeted almost everywhere.

Energy Supplies

Coal

Solid fuels account for approximately one-third of world energy consumption, although over the last forty years the share of solid fuels in the world energy picture has decreased considerably. This trend could change, however, since the United States now intends to make coal (and gas and oil manufactured from coal) a key element in future energy supply.

Total identified coal reserves in the world total about 8000 billion tons, with hypothetical resources now estimated at 6500 billion tons. Approximately 70 percent of identified resources are in the U.S.S.R., 18 percent in North America, and 6 percent in Western Europe. But China has considerable hypothetical assets and may be as well endowed as North America. It is believed that the total amount of recoverable reserves are at least one thousand times the current world output, and that their energy content is more than five times the known and postulated reserves of conventional oil and gas.

The basic technical problems of coal gasification and liquification have been solved for a long time, but a few imposing technical and economic issues remain. Not least among these are environmental issues; the sulphur dioxide emission standards that have been proposed in various parts of the United States effectively disqualify the unlimited exploitation of coal reserves using today's technology.

During World War II the German synthetic oil industry processed 600 tons of coal per day, producing about 12,000 barrels of oil per day. The Sasol installations in South Africa process about 3,500 tons per day, turning out more than 300 million cubic feet of gas daily and converting it into liquids similar to petroleum. Any facility operating in the United States would presumably handle at least 25,000 tons per day, producing a product whose oil equivalent could sell for between $14 and $18 a barrel. This figure has also been quoted in Germany, where it is said that plans are being made to restart the manufacture of synthetic oil if the oil price goes much above $14 per barrel.

Cochran (1976) has provided an excellent scenario for the buildup of an American synthetic fuel industry, where the output would be "substitute" natural gas and nonpolluting liquid fuel. The coal processing installations would be located near the mines to avoid having to move the astronomical amounts of coal feedstocks. As pointed out by Cochran, 100 plants producing about 30 percent of the U.S. consumption of energy in 1975 could be operated for 30 years on approximately 1 percent of U.S. coal reserves.

The total capital investment would be about $30 billion, which could be spread out over a number of years. Assuming that the output of these plants would sell for $2.10 per million BTUs, the rate of return would be about 12 percent, which is greater than the average for U.S. industry today; but it could be argued that the rate of return to these synthetic fuel facilities is actually much higher. The United States imports almost 40 percent of its fuel supply, at a cost approaching $40 billion, and a scheme that would eliminate about $30 billion per year in fuel imports would lead to savings of the type described below in connection with Britain and North Sea oil. Furthermore, the American dollar would tend to appreciate, thus making all American imports less expensive, and as an added bonus the United States would no longer be dependent on foreign suppliers.

Petroleum and Natural Gas

Proven reserves of conventional oil were 630 billion barrels in 1973. Published estimates of ultimate reserves average around 1.75 trillion barrels, although a figure as high as 4 trillion is occasionally mentioned. It would probably not be an exaggeration to say that no individual or organization anywhere can precisely calculate just how much oil is available in one form or another; but even so we must start looking forward to the demise of oil as the keystone of the world energy economy.

To be sure, major petroleum discoveries are undoubtedly still to be made, and these could just as easily happen sooner as later; but where the major industrial countries are concerned, the day of easily won conventional oil within national boundaries is about over. Most of the reserves of Canada, Russia, and the United States seem to be located in the arctic, where drilling costs alone may be greater than ten times those in more moderate climates. The greatest expense associated with this energy, however, is the cost of transporting it to the localities where it will be consumed.

Offshore resources are also expensive, and they will not become less costly in the future. Even so, the offshore oil in the North Sea must be regarded as an extremely valuable asset to both its owners and other countries in the area. Western Europe is in a very delicate position where energy is concerned, and requires a high production capacity in the North Sea and in politically less sensitive areas in case of another oil boycott by OPEC. Unfortunately, however, many European politicians seem incapable of understanding the full implications of an energy shortage, and as a result they treat the North Sea as a United Kingdom or Norwegian sideshow.

Given the enormity of the United Kingdom's economic problems, it has often been suggested that the rosy expectations of huge revenues from North Sea oil displayed by various individuals and organizations in that country are a malicious form of self-deception. However, estimates of North Sea reserves are constantly being revised upward instead of downward, and the cumulative effect of this oil on the current account of the foreign sector may come to 50 billion pounds. According to National Institute calculations, the production and consumption of oil may balance by 1980, and for some years after there can be a growing surplus. Table 2-3 shows some balance-of-payments effects of North Sea oil over the next few years.

Table 2-3
Balance of Payments Effects of North Sea Oil (estimated)

	1976	1977	1978	1979	1980	1985
Consumption[a]	92	94	97	101	105	
Production[a]	13	44	69	92	104	
Import Saving/ Export Gain	1090	2250	3400	5150	6600	14300
Additional Net Imports	−860	−600	−550	−500	−350	−100
Interests and Profits Repatriated	−200	−750	−750	−1250	−1750	−2600
Interest on Extra Reserves	60	150	350	550	900	4300
Net Effect	90	1050	2451	3950	5400	15900
Net Effect/GNP	0.1	0.80	1.80	2.50	3.10	5.210

Source: Treasury, Department of Energy, and National Institute estimates
Note: All figures except consumption and production in millions of pounds at current prices.
[a]In millions of tons

The first two lines of table 2-3 give the United Kingdom's estimated production and consumption in millions of tons; the next line shows import saving or the value of exports of North Sea oil. Then we have two lines with debit entries. The first gives the amount of imports of equipment that are being used in the North Sea project, and these taper off after the principal investments are completed. To this must be added interest and amortization on the foreign loans that were involved in exploiting these reserves, and also the profits (net of tax) of those foreign companies participating in the enterprise. Finally there is interest gained due to the accumulation of foreign exchange reserves, or interest outlays saved because of a reduction in foreign indebtedness. The net effect of these components is shown in the next to the last line, and this is followed by the ratio of this net gain to expected gross national product.

Although the casual reader may not realize it, 5 percent of the United Kingdom's gross national product represents a substantial amount indeed. Among other things this means that the United Kingdom's government could be obtaining up to 9 million pounds in annual revenues from North Sea oil by 1985, which could not only relieve some of the stress on British taxpayers, but also permit various social reforms to continue. The United Kingdom banking system might also find itself stabilized, with the long downward slide of the exchange rate finally checked. Although these things, by themselves, will not restore competitiveness to British industry, a return to normality in the monetary climate may help to create conditions favorable to solving various industrial problems.

With North Sea oil production increasing and Britain and Norway already contemplating self-sufficiency in energy, some thought will soon have to be given to how rapidly this new source of energy should be exploited. It might be argued that this depends upon technical developments in the nuclear field. The difficulty with nuclear energy is the rapidly growing inability of people from every walk of life to trust their duly elected representatives to satisfactorily manage the various aspects of nuclear security, in particular the disposal of nuclear waste. However if waste disposal technology moved rapidly enough to create a general feeling that this matter could be settled, then there is hardly any point in Britain and Norway going slow in the exploitation of their North Sea properties. If there is such a thing as a safe nuclear technology, and it is discovered, then both cost and environmental considerations probably call for the abandonment of the present fossil fuel technology as rapidly as possible.

This leads us to ask what strategy should be followed if nuclear equipment continues to be found objectionable and its large-scale deployment is deemed inadvisable. North Sea capacity should still be built at a very rapid rate, but energy-poor but otherwise affluent potential customers should give Britain some assurance that she will not have to worry about becoming a ward of the IMF should things take a bad turn. The Department of Energy in the United Kingdom believes that production could be sustained at 100 to 150 million tons a year after 1982, while Renton (1976) reports estimates which indicate that this could run as high as 300 million tons which, given estimated reserves of more than 5000 million tons, would mean being able to produce for about 20 years. Since Britain will be using only about 110 million tons of petroleum in 1982, she could conceivably export to Western Europe considerably more than she uses. Norway has similar possibilities, and thus the European energy equation may not be looking so bad as the Orwellian milestone of 1984 rolls around.

Natural gas is found in a geological environment similar to petroleum, and they are often found together. Given the ease with which gas can be handled and used, and its comparatively low cost, it has become an important fuel; on the basis of its cleanliness and the increasingly rigid pollution standards being introduced around the world, it should definitely retain its importance. Total recoverable world reserves of natural gas probably exceeded 1725 trillion cubic feet in 1972, and based on world consumption of approximately 40.5 trillion cubic feet per year, and a 5 percent growth rate, these could last about 22 years. However, the discovery rate for natural gas is high, and ultimately recoverable reserves will probably turn out to be at least six or seven times as high as the figures given above. A number of experts see gas playing a much more important role in the future energy picture.

Shale and Tar Sands

The rise in price of conventional oil has removed most of the economic barriers to exploiting large supplies of shale oil and oil from tar sands. The oil contained in tar sands would increase Canada's reserves at least ten times. Put another way, there is about two-thirds as much oil in various tar sand deposits in Canada as there is in the Middle East. Getting most of this oil out, however, will not be easy, since the areas in which it is located are both remote and extremely cold. The total cost of this oil, for a typical deposit, is now somewhat above North Sea oil; but as more experience is gained in exploiting these sources, this oil may become less expensive, particularly if in situ techniques can be introduced.

The largest deposits of shale oil are probably in the United States and are about as large as reserves of conventional oil. The cost of oil from high-grade shale is about the same as North Sea oil, but there are still a number of factors making it unattractive. With present technology an output of one million barrels a day would call for the processing, by surface means, of 5.7×10^8 tons of materials, which in turn would give rise to huge disposal and water supply problems. Under the circumstances, the large-scale exploitation of shale may have to wait until in situ techniques are better developed.

Hydroelectricity and Geothermal Energy

Hydroelectric power is an exceptionally clean source of energy. The unrealized potential of hydroelectricity is very large, but most of this potential is in underdeveloped regions where a general lack of demand and the availability of other sources of energy tend to prohibit the huge investments that would be necessary. Still, vast areas of Africa and Latin America could satisfy an enormous increase in the demand for electrical energy without requiring further resources of fossil fuels. On the other hand, North America and Europe have developed less than one-half of their hydroelectric potential, but exploiting the remaining sites would lead to conflicts about the use of land and water.

Geothermal energy is also exceptionally clean, and where available can be exploited for a moderate capital cost. In 1973 geothermal energy was being used in eight countries to generate electricity, and was also used directly for space heating, air conditioning, etc. Table 2-4 shows approximate capital costs for geothermal and various other energy sources.

Not much geoghermal energy is available in the main geothermal areas of the world at the present level of technology. However, it has often been claimed that if it were possible to get down ten or fifteen kilometers under the surface of the earth, where temperatures are up to several hundred degrees above those at sea level, geothermal power could become a key component in the definitive solution of the energy problem: the medium through which this energy would be obtained is the generation of steam. Professor Peter Kapitza (1976) is very impressed by the advantages of geothermal energy, and has suggested using underground atomic explosions to facilitate access to these supplies.

Table 2-4
1974 Capital Costs of Various Energy Sources (Estimated)

Source	Capital Cost (Dollars/Kw)
Tidal[a]	106
Geothermal	170
Oil and Gas	260
Gas	270
Coal and Gas	300
Coal	325
Oil	370
Wind[b]	500-700
Light Water Reactor	740
Breeder Reactor[c]	1000

[a]Estimated, the Bay of Fundy
[b]For Northeast United States
[c]For 1976; probably higher now

Solar and Wind Energy

Solar energy provides about 4 percent of the 75 quadrillion BTUs of energy consumed in the United States today. Various estimates suggest that about 25
percent of the United States' consumption of energy in fifty years will be
accounted for by solar technologies, although if goodwill toward an energy
source can influence its use, this figure will be considerably higher.

Since the economics of large-scale power generation still leave something to
be desired in most localities, the initial applications of solar systems will tend to
be concentrated at the household level, providing water and space heating.
Hippel and Williams (1975) have discussed some economic aspects of solar
energy and concluded that its advantages will soon be evident to most
households; for an average dwelling in the United States (except the northern-
most parts), that time may already be here. The same is true of southern France.
Solar energy along most of the Mediterranean coast is almost certainly competitive with other sources of energy today, and in most places this must be true a
hundred kilometers or more inland. Moreover, the costs of solar equipment can
probably be cut by 20 to 25 percent in the near future because of the economies
of large-scale production.

Generically, windpower also belongs to the solar technologies. According to
Hippel/Williams (1976), and Banks (1976), the economics of windpower are
attractive now, although aesthetic reasons limit enthusiasm for expanding its use.
A noise problem can make this medium unsatisfactory for generating electricity
for individual small houses, but this difficulty may not be important for
apartment buildings where the height of the installation would also give it some
advantages.

Because of the impossibility of predicting how much energy will be available
from wind or sun during a given period, backup systems to furnish other types
of energy would be essential; but in northern Europe and the northern United
States both wind and sun could be exploited in a single energy-producing
system, where the need for backup arrangements would be minimal.

Nuclear Energy

Nuclear energy falls under two headings: fission and fusion. Fission involves
splitting the nuclei of heavy elements such as uranium 235. (Uranium can thus
be considered fuel for a fission reactor.) As things now stand, if the reactor
programs that were projected several years ago had actually been undertaken, a
serious shortage of low-cost uranium reserves would have come about before the
end of this century.[9]

The specific answer to the potential shortage of nuclear fuel is the breeder
reactor which, by creating more fuel than it consumes, multiplies the available
supply of fuel by about twelve. In the breeder, thorium 232 becomes fissionable

uranium 233 or, more commonly, uranium 238 is transformed into fissionable plutonium 239.

The trouble is that the breeder is a little too hot to handle. It is hardly conceivable that a more dangerous substance than plutonium could be manufactured by mortal man and, as noted previously, there is no evidence that modern societies are administered by people with the kind of competence needed to keep this deadly material out of the wrong hands. The movement toward the plutonium economy is largely a panic reaction, based on the failure of responsible authorities to ascertain the nonplutonium energy supplies available and conserve them. What is needed is not only a sense of urgency, but also a sense of balance, and a little imagination—items that in some countries seem to be distinguished by their absence. Table 2-5 shows energy supplies for the United States and how they relate to the rest of the world.

Fusion energy is supposedly related to the source of energy for the sun and stars. Thus using it on earth means duplicating conditions similar to those found in the sun—including a temperature of 100 million degrees. The solution being considered at present involves a thermonuclear fusion of deuterium and tritium in a process similar to a hydrogen bomb. If this could be done, our troubles would be over. Thermonuclear fusion does not produce a significant amount of radioactive waste; the fusion reactor cannot explode, nor can its wastes be used in a bomb; and the almost inexhaustible supply of deuterium in the oceans can be extracted easily and inexpensively.

When do we have access to this equipment? Some people say never, but scientists of the caliber of Kapitza and Lehnert are more optimistic. They admit that it will take some time, but claim that eventually thermonuclear energy will be usable.

Table 2-5
United States Energy Supplies in Quads
(1 quad = 10^{15} B.T.U.)

	Normal Recovery	Enhanced[a] Recovery	Total	World/United States[b]
Gas	775	225	1030	4.44
Petroleum	800	300	1100	5.55
Oil Shale	1200	4600	5800	
Coal	12000		12000	4.30
Reactors	1800	128000	130000	10.00

Note: U.S. Energy Consumption in 1973 was 73 quads

[a]Enhanced Recovery with reactors means introducing the breeder.

[b]Ratio of world supplies to those of the United States, but *only* considering economically recoverable supplies. Otherwise these ratios would be much larger.

Conclusion

The choice facing decision makers is not so much what, but when—now, or after it is too late. This question is particularly pertinent to the United States, because with its huge reserves of coal and technologies that can exploit them, the United States can reorder the world energy scene. The promise of solar and wind power is also clear, but things are moving very rapidly in this field, and considering the capital costs of "going solar," it does not make sense to succumb to the lure of premature technologies.

Another energy resource that has not been discussed yet is energy efficiency. Ross and Williams (1976) give the following example. Consider a house with solar equipment that provides two-thirds of the required heating and which, together with an oil- or gas-fired backup system, is apparently superior in economic performance to a typical house. Compare this to a "fuel conservation house," which has a more or less conventional heating system but comes equipped with thermally massive walls, substantial insulation, sophisticated thermal controls, etc. The latter structure is superior from a cost standpoint. The point made by Ross and Williams is that merely raising the efficiency of the various components used in heating and insulation systems 20 and 50 percent would give at least the same savings as a well-designed, economical solar heating arrangement. Using the two together would probably be even more satisfactory.

Along the same lines, there has been a breakthrough in the design and use of glass for insulation, and even now tremendous savings can be realized simply by installing the right type and amount of insulating glass. Similarly, the use of fast-acting automatic doors has substantially reduced heating costs for industrial structures such as factories and warehouses.

On another level we find such thing as built-in obsolescence and careless engineering—both of which waste energy by necessitating more manufacturing than is necessary. There is also sheer waste on the part of consumers. It is difficult to say just how much electricity is wasted in households and factories, but it may be possible to provide incentives to save energy, or penalize waste. Electrical rates are now fairly high in most countries, and as an incentive they should be lowered for consumption below a certain level, and raised drastically above that point. The success of programs of this type undoubtedly depends upon consumers being informed of just how much they personally have to gain if they save energy. For instance, they could be sent detailed notices telling them how much they spent for electricity the previous year, and how much they would save if they reduced consumption by 25 percent, 30 percent, etc.

There is also enormous scope for the more widespread use of industrial waste heat, or cogeneration. The production of steam squanders a large part of the energy in fuel, and instead of fuel being used to generate steam it should first produce electricity, with the waste heat from power generation being transformed to process steam. In an important article Lovins (1976) points out that cogeneration provides about 4 percent of electricity in the United States, but about 29 percent in West Germany. As a result, an optimal use of cogeneration combined with a more efficient use of electricity would reduce the direct use of electricity in the United States by one third, and central station operation (which Lovins regards as an element of an inefficient system) could be cut by 60 percent.

One further point must be made in this chapter. Under no circumstances must the industrial world turn its back on nuclear energy. The present strategy of keeping the increase in nuclear installations to a minimum and emphasizing conservation is undoubtedly correct. But everything considered, the environment cannot tolerate much longer a continued exponential growth in the use of fossil fuels.[10] Of course if, as Cochran (1976) maintains, it is possible to manufacture nonpolluting fuels from coal, then this could be the medium run solution to the energy crisis; however, the evidence on cost and environmental effects has not yet been completely evaluated. Most important, the major industrial countries must not permit a situation to come about such as that in Sweden since the recent elections, where incompetent politicians in search of short-run political gains are trying to close the door on nuclear research. At the same time that barriers must be raised to a panicky introduction of the nuclear community, nuclear research must go forward faster than ever before.

Notes

1. Toffler seems to have retracted a great many of the predictions he offered in *Future Shock* in his new book *The Eco-Spasm Report* (1975). Despite a certain regrettable tendency to quote economists who do not know anything about economics, Toffler's book is rich in ideas.

2. The psychology of scientific invention is a fairly old subject, but what we need now is a little research into the psychology of reception. We do know that most articles in the leading economics journals are read only by graduate students, who quite wisely forget their contents as soon as they are examined on them. The few absolutely top articles published every year get about half a dozen readers from among members of the profession—assuming word is out that they are "must" reading. Professor Corden's paper (1976) was prevented from obtaining a general readership because Corden unwisely used a diagram on the second page of his article which implied that the reader needed some knowledge of consumer's surplus in order to follow the exposition. What is more interesting is the failure of those economists reading and understanding Corden's paper to disseminate its contents more widely. One reason for this is that Corden showed that the basic macroeconomics of the oil crisis was very simple indeed; as a result, the foundations and research councils might hesitate to fund a great deal of expensive research on what was obviously an open-and-shut matter.

Therefore the recycling issue was blown up out of all proportion, and thanks to a number of popular misconceptions about the importance of monetary as opposed to real factors, the research money began flowing in that direction. For the best nontechnical summary of the oil crisis, see "How OPEC's High Prices Strangle World Growth," *Business Week*, December 20, 1976.

3. In 1975 oil imports cost the United Kingdom approximately 3 billion pounds, of which 2 billion represented the increase in oil prices. Of this 1 billion was offset by exports to the OEC, while the other 1 million represented a decline in money demand.

4. This does not mean that the real income of every individual in the OIC would remain the same. If the government were to print and pass out money on street corners one day, the people who stayed home on that occasion would be losers.

5. See the appendix to this chapter for an example of how this could work.

6. In the United States comprehensive public employment schemes are implicit in the controversial Humphrey-Hawkins bill, and were made explicit in a proposal some years ago by Daniel Moynihan, which envisaged the government as "the employer of last resort." Many businessmen in the United States resent such programs, although the opinion here is that it would be more logical if they supported them—in fact, supported them with the same enthusiasm and tactics of the antiwar demonstrators of the 1960s and early 1970s. The recent high unemployment in the United States may have raised productivity somewhat, and perhaps decreased absenteeism, but everything considered the high unemployment community can hardly be regarded as a pleasant place to live. (In Europe, of course, the high unemployment of the young is rapidly developing into a direct threat to democracy.) The interesting thing is that if from the cost of a full employment program we were to subtract the cost of some welfare programs, a part of the cost for crime suppression, the implicit social costs associated with the demoralization of the families of the unemployed, the earning power lost later in life and various social costs due to the change in attitude of the unemployed toward work, and a few other things, we would find this to be one of the best investments any society could make.

7. A logistic curve has the equation $\log Y = a - b/X$, or $Y = e^{a - b/X}$. Its slope is:

$$\frac{dY}{dX} = e^{a-b/X}\left(\frac{b}{X^2}\right) \text{with} \quad \frac{d^2Y}{dX^2} = e^{a-b}\left(X\frac{b^2}{X^4} - \frac{2b}{X^3}\right)$$

The slope is positive for positive X; there is an inflection point at $X = b/2$; and as $X \to \alpha$, $Y \to e^a$. X and Y might be taken as time and energy consumption, respectively. The curve is shown in figure 2n-1.

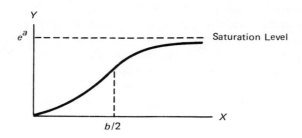

Figure 2n-1.

8. It is difficult to prove this for the general case (n factors), and in truth a general case proof is required; but the two-factor case is suggestive. Assume a neoclassical production function $Q = F(K,L)$ with homogeneity of the first degree; and also assume capital complementary with energy. We then have $Q/L = f(K/L) = f(k)$ and $\partial Q/\partial K = f'(K/L) = f'(k)$, with $k = K/L$. From EulersTheorem we immediately get $\partial Q/\partial L = w_L = f(k) - f'(k)k$. If the real wage w_L is fixed, then k must also be constant to satisfy this relationship; and so if we decrease the amount of K (because of decreasing its complement energy) then to keep k (K/L) constant, L must also decrease.

9. For some countries the shortage would come much later, and for others much earlier since, in all likelihood, their suppliers in other countries would probably be persuaded to cut them off. Table 2n-1 indicates the cutback in nuclear programs.

10. Environmental problems associated with fossil fuels may or may not include such things as the Torrey Canyon accident, or the recent offshore catastrophe in the Ekofisk area of the North Sea. The opinion here is that there is no more reason for an oil disaster to take place in the North Sea than for a skyscraper or bridge to collapse in downtown Oslo. The reason this accident took place, and similar accidents will probably take place in the future, is that

Table 2n-1

Country	Nuclear Capacity	Target 1985, as of 1/1/1975	Target 1985, as of 1/6/1976
Italy	0.60	26.00	17.0
Germany	3.30	52.50	39.5
France	2.92	55.5	42.6
United Kingdom	5.70	15.2	14.5

Figures are in thousands of megawatts. Recently most of them have been adjusted downward substantially.

the parliament of Norway—only slightly less than those of Denmark and Sweden—is obsessed by abstractions and irrelevances instead of meaningful issues, and thus did not pay enough attention to the possibility of a serious mishap in the North Sea. In fact, oil was pumped for six years in the Ekofisk belt without adequate emergency equipment.

Appendix 2A

We can examine one possible result of increased import prices by considering the two-sector input-output scheme presented in figure 2A-1.

To keep the exposition simple, we assume that only sector one requires imported inputs (of oil, for example); and that only the output of sector two is exported. There is a domestic final demand F_1 and F_2 for both products, and both use some of the domestic resource $\bar{R}$ in their production. Taking P_r as the rental rate of the domestic resource, and P_m as the price of the imported input, we get the following input-output relationships:

$$a_1 P_r + b P_m = P_1 \tag{2A.1}$$

$$a_2 P_r = P_2 \tag{2A.2}$$

$$b T_1 = M \tag{2A.3}$$

$$a_1 T_1 + a_2 T_2 = \bar{R} \tag{2A.4}$$

$$P_m M = P_2 E_2 \tag{2A.5}$$

$$F_2 = T_2 - E_2 \tag{2A.6}$$

$$F_1 = T_1 \tag{2A.7}$$

The exchange rate will be put equal to unity; as shown in equation 2A.5, it is assumed that trade always balances; and full employment will be assumed for the domestic resource. We now get from equations 2A.4, 2A.6, and 2A.7:

$$\bar{R} = a_1 F_1 + a_2 (F_2 + E_2)$$

Similarly we have $E_2 = P_m M / P_2 = b P_m T_1 / P_2 = b P_m F_1 / P_2$ from equations 2A.3, 2A.5, and 2A.7. Thus we get:

$$\bar{R} = F_1 \frac{a_1 P_r + b P_m}{P_r} + a_2 F_2 \tag{2A.8}$$

Using equations 2A.1 and 2A.2 we can write 2A.8 as:

$$F_2 = \frac{\bar{R}}{a_2} - \frac{P_1}{P_2} F_1 \tag{2A.9}$$

49

	(1)	(2)			
(1)	0	0	0	F_1	T_1
(2)	0	0	E_2	F_2	T_2
Domestic Resource	a_1	a_2			
Imported Input	b	0			

E: Exports
F: Final demand
T: Total demand

Figure 2A-1. Simple Input-Output Table for an Open Economy.

This is analogous to what Dorfman, Samuelson, and Solow (1958) call a social transformation curve: it shows the tradeoff between F_1 and F_2. We now need some means of choosing a point on this curve. One possibility is to define a utility function $U = U(F_1, F_2)$, and solve the following nonlinear program.

$$U = U(F_1, F_2) = \text{Max}$$

$$F_2 = \frac{\overline{R}}{a_2} - \frac{P_1}{P_2} F_1$$

$$F_1, F_2 \geqslant 0$$

If we make neoclassical assumptions about the utility function, the solution of this simple program is obviously $U_1/P_1 = U_2/P_2$. Diagramatically this result takes on the form shown in figure 2A-2(a).

We can now investigate what happens when the price of the imported input increases. From equations 2A.8 and 2A.9 we see that P_1 increases, and so the social transformation curve swings inward. Thus, in figure 2A-2(a) we move from utility curve U_0 to curve U_1. This is equivalent to a fall in real income.

Another way of approaching this is to note that from the above equations we have:

$$\frac{\partial F_2}{\partial P_m} = \frac{\partial F_2}{\partial P_1} \frac{\partial P_1}{\partial P_m} < 0 \qquad \text{since} \qquad \frac{\partial F_2}{\partial P_1} < 0, \frac{\partial P_1}{\partial P_m} > 0$$

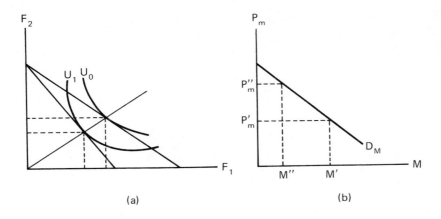

Figure 2A-2. Social Transformation Curve and Import Demand Curve.

The next step is to draw a demand curve for the imported good. This is shown in figure 2A-2(b). According to this curve, an increase in the price of the imported input results in a decrease in imports. We now notice from equation 2A.3 that a decrease in imports means a decrease in T_1, and from 2A.7 this results in a decrease in F_1. Again, with both F_1 and F_2 at a lower level, the real income must decrease.

If the reader desires, this effect can also be obtained from macroeconomic considerations. The money income Y in this model is constant, since $Y = P_1 F_1 + P_2 F_2 = P_r \bar{R} =$ Constant. Real income Y_r is, however, Y/p, where p is an aggregate price index or the aggregate price level deflator. One method of forming this deflator is by taking $P = w_1 p_1 + w_2 p_2$, with $w_i = T_i/(T_1 + T_2)$ and $i = 1,2$. The results obtained with this approach are roughly similar to those presented by Tumlir (1974) in his "Case 1."

3

The Political Economy of Primary Commodities

In a recent issue of a well-known scholarly journal, the editor, in introducing a memorandum written by John Maynard Keynes, assured his readership that Keynes's meditations should be of interest to all international economists engaged in contemplating and designing the "future international economic order." As luck would have it, this scholar did not choose to tell us why he thought economists should be engaged in this challenging and important work. Nor, for that matter, did he reveal his private roster of who these fortunate scholar-statesmen should be. However, these oversights may be unimportant in the cosmic scheme of things. While mankind may have yet to learn that war is too important to be left to generals (at least some generals), there seems to be a growing consensus that international economic affairs must at all costs be kept out of the hands of academic economists.

One explanation for this regrettable state of affairs can be found in the way economists have approached the rather serious matter of economic development. The interested noneconomist knows instinctively that the standard of living of the industrial world is based on the building of societies in which the highest premium is placed on technical skill and training, and in which even a sizable percentage of those people educated in the liberal arts and humanities do not turn up their noses at the thought of doing some productive work. For diverse academic economists and diplomats busily fabricating the "New World Economic Order," as the United Nations Special Assembly of 1974 chose to designate the glorious new era into which the less fortunate countries are supposed to emerge, economic development is largely a cerebral concept. It involves convening the right meeting, at which the right phrases are coined and the right speeches are made, and if possible arranging to convene another meeting. Unfortunately, although very few people have any faith in this particular approach, it is still easier to recognize the existence of nonsense than to introduce a remedy against it.

In case the reader is not up to date in these matters, the New International Economic Order is only the latest slogan concocted by the bureaucrats and aid experts trying to gain support for further misadventures in international philanthropy. Fifteen years ago it was the "Revolution of Rising Expectations," followed by the "First Development Decade," and then the Second. None of these could truthfully be called fiascoes, since they served their real purpose. This real purpose was to provide some upper-class welfare for the superbly fed men with tax-free incomes who, as the result of the application of a kind of inverted Darwinism, have been appointed by Fate to sit in elaborate conference halls and ponder various questions having to do with the future of the world economy.

At the present, however, not only is there not going to be a New World Economic Order, but the time and energy wasted in talking about one is going to increase the possibility of Malthusian calamities like those recently seen in Bangla Desh and the Sahel. Despite the reluctance of all parties to express themselves on the subject, the starvation and malnutrition in these places were not just the result of simple economic backwardness, but can explicitly be attributed to corrupt and inefficient governments and international agencies attempting to substitute grandiose rhetoric for elementary economic logic and unremitting hard work. Moreover, chimeras like the New World Economic Order encourage the proliferation of this type of situation, since they deemphasize technical proficiency and productive work, and picture development as the abstention of the industrial countries from a portion of their worldly possessions, and the transfer of these goods to the less-developed world.

This chapter will briefly examine some of the issues raised at the sixth and seventh special sessions of the United Nations, the first such sessions to be exclusively concerned with international economic affairs and cooperation. Among the pronouncements of these august assemblies and the various kangaroo congresses they summoned to straighten out the international economic scene, we find one which insists that 25 percent of the world's industry must be located in the LDCs by the year 2000, and that the role of these countries as exporters of primary commodities must be altered. It now seems more likely than ever that exports of primary commodities from the LDCs will continue to increase, even though more of them may receive more processing domestically. The principal reason for this is the lack of productivity of many LDCs outside the primary commodity sector; if they do not produce primary commodities, they may find it difficult to produce and export anything significant. What should be done, then, is to attack the reason for this regrettable state of affairs, and this means—as pointed out by Berg (1977)—that these countries need a New Internal Economic Order.

Commodity Power

The realities of commodity power are considerably less drastic than the informal rhetoric surrounding the subject suggests. The "demands" of the LDCs, which make up the agenda of commodity power, are no more pernicious than the demands the industrial countries periodically make of each other: higher prices for their products, guaranteed access to markets (particularly for their light manufactured goods), and stabilization of export earnings. According to Mc-Culloch (1975) what is revolutionary in all this is the belief of these countries that such measures will constitute a major channel for the redistribution of wealth from the industrial to the less-developed countries. Perhaps it is a matter of terminology, but what McCulloch labels revolutionary strikes me as a mere mistake in elementary arithmetic. Given the comparatively small value of nonfuel items traded internationally, no genuine redistribution of wealth could come about through acceding to the LDCs' demands.

The influence of OPEC as a precept and example for the partisans of commodity power should not be underestimated, but OPEC's main impact has been on its customers in the industrial countries. An organization that was born merely to protest the loss by producing countries of a few cents of revenue to some multinational oil companies eventually achieved an extraordinary increase in both its earnings and power without the permission of the oil companies or the developed countries. With this in mind, the developed countries (with Dr. Kissinger as their mentor and spokesman) suggested in May 1975 that the time had come for the regulation of commodity questions. Just what regulation they contemplated cannot be discussed here, since once it became clear to Kissinger & company that the nonfuel producers were more mouth than muscle, the project was allowed to wither on the vine. Eventually a semipermanent talk shop was established in Paris under the name "North-South Dialogues," where high-salaried people could exchange illusions and memoranda and receive journalists in an atmosphere of genteel animosity.

There are a number of interesting paradoxes here. The underlying rationale of the New International Economic Order is that the international distribution of wealth can be changed through intercountry transfers of cash and goods, rather than through a conscientious and systematic elevation of international productivity. We would therefore expect it to be denounced by anyone at the giving end of this arrangement. But in fact, in countries like Holland and Sweden it has been greeted with sympathy and occasional enthusiasm, even though the well-educated or well-read know that for every 100 florins or crowns going to a worthy cause in a poor country, at least another 100 must be contributed to the price of a plane ticket, cocktail, or luxury hotel room for some corrupt official of that country or the unproductive employee of an international or aid organization.

However, a number of real economic advantages might accrue to all parties if some of the inequities of the primary commodities markets could be rectified. The raw materials industries in the LDCs have contributed much to the development of the international economy, and conceivably they have an even greater role to play in the future. The rules of comparative advantage could probably be best served if many manufacturing and processing industries were relocated in the Third World, where there are large potential supplies of energy and raw materials. The continued poisoning of relationships between the developed and less developed parts of the world has, however, made developed countries afraid to relinquish direct control over the supplies of various products. Even if this were not so, many LDCs no longer welcome foreign firms and investments if they can avoid it. One of the problems here is that the decision makers in the developed countries are not prepared to make the comparatively modest financial commitment necessary to turn the primary commodity industries in the LDCs into a base for general economic development until they must. On the other hand, they have nothing against lavishing untold millions or billions on untied development aid and military assistance, with its vast complex of rakeoffs and pretentious waste.

The Actors

At this point some attention must be paid to various characteristics of the actors appearing in our drama. Among the industrial countries, the United States, Canada, Australia, and perhaps one or two others are basically different from Japan and most of Western Europe.[1] The principal difference turns on the availability of natural and energy resources, either at hand or latent. Despite the depth and brilliance of European and Japanese technology and the vigor and skill of both labor and management, which have resulted in record increases in the standard of living outside the United States, these parts of the world are quite vulnerable to sundry turbulences like the energy crisis. In the long run technical progress may overcome this shortcoming, but for the time being most of these natural-resource-deficient countries must try to reach some sort of accommodation with the raw-material-producing countries. At the same time some of them must hope (and perhaps pray) that their domestic political situation does not deteriorate to a point where politicians cannot look after external economic relations.

On the other hand, the United States is under no long-run compunction to bend over backwards in its relationships with the Third World or, by extension, its European or Japanese colleagues. The United States still possesses enormous supplies of natural resources and the technology needed to exploit them; their agricultural sector has never been more efficient; and their political stability seems to be returning at a time when several key industrial countries in Europe are showing a tendency to come apart at the seams. It is thus not surprising that the United States felt strong enough to agitate against a generalized system of preferences when many of its European friends favored such an arrangement.[2]

Even more heterogeneous in economic strength and political leverage, however, are the LDCs, even though both they and their patrons in the developed world encourage acceptance of the myth that these nations speak with a single voice. This issue is so vast that it can only be skimmed at this point, but it does no harm to single out four main groups of countries. First there are those with definitely sound economic prospects, such as Brazil and perhaps Iran; second, there are those whose prospects are based almost exclusively on the outcome of the world energy situation. Just what the future holds for them is difficult to say, but in the next ten to twenty years some of these nations may drastically revise their expectations in one direction or the other.

Third, there are the very poor "Fourth World" countries, for whom an extended dose of benign neglect would undoubtedly be the best remedy. These countries need cultural revolutions to replace their present stone-age lifestyles with postures more in keeping with the development goals so highly touted by their leaders in diverse international forums. Finally, there are those countries that seem to have both the human and material prerequisites for rapid economic growth, but where corruption has been institutionalized.

To illustrate the quandary in which some of these countries find themselves, we can consider the less-developed copper producers. After eight years of refusing to enter into a dialogue with the major consumers, and only two years after the OPEC initiative that signaled to many a new aggressiveness on the part of all primary producers, the Intergovernmental Council of Copper Exporting Countries (CIPEC)—the organization of the less-developed copper producers—requested talks with the industrial countries. The explanation here is not simply that, because of the reduced demand for copper, several CIPEC countries found themselves facing bankruptcy, but that these producers could not devise and coordinate a program of reduced production, even though there has been a severe oversupply for the past eighteen months. Since they could not work with each other in this matter, what was more natural than to attempt to establish a new type of relation with the "other side"?

The Tools of Commodity Power

The present objective of commodity power is for various countries to control market variables related to the commodities they produce—although UNCTAD, in its more expansive moments, looks forward to the day when it can control the trade of all primary commodities. The device for this control is an international commodity agreement signed by both producers and consumers. A much more straightforward arrangement is a commodity cartel such as OPEC, which proceeds with or without the support of consumers.

The purpose of a cartel or commodity agreement is to increase the price of or revenue from certain products or to "stabilize" price or revenue. When used by producers, "stabilize" is generally a euphemism for "raise," although McCulloch feels that increased prices might also be stabilized prices. A cartel usually sets a price, leaving it up to the consumer to buy the amount he desires; but a cartel occasionally wants to determine the quantity it sells. OPEC has successfully used export taxes to restrict the amount sold, and some bauxite producers have used these levies to attempt to raise world prices.

On the other hand, since an international commodity agreement is signed by consumers, its mechanism must be somewhat more sophisticated than that of a cartel. The tin agreement provides for export controls, for example, but only under certain well-defined circumstances. The principal subjects of a commodity agreement would most likely include buffer stocks, buffer funds and compensatory financing measures, import-export agreements, and proposals for reducing tariffs and establishing manufacturing capacity in LDCs. Since buffer stocks seem to have a high priority in the thinking of those consumer countries inclined to go along with commodity agreements, the next section of this book will discuss the tin agreement, the tin buffer stock, and UNCTAD's integrated program; the following section will take up the possibility of a bauxite cartel. But first some general background will be provided.

Buffer stocks are supposed to restrict supply when the price is too low and increase supply when the price is too high. They do this by purchasing the commodity in the first instance, and selling it in the second. In the case of tin a *floor* and *ceiling* were established: when the market price is near the floor, a buying mechanism is supposed to be automatically activated, and the opposite happens at the ceiling. There is also a band that surrounds what is known as a middle price, which is a kind of datum; within this band, the buffer stock management can follow the dictates of its conscience.

Buffer stocks are not supposed to make a profit, but merely to cover their own costs. The effectiveness of the buffer stock is largely a matter of the amount of resources (commodity and money) at its disposal. The contention in the sequel is that the ceiling price is basically uninteresting, while the tin buffer stock, for example, does not possess enough financial resources to support the floor price through conventional buying; its real weapon on the down side is the export stop or export quotas that it can impose, or the threat of these measures. The results of the tin buffer stock over the years have been inconclusive at best. They may have smoothed out some minor fluctuations from time to time, but they do not seem to have had any effect on larger price movements. Of course it would be difficult to find anyone prepared to claim that this buffer stock has stimulated economic or social progress in the tin-producing countries. It has, however, provided some pleasant and not very strenuous employment for the staff of the Tin Council in an interesting part of London, far from the sweat and clamor of the mines and pits where the tin ore is being dug up and processed.

Buffer funds, revenue supporting schemes, compensatory financing arrangements and so on are intended to provide the seller with the equivalent of a certain price or revenue. Naturally, even a high price will not mean much when the amount sold is small, and so producers would prefer revenue or income maintenance schemes. Import-export agreements are supposed to stipulate minimum prices for sellers and maximum prices for buyers, depending upon the amount traded. The sugar agreement, which is a part of the Lomé Convention, includes an export-import commitment.

A typical compensatory financing arrangement is operated by the IMF, and between 1963 and 1975 thirty-two countries made fifty-seven drawings totalling about $1.25 billion. Because of the special nature of the IMF, a number of stipulations are attached to its use. The country in question must have an overall payments need; if low earnings from one commodity are balanced by high earnings from another, the country may be ineligible. The predicament which led to the drawing must be essentially short-term, and if possible caused by circumstances beyond the control of the country, such as a natural catastrophe. The IMF also requires a country using the facility to try to improve its balance of payments.

The formula used by the IMF to calculate effective export earnings involves a five-year average centering on the year in question. Actual export earnings for the first three years are averaged with projected values for the next two years. If the value obtained is under a certain datum (computed from a trend of export earnings), then the country is entitled to make a drawing. The amount of financing available to a country is related to its quota—the amount it has deposited with the IMF—and is determined by factors such as the country's size and wealth. Up to one-half of the quota can be drawn under the compensatory financing facility, with not more than one-quarter drawn in a given year. Interest must be paid on these drawings, and repayments are to be made within three to five years (as is the case with regular drawings).

There are a number of variants on the IMF compensatory financing arrangement, and because some fairly comprehensive commodity agreements might be concluded in the not-too-distant future, we must ask what type would be desirable. As far as I am concerned, the essential thing is to encourage producing countries to restructure their economies more efficiently, which probably means introducing some kind of scheme that rewards success. This, by itself, rules out playing games with a buffer stock. What is needed is an import- or revenue-supporting scheme with regressive repayment provisions: if transfers over a period of time improve the economic performance of a country, then that country need not repay the transfers. Because economic performance can be difficult to measure, it might be preferable to use export success, as measured by a series of indicators.

As quoted by Rose (1976), Professor J. Michael Finger of the United States Treasury has cast his vote for some kind of direct assistance, although Dr. Finger and apparently Mr. Rose seem to think the main issue is whether consumer-taxpayers in the industrial countries would be willing to make, or could be fooled into making, transfers in what they call an inefficient and indirect form (via commodity agreements) when they were unwilling to make them directly as foreign aid.

This is an interesting observation, but hardly the "real" issue. Willing or not, the consumer-taxpayers of countries like the United States have contributed scores of billions of dollars to inefficiencies and various forms of nonsense in remote parts of the globe without thinking twice about it; it seems likely that they are prepared to continue this practice to some extent. What must be done now is to eliminate the more obvious extravagances. Despite the implication that conventional foreign aid exhibits some merit, the truth is that except for that portion which goes directly into Swiss banks, much aid usually turns out to be an unameliorated curse. A positive side of commodity agreements is that they may allow the financing countries to insist that the primary-product-producing countries use at least a portion of these transfers for sensible investment activities rather than luxury consumption or showy projects.

Another commodity agreement of sorts, the Lomé Convention, is an export stabilization plan for twelve primary commodities; the conditions for sugar are in a special agreement.[3] The convention is between the EEC and forty-six African, Caribbean, and Pacific LDCs, and covers a number of issues related to trade and aid. This convention seems to be regarded as a model by various personalities in the EEC, and lately some talk has originated from the high councils of that organization about an analogous convention to cover minerals. The leader in all this is of course Holland; there is apparently no limit to the welfare projects that the Dutch bureaucrats want to see financed—both at home and abroad.

The purpose of the Lomé Convention is to protect primary product exporters against export losses involving the EEC. Under the "Stabex" system, Third World members of the convention are eligible for monetary transfers whenever earnings from one year's exports to the EEC fall below a certain level. Stabex takes a commodity-by-commodity approach, and financing tends to be automatic rather than any complicated administrative procedure. For the thirty-four least-developed countries associated with the convention, the funds received need not be repaid, while the others receive interest-free loans which are supposed to be repaid if and when export proceeds increase. On the whole, repayment provisions are fairly obscure, and what it comes down to is that Stabex is a kind of public relations stunt. In most respects, though, it is a fairly harmless gesture, since its financing involves only about $75 million a year.

The International Tin Agreement, and the UNCTAD
Integrated Program

As a result of the Fourth International Tin Agreement, seven producer and twenty-two consumer countries are now members of the International Tin Council. (The best-known nonmembers are China and the United States.) Among other things, the agreement provides for a buffer stock, where contributions are mandatory for producers, and voluntary for consumers.

Of the major tin producers, Bolivia obtains about 42 percent of its export revenue from tin, Malaysia 15 percent, Thailand 6 percent, and Indonesia 2.5 percent. Tin producers are also geographically concentrated, since Malaysia,

Indonesia, Thailand, and Bolivia account for 79 percent of world production. There are approximately forty-five different brands of tin available from twenty countries; thirty of these brands are registered for delivery on the London Metal Exchange.

Establishing the right tin price has always been a bit of a problem, since it is only rarely possible to satisfy both consumers and producers. The psychological factors that led to the approval of a tin buffer stock are difficult to pinpoint, although on the basis of the facts noted above, the tin-producing countries today are in a fairly good position to operate a successful cartel. However, in its twenty years of existence the International Tin Agreement (ITA) has convinced many individuals and organizations that it is a genuine success, and in at least one sense it is: tin consumers have not called for its abolition and producers have not threatened to come with something more radical.

When we examine the tin buffer stock's results, it is difficult to be impressed. The simulations of Smith and Shink (1976) and the econometric model of Desai (1966) provide considerable evidence that buffer stocks have had little effect on the stability of the price of tin. Banks (1972) has argued that instead of the buffer stock, the main device for safeguarding the floor price has been the use or threat of export or production controls. The buffer stock management has never had much luck in defending the ceiling price; however, few people connected with the industry really care about this. In reality, the producing countries do not want the ceiling price defended, and since this price is usually exceeded during periods of economic prosperity, tin buyers do not usually feel put out at having to pay higher charges, especially since they know that in good times these can be passed on to the final users of the product.[4]

The simulations mentioned above indicate (but do not prove) that to have kept price movements between 1956 and 1973 to within ±15 percent a year, a tin buffer stock of about 120,000 tons (with a value of more than $1 billion at present prices) would have been necessary. Actually, the tin buffer stock has never been larger than 20,000 tons and has averaged less. By the same token Finger and Kreinin (1976) state that to have kept copper price movements within a range of ±15 percent over the same period, a buffer stock of nearly 4 million tons would have been necessary. At the present low prices such an inventory would cost about $6 billion.

There is also the matter of the United States Strategic Stockpile, which is also called the General Services Administration (GSA) Stockpile. Virtually since its formation it has played an important role in stabilizing metal prices in the United States, and given the position of the United States as a tin consumer, it has had an important effect on the world price of tin. Since the early 1960s the policy of the GSA stockpile's management has been to reduce gradually its holdings of such commodities as tin; since at one time it maintained an inventory that was more than twice the annual consumption of the non-centrally planned countries (and more than 4 times the annual consumption of the United

States) it could obviously place considerable downward pressure on the price of tin. In recent years it has not been overly considerate of the feelings of tin producers but, prior to 1973, whenever tin prices were low and displayed a tendency to fall, the GSA stockpile management limited its selling. This can be inferred from table 3-1. In addition, the buildup of the GSA stockpile took place when the United States dollar was a premium monetary unit in the world economy, and sales to the stockpile enabled many tin producers to carry out important investment programs. This did not, however, keep them from leveling intense criticism against the stockpile management for the disposal policy they have followed in recent years.

Among its various strategies, the ITA buffer stock has usually tried to fix the floor price so low that it would not require a great deal of defending. Fox

Table 3-1
The Consumption and Stockpiling of Tin, 1956-1973

Year	Price[a]	Consumption[b]	ΔS (ITC)	ΔS (GSA)	Stockholding[c] (GSA)
1956	101.4	153.7	0	−19.5	347.0
1957	96.2	150.4	−15.5	−4.0	351.0
1958	95.1	143.1	−8.2	0	351.0
1959	102.0	149.9	13.5	−1.8	352.8
1960	101.4	159.7	0	−5.2	357.8
1961	113.3	158.8	10.2	2.8	355.1
1962	114.6	163.3	−3.3	2.2	352.9
1963	116.6	166.9	3.3	10.0	342.8
1964	157.6	172.3	0	29.1	313.7
1965	187.2	171.5	0	24.4	289.3
1966	164.1	172.7	0	16.4	272.9
1967	153.4	172.2	−4.8	7.4	265.5
1968	148.1	175.5	−6.6	3.6	261.9
1969	164.5	183.5	6.8	1.7	260.2
1970	174.2	183.4	3.5	3.5	256.7
1971	167.3	185.7	−5.4	1.8	254.9
1972	177.5	186.4	−5.8	0.2	254.7
1973	227.5	202.4	11.5	19.5	235.1

Source: International Tin Council; United States Government Stockpile Reports; Banks (1976); *Commodity Year Book*, various issues.

Note: For changes in inventories ΔS, (−) indicates sell and (+) buy (in metric tons).

[a]In cents/pound

[b]Non-centrally planned economies

[c]End of year figures (metric tons)

(1974), himself a buffer stock official, states plainly that the tin council followed rather than anticipated market forces when fixing its price. This was inevitable, because just as the inventories of tin controlled by the buffer stock management were never sufficient to make more than token effort to defend the ceiling price, the financial resources of the council never really amounted to much.

One final point. In their assessment of the tin buffer stock, Smith and Shink conclude that export controls have been a rather minor factor in the market. This may or may not be so; but even though supply restriction is considered in bad taste (and as a result there has been a febrile and time-consuming search for reasons why it cannot work), in theory it can always work—at least for a short time.

The UNCTAD Integrated Program

The UNCTAD integrated program was launched in 1975, partially as a reaction to UNCTAD III—the 1973 congress in Santiago that was called a "farce" by the *London Economist*. It is constructed on five basic proposals:

1. Establishment of international buffer stocks for eighteen commodities
2. Creation of an international fund to finance the buffer stock
3. Negotiation of supply and purchase agreements by individual countries
4. Compensatory financing to stabilize export earnings of producing countries
5. Expansion of raw materials processing activities in producing countries

The novelty of this plan is its ambitions: it would be working with a broad group of raw materials produced in over 100 countries, and the guiding mechanism would be in the hands of international bureaucrats whose technical and administrative abilities are limited, to say the least. Professor Johnson (1976) has traced some of the background of the integrated program in terms of his own association with UNCTAD. In his opinion the program is without meaning, containing as it does mutually inconsistent goals.

The way to put some meaning into it is to introduce the word equity. This requires insuring the raw-material-producing countries against having their economies ruined and their development programs set back indefinitely because of a sudden, temporary fall in demand for their products. In addition, work should begin immediately to make it possible for the LDCs to expand their processing capacity. (This rather extensive topic will be treated later in the chapter.)

Insofar as these suggestions are a part of the integrated program, so much the better, because I believe that two aspects of the integrated program should make it unacceptable to anyone not directly benefiting from its patronage. The first is that it will serve as an instrument of confrontation between the Third World and the industrial countries. The secretary general of UNCTAD has spoken at least once of the value of having muscle behind UNCTAD's aspirations, and presumably within his thinking six or seven billion dollars of commodity stocks will provide a means for "redressing the balance between the developed and developing countries." Then, too, the idea stands an excellent chance of becoming still one more system of indoor charity for the nepotists and professional idealists on the U.N. conference itinerary. The immediate result of accepting this scheme will be a sprouting of high salaried jobs and expensive structures near the Place des Nations in Geneva, and these will remain long after the integrated program, with all its theatricality, waste, and economic irrelevance, has been relegated to the scrap heap.

Other Stockpile Schemes

The most important national stockpile scheme has already been mentioned: the United States Strategic Stockpile. This has, at one time or another, contained 50 different items, and even in its present depleted form it has a value of more than $7 billion. In October 1976, it was decided to restock this inventory, bringing the value of its contents up to between $13 and $15 billion. Purchases are scheduled to begin in the autumn of 1977.

Included in this stockpile will be 1,180,000 tons of copper; the earlier maximum was about one million tons. The intention is that this inventory is intended to enable the United States to withstand a temporary interruption in imports, and given that the United States has a large domestic production which could be increased if necessary, the contemplated inventory—together with conservation and increased recycling—should provide a respectable buffer in an emergency.

Japan is also in the market for a large buffer stock, and Spain and France have also made plans to stockpile various items. A problem for Japan is that she is so completely dependent on imports that she is afraid to give the impression that the primary-commodity-exporting countries would be capable of a hostile action. Some Japanese sources have also proposed national stockpiles as an alternative to an UNCTAD stockpile. Just what UNCTAD thinks of this suggestion is not now known, but it is not likely that they are impressed.

A Bauxite Cartel

The topic just now is the effectiveness of a bauxite cartel. Bauxite is chosen instead of iron ore, copper, or one of the other key minerals because a leading commodities economist, C. Fred Bergsten (1976) believes that the bauxite producers association (IBA) qualifies as a coming OPEC.[5]

To understand this problem we must first comprehend that almost any producers association involving a major nonfuel mineral can engineer a large price rise, and can probably make it stick for a short time. The question is, can they retain control over the price for a longer period, and will the day come when they regret their decision to take price matters into their own hands?

Optimists feel the day will arrive when there is a sufficiently large supply of energy resources outside OPEC so that the threat of catastrophic unilateral price increases by OPEC will decline and eventually fade away. When that happens OPEC will still be important and will receive a large annual income, and so it is unlikely that an impartial observer will be able to claim that, from the point of view of its own self-interest, OPEC acted incorrectly in jacking up the price. In gambling parlance, OPEC possessed what is known as a "middle"; the only relevant question is, "What made them wait so long?"

Just the opposite is true for bauxite. The LDCs producing bauxite tend to be among the poorer of the LDCs, and if they are not "Fourth World," then several of them seem to be heading in that direction. Of the active as opposed to potential producers, only Jamaica could be considered as firmly established in what the World Bank calls the middle-income bracket of the developing countries. But Jamaica is now highly dependent on bauxite. If it became impossible to sell this resource, then Jamaica would become just another island in the sun, dependent on the generosity of tourists.

This means that the bauxite producers must be extremely careful that their customers continue to use bauxite. If substitutes were developed, and if as usual when customers abandoned a specific mineral input they did not return, then the economies of these bauxite producing countries would be ruined—perhaps permanently.

We might thus ask why a government like the Jamaican government, composed of highly sophisticated politicians and able to call on first-class economic advice, would decide to impose levies on bauxite that would more than double its price to consumers and encourage other producers to do the same. To begin, it was the right moment from a psychological point of view. The oil price increases had sent the industrial countries reeling, and they were expecting more of the same from the other primary product producers. Hence, there was no indignation when, in March 1974, the first price increases arrived.[6] Then, too, according to United Nations statisticians and World Bank experts, the Jamaican economy was decelerating, and it was not helped by having to pay an additional $150 million for oil imports as a result of the rise in oil prices. The Jamaican move may thus have been an act of desperation, because the amount they recovered by raising the price of bauxite was also about $150 million.

It should also be appreciated that the bauxite-consuming countries had neither the time nor the energy to be bothered with Jamaica or even the IBA in 1974, since by OPEC standards, IBA was and is small beer. The oil import bill for the United States increased by $14 billion in 1974, but bauxite increased only $200 million. In addition, the main aluminum companies are locked into specific types of bauxite; a plant that produces aluminum from Jamaican bauxite, for example, cannot handle Brazilian bauxite with modifying its equipment. Most important, in a period when there are very high price rises, as there have been over the past few years, these price increases could always be passed along. Remember that bauxite is only one of the many inputs needed to produce aluminum, and a 100 percent increase in the price of bauxite in 1974 increased the price of aluminum only a few percentage points.

But in the long run, as most people realize, a bauxite cartel's ability to increase prices will be limited by the enormous amount of alternative clays out of which aluminum can be manufactured. A bauxite boycott or even a very large price rise would simply mean that governments of the bauxite-consuming countries would have to become involved in producing aluminum—probably through subsidies, but conceivably otherwise. Once this happens the large-scale production of aluminum without bauxite is probably less than a decade away—although many people say much less; afterwards there would hardly be any reason to return to bauxite. In the United States the quantity of anorthosite was estimated at 600 billion tons in 1967. Given a reduction ratio of ten tons anorthosite per ton of aluminum, the potential reserves of aluminum in the United States would be about twenty times the estimated aluminum content in the known global bauxite reserve. Note that we are not talking about potential technologies: aluminum is already being produced from alunite in the Soviet Union, and the French government has indicated to the Péchiney Aluminum Company that it would be pleased if Péchiney would begin manufacturing aluminum out of local clays.

We can now look at another aspect of this matter. A major reason that bauxite has become a problem is the inability of the consuming countries to shift a certain amount of processing capacity to countries like Jamaica. Value added in mining is much less than value added in smelting and refining, where value added includes such things as wages and profits. Furthermore, the aluminum industry in countries like the United States, with its huge investments in processing capacity oriented toward specific sources of foreign bauxite, seems to a certain extent a captive of these foreign producers. The aluminum companies understand this situation, and it usually makes them willing to cooperate with bauxite sellers by passing along price increases. This is convenient for bauxite and aluminum producers, but not particularly pleasant for the general public. It might be better for the public if the bauxite-producing countries also owned some bauxite processing facilities, which would give them a vested interest in continuing to supply ore.

The question that might be asked here is why the price increases practiced with bauxite could not be attempted with smelted products. They could, but it would not be particularly easy for a typical LDC to accept large unemployment and loss of sales in a processing industry while customers drew down inventories and worked harder on perfecting alternative technologies. Of course, it would hardly be logical for the industrial countries to consider dismantling their processing industries until they get some definite assurances about supply—and these would probably have to come from individual countries rather than a cartel. In addition, in place of heroic pronouncements about how much processing capacity should be placed in this or that part of the world by such and such a year, the LDCs could make some constructive suggestions about where increments to existing processing facilities should be located to get an optimal global allocation of scarce resources of such things as capital and energy.

At one time the principal arguments for retaining aluminum processing capacity in the consuming countries had to do with scale economies and the cost of energy. Even Australia ships bulky bauxite to Japan rather than processing it locally. But now it is apparent that American aluminum manufacturers must receive a subsidy of some sort on the electric power they consume if they are to maintain the present level of production and not escalate their prices. Because of the increases in the price of petroleum, the most favorable locations for processing bauxite are probably on the west coast of Africa, in Guinea or Ghana, where the large potential hydroelectric capacity makes the cost of oil more or less unimportant. On the other hand, Jamaica is still vulnerable to higher oil prices, but wages are lower on Jamaica than in the United States and Europe, educational levels are higher than in most LDCs, and technically trained personnel would be easier to obtain. It may therefore be possible to construct very large installations and thus take advantage of scale economies.

Tariffs and Further Processing

Many economists feel that the only way to assist the less-developed world is to expand international trade and probably change its structure. As indicated in the previous section, there is little or no future for a country that merely produces primary commodities. What has to be done is to transfer some processing facilities for raw materials to the nations producing them.

But this is not all. The tariff structure facing these processed products must be altered. Take manganese. Tariffs on manganese ore are trivial if they exist at all. Japan has no tariffs on the amount of manganese ore needed to meet domestic demand, although imports exceeding this have to face a tariff of between 10 and 40 percent ad valorem.[7] On the other hand, almost all industrial countries subject manganese products such as alloys to tariff and nontariff barriers. These barriers, while ostensibly intended to help domestic manufacturers, make it impossible for LDCs to enter this market. Of all the LDCs that produce manganese ore, only India is an important exporter of manganese products and is experiencing great difficulties in maintaining its competitive position.

There are actually two points here. The first has to do with the general decline in price of many ores relative to manufactured products. In 1974 the price of a unit of ferromanganese was about four times the value of the manganese ore it contained, and this ratio is increasing. (Manganese ore is given a ferroalloy form before it is used for steelmaking, and the most common ferroalloy is ferromanganese, which contains 80 percent manganese.) The price of the manufactured goods for which manganese ore is exchanged is also increasing rapidly. In 1970 manganese-exporting countries had to export 1.8 tons of ore to obtain the same purchasing power that was realizable from 1 ton in 1950, and it now requires more than 2.5 tons.

As for tariffs, if we merely look at face values we see how the basic tariff structure discriminates against semifabricates and final products. Some tariff rates are given in table 3-2.

However, this is only the beginning of the trouble. The main problem is tariff escalation, where in extreme cases the effective tariff rate can amount to several hundred percent. To see this, the reader should examine the following simple example.

Assume that a product selling for $100 contains $50 worth of imported raw materials and $50 worth of payments to the primary products, capital and labor. Then assume that the good can also be imported for $100 (which means in this artificial case that local production and imports share the market in some manner). Now place a tariff of 10 percent on the imported good, bringing its price to the final consumer to $110. Under certain conditions, domestic producers would simply leave their price at $100 and take over the entire market. But note that if the home country has no duty on the imported raw materials, then the domestic producer can raise his price to $110. His value added on every unit sold now becomes $110 − $50 = $60, and we say that the effective protection is 10/50, or 20 percent.

Of course he would not raise his price to *exactly* $110, because then he would have to share the market with the imported good. Assume instead that he raises it to $109.99. His value added now is almost $60, and his effective protection almost 20 percent.[8] According to World Bank calculations, the average nominal tariff on manufactured goood is 11.8 percent, while the

Table 3-2
Tariff Rates on Varous Products (1959)

	Raw Materials	Semifabricates	Finished Products
European Economic Community	0.8	8.0	11.7
Japan	1.6	10.1	14.6
United Kingdom	1.5	8.5	18.0
United States	3.6	8.3	20.8

Source: United Nations World Economic Survey

effective protection rate is 22.6 percent. The interesting cases in the real world are probably not metals but textiles. Many industrial countries display extremely high effective tariff rates, to protect industries that should be closed down immediately and their highly efficient employees transferred into science-based or similar employments in which these countries have a comparative advantage.

But there is no point in insisting that the governments of the industrial countries immediately remove trade barriers without saying something about the ills these barriers are supposed to remove. Economic theorists like to think they can prove that in the long run even the tariff-imposing country will gain by the removal of these devices; however in the long run politicians who make what appear to be bad decisions in the short run have a way of finding themselves out of public life. A tradeoff thus seems in order, and it amounts to the following.

The industrial countries should pay for the retraining of employees and the establishment of new industry out of the money now being squandered on development aid. The losers will be a few big bureaucrats in the United Nations, a large number of small bureaucrats in the various aid organizations, and undoubtedly some corrupt politicians and functionaries in the LDCs; but from the gains eventually accruing to all parties, it might be possible to provide these citizens with some kind of direct welfare payment instead of the roundabout type they now receive for the elaborate idleness they call work.

Conclusion

One of the more controversial proposals now making the rounds concerns the possibility of indexing raw materials prices to the price of industrial goods. The oil producers in particular have paid a great deal of attention to this matter, framing most of their complaints around the high inflation rate in the industrial countries. With these countries, of course, the issue is not only the terms of trade of oil, but the declining purchasing power of the large financial balances they have accumulated. Where trade by type of commodity is concerned, the figures in table 3-3 are relevant for 1971.

These values have been altered considerably by the oil price rises, which have led to greatly increased imports of capital goods by the oil-producing countries and extremely large increases in the value of petroleum exports. The terms of trade between oil and industrial products may have deteriorated slightly to the disadvantage of the former, but far from enough to wipe out the huge gains that resulted from raising the price of oil almost 400 percent. As for the nonfuel primary product producers, in addition to a terms-of-trade deterioration caused by such things as inflation, the popular belief is that the demand for primary products tends to grow less than proportionally to the increase in income, and thus the rapidly growing industrial countries have tended to spend less for this type of import than they do on manufactured products. With

Table 3-3
Exports from and to Developed Market Economies and Less-Developed Countries (LDCs) (1971), and Some Commodity Exports from LDCs (1973)
(in billions of dollars)

(a)		
Exports To	Developed Market Economies	LDCs
Developed Market Economies		
Manufactures	144.8	36.6
Primary Commodities	45.1	7.6
LDCs		
Manufactures	8.3	3.4
Primary Commodities	34.7	8.2

Source: United Nations Statistical Yearbook

(b)				
Minerals			Nonminerals	
1. Fuels	(41,318)		1. Coffee	(3,990)
2. Copper[a]	(3,882)		2. Sugar	(3,181)
3. Iron Ore	(1,219)		3. Timber	(2,421)
4. Tin[a]	(847)		4. Cotton	(1,993)
5. Phosphate Rock	(336)		5. Cocoa	(938)
6. Bauxite	(244)		6. Tea	(602)
7. Aluminum	(293)		7. Bananas	(591)
8. Zinc[a]	(184)			
9. Lead	(131)			
10. Manganese Ore	(96)			

[a]Includes semiprocessed items

everything else the same, this would cause the price of primary products to fall relative to those of manufactures.

Investigators do not agree on this question, although over the last few years the terms of trade of almost all nonfuel primary products have deteriorated rapidly.[9] Strangely enough, even U.N. experts and consultants cannot agree on just what has happened to primary commodity prices vis-à-vis other prices over the past two and a half decades. The expert group recently convened by UNCTAD to examine this situation reported that they could present no indisputable evidence that long-term price movements have gone against LDCs.

The principal argument against indexation now being presented in non-academic circles is that indexation perpetuates inflation. Unfortunately it is seldom pointed out that, at least theoretically, noninflationary indexation schemes could probably be designed; and that if, during business cycle downturns, primary-product-producing countries were willing to accept industrial goods in return for a small part of their exports, they could have an important stabilizing effect on the world economy. On the other hand, the academic argument against indexation mostly turns on the distortion of relative prices. Ostensibly this distortion would prevent producers and consumers from making optimal substitutions between goods. As things stand now, the opposition to indexation is so strong that it would be difficult to imagine its introduction on any but the most paltry scale.

LDC debt is also an important item. At the end of 1975 the official external debt of eighty-eight non-oil-producing LDCs came to $90 billion, and total debt was about $135 billion. Approximately one-quarter of this debt is held by private banks, and servicing requires, on the average, an estimated 10 to 13 percent of the value of exports of these countries.

For some time now there has been considerable agitation to cancel this debt, or at least to change the conditions for its servicing. For the most part the response on this has been negative, with the debt-holding nations usually falling back on arguments having to do with moral law, since the present cycle of aid, loans, repudiation, and deepening underdevelopment for many countries hardly makes economic sense; but again we should ask whether a debt relief program could not be worked out to reward high performances and penalize low ones. If the developed countries intend to eliminate some of the poverty and backwardness in the LDCs by helping them modernize their economies, then those LDCs who prove that they mean business should have their debts scaled down.

Notes

1. This is true even though a recent prime minister of Australia seemed to feel that Australia had more in common with the Third World than with the industrial countries.

2. Although it may appear that the purpose of these preferences is to give the LDCs an unreasonable advantage over the industrial countries in certain markets, the LDCs also maintain an impressive structure of tariffs that many of the industrial countries would like to see lowered, and which perhaps could be lowered as part of a more extensive "deal." It could also be reasoned that in conjunction with the introduction of preferences of one type or another, many of the industrial countries could begin to rid themselves of the onerous and absurd burden of development aid in its present form and to replace it with forms of cooperation capable of making a real as opposed to an illusory contribution to the development of the Third World. As even many LDCs are beginning to realize, trade is often better than aid as a vehicle for getting the best

out of foreign assets. For reasons that cannot be discussed here, trade facilitates the acquisition of modern techniques and also mitigates a large part of the corruption that cash transfers promote.

3. The commodities covered are peanuts, cocoa, coffee, cotton, coconuts, hides and skins, timber products, bananas, tea, raw sisal, iron ore, and sugar.

4. To see this passing along, we can note that a few years ago an average automobile contained about thirty-five pounds of copper. Even if we take a price of one dollar per pound for copper, this comes to only $35 in a vehicle price of $4000 or so. If the price of copper tripled and the entire increase was passed along, the automobile would cost $4070. It is doubtful that a price increase of this magnitude would cause much of a change in buyer preferences.

5. The main LDC producers of bauxite are Jamaica, Surinam, Guyana, and the Republic of Guinea. Guinea and Australia are the countries possessing the largest share of reserves; and Australia also produces about 20 to 25 percent of the world's bauxite. Total LDC exports of bauxite amounted to $218 million in 1972, as compared to $13 billion for oil.

6. A bauxite tax that was a percentage of the United States producer price was later supplemented by royalties on each ton of bauxite mined.

7. A sales tax can be specific or ad valorem. If it is specific then we can write for an item Cost $= FC + VC(q) + tq$, where FC and VC are fixed and variable costs. If the tax is ad valorem we have Cost $= FC + VC(q) + t'pq$, where t and t' are tax rates.

8. The algebra in this example is simple. To begin take p_0 as the free trade price, p_1 as the price after imposition of the tariff, p_i the price of the imported raw material, and a_i an input-output coefficient giving the amount of the import required per unit of output. Then we have, with v_0 the original value added and v_1 the value added after imposition of the tariff:

$$p_0 = v_0 + a_i p_i$$

and:

$$p_1 = p_0(1 + t) = v_1 + a_i p_i$$

With the effective rate of protection defined as $(v_1 - v_0)/v_0$ we get from the above equations:

$$\frac{v_1 - v_0}{v_0} = \frac{tp_0}{p_0 - a_i p_i} = \frac{t}{1 - \theta}$$

In this last relationship we have defined $\theta = a_i p_i/p_0$ as the share of imports in a dollar's worth of final output at free trade prices. If we take the example given in the text we might have a_i = ½, p_i = 100, and p_0 = 100. We can thus calculate θ = ½, and if we also take t = 0.10, then the effective protection rate is equal to 20 percent.

But also note that in this example the amount the domestic producer would actually raise the price depends upon the elasticity of demand for the product. If the demand were completely inelastic then he would, of course, raise the price to just below $110. But raising the price could decrease demand. If so, he might not raise the price at all, or perhaps raise it but not all the way to $110.

9. The following estimates are valid for non-oil producing countries over the period 1973-75. Index numbers are used, with 1973 = 100

	1973	1974	1975
Exports	100	98	95
Imports	100	108	103
Purchasing Power of Exports	100	96	86

Appendix 3A

Earlier in this chapter it was said that the income of producers of manufactured goods tends to increase relative to that of the producers of primary products if we just look at demand. Proving this in the context of the international economy is fairly complicated, but the following simple algebraic exposition gives a small idea of what is involved. If, to begin, we write as the demand for various manufactured goods $D_1 = D_1(Y), D_2 = D_2(Y), \ldots, D_n = D_n(Y)$, where Y signifies income or a similar variable, and if we take θ as the input-output coefficient relating the value of primary product input to the value of the finished product, we get as the income of primary producers:

$$I = \Sigma \theta_i D_i(Y)$$

or

$$I/Y = \Sigma \theta_i \frac{D_i(Y)}{Y}$$

then:

$$\frac{d}{dt}\left(\frac{I}{Y}\right) = \Sigma \frac{\theta_i}{Y} \frac{\partial D_i}{\partial Y} \frac{dY}{dt} - \Sigma \frac{\theta_i D_i(Y)}{Y^2} \frac{dY}{dt}$$

$$= \left[\Sigma \theta_i \frac{\partial D_i}{\partial Y} - \Sigma \theta_i \frac{D_i}{Y} \right] R \ \ (\text{with}) \ \ R = \frac{1}{Y} \frac{dY}{dt}$$

This expression is negative if:

$$\frac{1}{Y} \Sigma \theta_i D_i > \Sigma \theta_i \frac{\partial D_i}{\partial Y}$$

or

$$\Sigma \theta_i D_i > \Sigma \theta_i D_i \frac{Y \partial D_i}{D_i \partial Y} = \Sigma \theta_i D_i e_i$$

In this last expression we have e_i as the income elasticity of demand of D_i. The simplification of this relationship becomes:

$$\Sigma \theta_i D_i (1 - e_i) > 0$$

75

Statistical studies seem to indicate that for the primary products sold by LDCs, which for the most part are necessities, the value of e_i is less than unity ($e_i < 1$). This means that the final equation above is greater than zero, which in turn means that $d/dt\ (I/Y) < 0$. The relative income of the primary producer falls over time.

4 Some Aspects of the Problem of Economic Growth: Money, Multinational Firms, Commodities, and Inflation

Three principal factors explain the current state of uncertainty in the world economic system. The first might be called fallout from the Club of Rome report and similar documents, which questioned the long-run physical viability of the global economic system. As some readers are undoubtedly aware, speculation of this type has a long history, but even within a conventional Malthusian framework it could be argued that there was always room to raise living standards gradually through technical progress. The notion of growth coming to an end because of the exhaustion of a finite supply of some irreplaceable input has only recently appeared.

Then, too, there is the so-called energy crisis. Among other things, this has confirmed for many people some of the Club of Rome predictions. An earlier chapter discussed energy problems, and the limits of growth will be taken up in chapter 7, so the only comment necessary here is that the oil price rise probably ranks just behind the outbreaks of the world wars as one of the most important events of the century.

Finally, there is the world monetary muddle. Academic economists disagree on how this began, but a good guess would be with the budget deficits used by the United States to help finance the war in Vietnam.[1] Whether the dollar would eventually have been in trouble without the war is a moot question, since one of the less recondite assumptions of the Bretton Woods conference was that the United States would always be able to outcompete all countries, all the time, in all markets. Apparently this is no longer true. Even so, had the United States become a merely average performer in the global economic league, its size, political stability, geographical position, and various psychological advantages over its competitors might have maintained the dollar on its pedestal; but the financing of a large part of an unpopular war with the printing press was bound to cause difficulties—the most pronounced of which was an unprecedented expansion of world liquidity. According to Professor Robert Triffin (1975), the growth of world monetary reserves in 1970-72 was greater than all previous history. The significance of this phenomenon for the present world economic crisis will be made clear in this and the following section. We begin with a little chronology.

The first key event took place in 1965, when the United States abandoned the gold reserve requirement for Federal Reserve liabilities to member banks, and later, in 1968, abandoned the requirement that United States notes must have gold backing.

Then the price level sped up in the United States in 1965, following the 1964 "Kennedy" tax cut. The escalation of the Vietnam War in 1966 was accompanied by the printing of between $20 and $30 billion. There was the cost inflation in the United States in 1967, and the devaluation of the pound, the big deteriorations in the United States foreign trade balance in 1969 and 1970, the resort to a two-tier gold system, and the introduction of the Special Drawing Right (SDR) in 1970. The Bretton Woods system (essentially based on fixed exchange rates) collapsed in 1971, and the dollar was devalued for the first time. Later there was the raw materials boom and a further devaluation of the dollar, topped off by the October War in the Middle East.

Intermingled with all this we have the explosion in both the size and influence of the Eurodollar market. This market contained $15 billion in 1963; 11 years later it had grown to more than $200 billion. In other words, it grew from one-twentieth of the world's money supply to about one-fifth. In addition, because of its size, it proved a convenient receptacle for dollars when various financial institutions found it necessary to put them to work rather than holding them as they traditionally had. As will become clear later, had the Eurodollar market not existed during this period, somebody would have been forced to invent it, because central bankers and governments would have found it quite difficult to explain why they allowed themselves to be lumbered with a currency whose decline in value became a certainty months, or perhaps years, before it actually happened.

The problem of getting rid of dollars was acute in 1970, when it became clear to many individuals that the war in Vietnam was not going to be concluded in a manner satisfactory to the United States government. Great suspicion would therefore be cast on the future of many American institutions, and by extension on that institution which foreigners esteemed before all others: the American greenback. This created a genuine dilemma, because during the Vietnam War most of Western Europe and Japan had absorbed tens of billions of dollars in return for real resources and diverse services; the issue now became one of being repaid for this altruism in other than more dollars, or requests for more altruism.

To begin, foreign central banks sent a large number of dollars back to the United States in return for gold; within two years, United States gold reserves were cut in half. They were not allowed to send more of them back, however, because although the banker was behaving quite irrationally, he was still influential enough to convince his clients that it was in their long-run interest to maintain the integrity and good name of his bank. In a sense this was understandable: had the dollar fallen completely from grace, governments outside the United States who were sitting on more than 100 billion of them would hardly have had reason to celebrate. Private individuals and institutions now sent their dollars to the central bank in their country in return for safer currencies, and the central bank rerouted these dollars into the Eurodollar market. Thanks to the special circuitry of this market and some peculiarities of the international financial system, the reserves of commercial banks all over the world were increased and the world's money supply was rapidly expanded.[2]

We can now inquire into what was going on in the United States during this period. In theory, the unprecedented loss in gold reserves should have led to some kind of monetary contraction, but two factors mitigated against this. First, the United States government removed gold backing for its monetary liabilities in 1965 and 1968. Second, countries at war are not inclined to play by the rules. Instead of a contraction, the printing presses kept the green wave advancing, increasing the United States money supply and boosting the quantum of Eurodollars. Then, in late 1971, almost without regard for the consequences, the United States Joint Economic Committee publicly recommended devaluing the dollar. The first result of this was a run on the gold reserves of Britain—whose position as a guarantor of the international monetary system might best be described as honorary—to the extent of $3 billion in "requests." The United States responded to all this by suspending convertibility, because convertibility could have fatally diminished the United States gold stock had it continued.

The next section will elaborate some of these topics, but it might be interesting to consider what the various economic conferences held during this period were doing. To begin with, they were not dealing with economics as such, but with trust or confidence. For the past twenty-five years the international economic system has been based on confidence in the dollar and, should that confidence prove unjustified, convertibility of the dollar to gold. However when it became clear that the dollars outside the United States were ten times the United States holdings of gold and seemed to be accelerating, it became clear that the only thing to do was close the bank. Forthcoming economic conferences will also essentially be dealing with this, with statesmen and quasistatesmen plumbing the virtues—or lack of them—of their colleagues, to make sure that in the next crisis they are not gulled into filling the vaults of their central bank with a debased coin. What many of us hope, however, is that someone will inform these VIPs that the standard of living of the industrial countries has always depended on what happens in factories and laboratories, and that the loss of confidence in a currency only reflects a loss of confidence in the production apparatus that stands behind it. This means, incidentally, that no government should place its trust in an organization like the IMF, or its liabilities (SDRs), since behind these liabilities we have not production but rhetoric—and insipid rhetoric at that.

Although vanquished in theory, the dollar still looms large in fact—primarily because of the high level of development of United States capital markets as compared to those of Europe and Japan. It is highly probable that the dollar and the pound will someday regain their former prominence—in fact, the pound may become stronger. The Nobel Prize-winning physicist Dennis Gabor has suggested abandoning gold and making production the basis of the world monetary system. In a sense, production was the informal basis of the world monetary system, because immediately after World War II the rationale for countries securing dollars was to enable them to import from the United States, the equipment needed to rebuild their economies. But now production seems to be linked, first and foremost, to energy. If this is so, then those countries that have the best chance to solve their energy problems are the logical candidates for sponsoring the new reserve currency, assuming that someday a traditional reserve currency will again be found desirable. At present, the best candidates for this role are Britain and the United States.

The World Economic Crisis

This section continues some of the themes taken up in the introduction to this chapter, which postulated a link between international reserves and prices: world reserves have grown at a very high rate, vastly increasing the global money supply and placing the world price level under a strong upward pressure.

Between 1950 and 1969 international reserves grew an average of 2.7 percent per year. In the three years beginning in January 1970, they increased by almost 21 percent a year, from $78 billion in SDR units to $146 billion; of this amount $59 billion can be credited to an increase in United States dollar reserves. Interestingly enough, Heller (1976) rejects the usual argument that excessive monetary expansion in the United States was the main cause of the escalation in world liquidity and the ensuing worldwide inflation, although at second remove his argument can be reduced to exactly that. According to Heller, the shift from dollars to other currencies led to the excessive expansion of world liquidity. However the shift from dollars only reflected the potential decline in the value of the dollar relative to other currencies, and the obvious fact that convertibility of the dollar to gold would have to be suspended if the United States could not or would not control the rate of increase of dollar liabilities.[3]

As noted earlier, when more and more dollars appeared and the rate of inflation in the United States began to pick up, it became clear that anybody concerned with his future standard of living could not afford to hold this currency. Corporation treasurers in particular made sure that their dollar balances were minimal, and United States commercial banks increased their foreign assets from $6.5 billion at the end of 1969 to $13.6 billion at the end of 1972. In many cases these foreign assets were obtained in exchange for dollars through transactions in which the access of foreign branches of American corporations and banks to the Eurodollar market played an important role.

One of the more lucrative puzzles that international monetary economics has furnished its practitioners in the last few years concerns the direction of causation between changes in the money supply and changes in prices. The so-called monetary theory of the balance of payments begins with price changes; in a brilliant article, Mundell (1976) has sketched a self-perpetuating inflationary process with a Wiksellian flavor. An increase in the price level causes an increase in the desire for liquidity, because more money is required to purchase a given quantity of goods. This causes a shortage of liquidity for various financial institutions, which eventually causes central banks to engage in open market operations, and governments to lean towards an expansive economic policy.

At the same time the Eurodollar market expands to meet the needs of customers engaged in financing the higher value of international trade. In other words, in light of our previous discussion, the Eurodollar market is not only a place to get rid of dollars, but must also produce dollars to make sure that goods costing more because of inflation can be purchased. As intriguing as all this may sound, Heller rejects it and, on the basis of his empirical work, states flatly that reserve changes cause price changes—and not the opposite. The issue is still open.

We mentioned earlier the inability of central banks to exchange dollars for gold, but most important in a discussion of this type is the exchange of dollars for goods. While the dollar "overhang" was building up, both productivity and quality in the United States manufacturing sector were declining. Along with incipient inflation, this made United States products less attractive than those of countries like Japan and Germany. This was the basis of the devaluations of 1971 and 1973; had those devaluations succeeded, confidence in the dollar might have returned. Moreover, these or further devaluations could have worked, but the October War and the rise in oil prices put the international economy in an entirely new situation.

The oil price rise meant a cost-push effect on the price level in the oil-importing countries. The Organization for Economic Cooperation and Development (OECD) secretariat estimates this at 1.5 percent on the average for all OECD countries, and 2.3 percent for the European OECD countries. This is not excessive in the light of the inflation rates that have become common over the past three years, although a decade ago it would have been considered scandalous; and of course it must be added to the other price rises.

By employing a monetarist approach, Swoboda (1976) reasoned that the initial impact of the oil price rise should have been deflationary. The increase in the oil price decreased the real balances of individuals and institutions, who tried to rebuild these by hoarding money. This in turn caused an excess supply of goods, whose price would normally tend to fall. Of course since much of the money transferred to oil producers also ended up in the same circuits referred to above, particularly the Eurodollar market, any deflation was immediately counterbalanced. Some idea of the changes that took place in prices and reserves between 1961 and 1975 can be obtained from table 4-1.

Some reference to exchange rates is also necessary. The argument for flexible exchange rates is both clear and appealing: when the exports of a country become less desirable to foreigners, then their price should go down. One way to bring this about is to depreciate the currency of the country in question, which makes exports more attractive and also makes it more expensive

Table 4-1
World Monetary Data, 1961-1974

Year	World Reserves[a]		M_1[b]	Percent Increase	M_2[c]	Percent Increase	Percent Change (price level)	Eurodollar Market[a]
1961	62.6	19.6	251	6.8	407	9.2	1.8	
1962	63.1	20.1	265	5.9	449	10.3	2.4	
1963	66.6	22.4	288	8.6	496	10.5	2.5	
1964	68.8	23.8	304	5.6	540	8.7	2.2	
1965	70.7	23.4	328	7.5	599	11.1	2.7	12
1966	72.6	25.4	312	4.3	645	7.5	3.4	15
1967	74.3	29.0	372	9.0	726	12.7	2.9	18
1968	77.4	31.9	406	8.9	810	11.5	3.9	27
1969	78.2	32.1	427	5.1	856	5.6	5.0	44
1970	92.6	44.6	472	10.6	973	13.7	5.6	57
1971	130.6	78.1	558	18.3	1176	20.9	5.1	70
1972	159.0	103.7	642	15.2	1384	17.7	4.4	92
1973	187.2	126.1	731	13.7	1660	19.9	7.4	130
1974	218	—	745	2.0	1767	6.5	13.9	—

Source: International Monetary Fund Documents, and Herin, Jan and Wijkman, Per M. "Den Internationella Bakgrunded," SOU 1976: 27.
[a]In billions of U.S. dollars (Reserves: Total Reserves and Foreign Exchange)
[b]Currency + Demand Deposits, in billions of U.S. dollars
[c]Currency + Demand Deposits + Quasi Money (mostly time deposits), in billions of U.S. dollars

for domestic residents to purchase the products of other countries. If things go well export revenue is increased relative to the amount spent on imports; but the domestic price level may also increase (due to an increase in import prices) and real consumption will probably fall. To hold prices down, and also to ensure that the domestic industry has adequate capacity to produce exports, it may be necessary to decrease domestic purchasing power somewhat. This could be done with the help of direct taxes, compulsory savings schemes, lower government outlays, and so on. In these circumstances we might get constant prices and adequate export capacity, but will also almost certainly end up with lower real consumption, or perhaps a lower rate of increase in real consumption.

It is precisely this last item that people will not accept in a devaluation or depreciation—at least not willingly. They prefer painless depreciations, although there is generally no such animal. Mundell cites the case of a British devaluation in which the value of the pound fell, raising the price of raw materials and food, which in turn created upward pressure on wages, and thus further increased the cost of living via price rises. Unfortunately, none of this was reversed when the position of the pound improved. Given the present institutional setting, flexible exchange rates have a kind of ratchet effect, leading to irreversible price increases. Neither in Germany, with its major revaluations, nor in Britain, with its occasional improvements in the exchange rate, has a strengthening of the mark or pound checked a rising price level. If to this catalogue of unfulfilled promises we add the extensive currency speculation that is now taking place, which appears both politically and economically destabilizing, then we might suspect that, like so many purported panaceas in economics, flexible rates are destined to be a flame without a tomorrow.

Multinational Corporations

Depending on the circumstances and the company, it can be as difficult to discuss multinational corporations as it is to discuss religion. Because they are a convenient focus of resentment, these organizations often serve the same purpose in polite society as various minority groups in not-so-polite society. Of course, they do have a great deal going for them—or against them—depending upon the viewpoint from which one inspects their activities. In GNP, General Motors is supposed to be larger than South Africa, Ford larger than Austria, Exxon larger than Denmark, and so on. The ostensible problem here is that unlike Kreisky or Jorgensson, the managing directors of Ford or Exxon did not have to convince their employees that they were worthy of office, which some people take to imply that multinational or transnational corporations are a kind of avant garde of high capitalist dictatorship.

The present section will consider multinationals in the context of LDCs, since it is sometimes felt that these companies are playing an insidious role in the Third World. Dion O'Banion, the celebrated Chicago gunman, once referred to his organization as "big business without top hats," and considerable effort has gone into portraying the multinationals as gangsters *with* top hats. Even a former associate editor of Fortune Magazine seems to feel that ITT was instrumental in "destabilizing" the Allende government in Chile, although insiders in that affair have gradually become convinced that the amateur economic policies of Dr. Allende and his fly-by-night advisers destabilized the regime. In any event, I have already recorded—in Banks (1974)—my opinion of what multinationals can and cannot do

in these days when a call by such companies for gunboats simply results in the phone being hung up on the other end.

The truth is that we now live in a world where the multinational or transnational company, regardless of its size and influence in the great capitals of the world, would do well to stay on the good side of national governments. We do not have to look very far across the nationalization battlefields of the 1960s to see a large number of corporate wounded—Annacott, Kenecott, Roan Selection, Union Miniere. The 1970s have brought new casualties, such as Shell, Exxon, and ITT. Of course, another problem is that these firms may not only stay on the good side of various governments, but ally themselves with these governments against individuals and political parties, other corporations, and other governments. As fascinating as this topic is, it cannot be taken up in this book.

The starting point for our discussion will be the contention of the Chilean economist Ricardo French Davis (1973) that foreign capital "cannot, has not, and should not" play a decisive role in the development of the Third World. It could be argued, of course, that since much of the foreign investment and loans destined for LDCs originates in industrial countries that are themselves in serious trouble, it might be more suitable to use these resources at home; but this is hardly what Dr. Davis and his well-wishers had in mind. Instead the position here will be that although foreign capital cannot, has not, should not, and probably will not play a decisive role in the Third World, it is senseless to maintain that it has no role to play.

Before going into my concept of this role, I will make a few unpopular remarks about some of the literature dealing with international corporations. Although the officers of some multinational corporations may have been inclined to ignore the overall social content of their decisions, do they belong in the quasi-criminal category in which much of the literature attempts to place them? However, in reality, the issue is not the function or activities of the leadership of the multinationals, but their wherewithal and authority. If these firms chained their employees to their working places, but their directors wore G-strings and traveled between continents by kayak, we would probably have been spared any number of pithy essays and books about multinationals, since much of what is now offered as impartial research on the subject is no more than the resentment and distilled envy of academics and journalists who take the privileges of the top executives of these companies as a calculated insult to their own modest place in the scheme of things.

Similarly, it is amazing that so many people from highly developed countries who are writing about international corporations are against all corporations, international or otherwise—in fact, against the industrial ethos in general. Many of the younger economists who rail against the sins of ITT or Standard Oil seem to idealize a stage of development which is a combination of Tahiti and fourteenth-century Hungary. This may seem trivial, but it is extremely important. It means that, as an alternative to the multinational corporation, many of these people would be perfectly willing to have no economic progress at all, and indeed seem to preach economic regression back to the pastoral society. These people, their sponsors, and their audience are the greatest existing obstacles to the modernization of the less-developed countries and the establishment of a rational international economic order.

Some Background

What follows is a short resumé of the activities of the copper-producing multinationals in Chile and Central Africa. In Chile the difficulty was always "returned value," or that part of copper revenue that stayed in the country via wages, taxes, and similar benefits. Two schools of thought were in vogue on this matter. The Chileans claimed that they were being cheated, because most of the income from assets with a comparatively short lifetime was going to the copper companies and their shareholders. The copper producers thought of themselves as educators and missionaries: missionaries with a dollar sign.

The antagonism over returned value began with the first shovel of copper that left the country and continued regardless of the government exercising power. This indicates that much of the controversy was personal. In both human and material resources Chile may well be the richest country on an extremely rich continent; thus the comic-opera aspects of cultural conflict that are never far away when East meets West, or North meets South, took on a special intensity. In particular, the culturally advanced Chileans could not tolerate playing the role of subordinates to the mining companies and their representatives. Thus the issue was not just nationalism, but nationalism and outraged vanity.

There was also the matter of the long-run instability of the Chilean economy. With industrialization, social changes increased the uncertainty of the middle- and upper-income groups. This shortened time horizons and increased capital exports and luxury imports—which drained away the resources needed to finance a competitive import sector. It also established a social framework conducive to widespread private and public corruption. Chilean authorities responded to this situation by running the printing presses at full blast in a desperate and absurd attempt to stave off a complete breakdown. Strangely enough, this was accomplished for the most part, though at the cost of perpetual inflation.

Successive Chilean governments tried to get the copper companies to increase the size and scope of their operations, to increase their tax base. This was a political as well as an economic goal, because given the debilitated condition of the Chilean peso, the copper industry was the government's lifeline to healthier currencies. Understanding this situation, the mining companies expanded capacity as slowly as possible. Largely through this artifice, various Chilean governments were, as they say, "kept on the hook." The possibility of nationalization was not taken seriously until the outbreak of an epidemic of nationalizations and proposals for nationalization some years after World War II. Of course, even if a Chilean government had seized the copper mines, it would have been unable to sell the commodity. However, seizing the mines would not have been easy, because as General Smedley Butler enjoyed pointing out after he retired from the United States Marines, one of the purposes of the Corps before

World War II was to ensure that the concept of property rights was understood by those unlucky persons who had not enjoyed a proper upbringing.

The presence of a multinational company with operations in disparate parts of the globe made it difficult for Chile to develop its economy in a capital-intensive direction. In other words, the companies developed standard techniques for doing certain things and applied these techniques automatically. At the major copper mining and processing installations, the output per unit of labor and the wage rate rose steadily from the early 1920s to at least 1960, but labor payments as a share in the value of production fell. In Britain or Germany this would have been fine, but it is difficult to applaud this situation in a less-developed country. Some of the capital destined for the copper industry should have been diverted into other industries, or even into the agricultural sector. Chile, as opposed to the large copper firms, needed less capital intensity in its industrial operations (including the copper industry) and more local suppliers of intermediate inputs. They got an industry that became increasingly capital-intensive and even less dependent on local inputs because local manufacturers could not match the technical sophistication of imported products. Furthermore, the "surplus" created by capital was basically unavailable for investment, since its owners were abroad.

Following World War II and the transfer of a number of colonies to their rightful owners, a new spurt of protest swept over the nonindustrial countries. In Chile the handwriting was on the wall from about the end of the Korean War. Taxes levied against the mining companies had been increasing since the middle of the 1930s, and from about 1953 until their departure from the scene, these firms may have invested more than they intended. Eventually the copper producers felt it necessary to tender the government its conditions for a major expansion program. These conditions included twenty years of noninterference in such things as taxes and exchange regulations. After a few years they received a reply. As it happened, it turned out to be nationalization.

The takeover of the copper companies was of couse inevitable. Through their hamhandedness and corporate evangelism, these firms lost the chance to take the lead in turning Chile into a kind of South American California and an economic model for the rest of the continent. For example, Chilean graduates wanted jobs; they received sermons and biographical sketches of presidents and vice presidents of Kennecott and Anaconda.

In Central Africa things moved toward their denouement in a much more leisurely fashion—which can probably be explained by the more leisurely drinking habits of the mining company and colonial government officials in that part of the world. The large international firms began operations in Central Africa slightly after the cresting of late nineteenth-century imperialism. Although there were excellent economic reasons for the appearance and expansion of these enterprises, such as proliferating industrialization in Europe and the growing need for raw materials, it is difficult to make a case for the existence of some sort of coordinated political and economic plan through which giant corporations operating in the colonies provided the economic basis for political domination at home or close to home. Apparently a mineral resource would be discovered, and subsequently enough would be removed to satisfy industrial demand in some developed country. No long-term global forecasts were made of the total raw materials available and the cost at which they could be removed. No optimal level of exploitation and resource development was worked out from the home country's viewpoint.

The arrival of these companies involved importing an entirely new technology into Central Africa. This consisted of European capitalists, technicians, and administrators, European skilled and semiskilled labor, and much African unskilled labor. For a while these elements formed a production apparatus displaying a fairly high degree of corporate efficiency; decisions moved fairly rapidly down the corporate chain of command, and the special social and psychological circumstances of the region prevented a great deal of backlash. When world consumption of minerals slumped, the unskilled African laborer could be furloughed back into the domestic subsistence economy, while European employees could usually be kept in line with threats of eventual replacement by Africans. Eventually, overall size and profitability made it possible to build up communities in Central Africa that were more European than African. These outposts of high consumption were to become in many respects a reminder to the local populations of just what they were missing materially. They also provided a view of what the future might look like.

According to the speeches that various company chairmen made to their stockholders and to the press, all that was being done—and would be done—in this part of the world was intended to further the economic and moral progress of the local population. But since from time to time these things included such irregular practices as forced labor, the arbitrary displacement and discharging of workers, and in particular the transfer from the industrial countries of many obtuse and socially wasteful industrial practices, the opinion grew that these companies were less altruistic than they claimed to be. Regardless of what they actually were, they eventually lost control of events. In the end they frittered away their time with what they had come to think of as major industrial projects but which, given the resources and possibilities of the region, were no more than pretentious trivia. Eventually, when it became apparent that they no longer had any economic purpose to serve other than furthering the career possibilities of their directors and paying the occasional dividend to stockholders, they simply disappeared from the scene.

By this time the technology of the area had changed considerably. In particular, Africans had moved into many of the so-called skilled jobs on a large scale. Most important, the psychological climate surrounding these occupations had changed somewhat: experience showed that Africans both could and would fill these positions without substantially losing efficiency. There had not, however, been a significant displacement of European technicians and administrators by Africans. This, in fact, explains why the controversy about multinational firms in Africa (and much of the Third World) takes the particular form it does. Economic development means industrialization; industrialization means large firms; and large firms mean large numbers of technicians. With certain exceptions, however (such as the United Arab Republic), nonwhite Africa is without technicians. A great deal of what has gone wrong and will continue to go wrong with economic development in Africa results from this situation—and this situation cannot be improved simply by making speeches at the U.N. or giving press conferences.

The Crux of a Solution

The previous discussion concluded that the economic development of underdeveloped regions such as Africa has not gone well because of a shortage of technicians. To some degree, this applies to all of the Third World. Where technicians are present they are in short supply, and thus the pace of technology transfer from the developed countries is inadequate. Consequently, the desirability and scale of foreign investment in the Third World should turn on remedying this shortage.[4]

Some people—perhaps even most people—feel that this assignment should go to the schools and universities. This point of view is at best misguided. One of the most catastrophic mistakes of the so-called experts in the early debates on economic development was to assume that the education of technical and managerial personnel in the less-developed countries could be carried out by the traditional instruments of the educational system; they continued making this assumption in the face of much evidence to the contrary. It should be apparent by now that eleven or twelve years of primary and secondary education, plus three or four years of higher education, followed by even a comparatively short period of unemployment, underemployment, or even the pseudo-full employment so common these days in both less-developed and highly developed countries, simply results in a kind of disguised welfare case rather than a motivated, productive individual capable of making a positive contribution to development. As in sports, proficiency in technical and administrative matters come from continuous training that includes frequent periods of high-tempo operations. Very few schools or universities in any part of the world provide this kind of activity. Experience indicates that only active participation in a fairly successful production process can supply this background.

Our purpose is not to denigrate all traditional education. Primary education and much secondary education is still necessary: insofar as the experts in the measurement of human capital have been able to determine, these continue to display a fairly high private and social rate of return. On the other hand, does the social rate of return on higher education actually justify the enormous resources being allocated to the universities? The question here is not one of abolishment, but of reform.

Under the circumstances it might be argued that in return for a competitive rate of return—which the host government would be a party in establishing, and perhaps even guaranteeing—the multinational firm should provide thorough industrial apprenticeships for an increasing number of workers in the host country, and should help complement the training of nationals whose academic backgrounds are technical or administrative. Many multinational firms prefer to use as few local nationals as possible in their operations, on the grounds that such individuals are less competent or loyal than their own nationals and therefore increase business risk. Leaving aside the question of loyalty, local personnel are often less competent and do increase business risk. But multinational firms will have to make allowances for this fact by providing facilities to train these locals up to what they regard as a minimum standard. By the way, recommendations of this type are strangely absent from the scholarly literature. There is no market for prescriptions which suggest that university graduates in less-developed countries should enter productive employment instead of occupying sinecures in the various bureaucracies. Unfortunately, however, productive employment and economic development go together, and the sooner development economists come to realize this the better.

In summary, while multinational companies may not be able to show a spotless record in much of the Third World, they are no longer capable of imperialism in the classical sense. In addition, they can play a crucial role in the training of technicians and administrators in many LDCs—and perhaps more. As Pierre Uri (1976) has argued, they could serve as bridgeheads for a better division of labor, more egalitarian development, and even for a more democratic organization of labor. Although many readers may not realize it, many LDCs have very little freedom to decide whether they are interested in playing host to foreign investment or multinational firms—if, that is, they are committed in fact as well as assertion to any sort of economic development at all. In the words of former President Alvarez of Mexico, they are free to take adequate precautions to ensure that the multinationals they accept do not enrich themselves on the backs of the local population. Everything considered, that should be enough.

The World Commodity Boom and Inflation

Between mid-1972 and mid-1974 the price of many primary commodities increased by huge and, in some cases, record amounts. Moreover, this boom came immediately after a period of oversupply, and during a time of great concern throughout the world about inflation. Then, in mid-1974, primary commodity prices began to slide; by the beginning of 1975 they were down to pre-1972 levels. Even now the slump may not be over for many nonfood items. Table 4-2 shows what happened to some commodities.

One of the most important price indexes is that maintained by the London Economist. This index, which has been compiled since 1860, reached its historical high in May 1974, when it was 115 percent above 1972 levels. Prices of industrial goods rose 127 percent over two years to their peak in April 1974, then declined by 40 percent in the period ending June 1975. During the 117 years that this index has been kept, prices have never risen so rapidly in a single year as they did from 1972 to 1973 (by 63 percent), nor ascended so fast in a three year period as from 1972 to 1974 (by 159 percent).[5]

The usual, and perhaps correct, explanation of the rapid rise and decline of commodity prices turns on world business cycle phenomena during the years 1972-1975: a sharp upturn during 1972 and 1973, and the onset of depression in 1974-75. In between there was a wave of panic buying as well as considerable speculation based on irrational expectations stemming from the oil price rise, and perhaps a desire to use primary commodities as a hedge against currency uncertainties.

The last chapter of this book will briefly discuss a stock flow model which, extended slightly, would normally explain many aspects of short-run pricing in the primary commodity markets; as mentioned in chapter 1, long-run pricing is a

Table 4-2
Some Commodity Prices: April 1973-April 1975

		April 1973	Peak Price 1974	April 1975
Sugar	U.S. cents/lb	9.06	56.63	24.06
Coffee	U.S. cents/lb	59.77	73.74	59.53
Cocoa	U.S. cents/lb	42.73	82.74	56.22
Tea	U.S. cents/lb	49.17	69.76	64.88
Cotton	New pence/kg	42.91	97.81	48.57
Sisal	U.S. dollars/ton	442	1093	760
Abaca	U.S. dollars/ton	359	893	501
Rubber	U.S. dollars/lb	24.6	49.2	24.4
Copper	Pounds/ton	638.8	1268	560.5
Lead	Pounds/ton	155.9	303	202
Zinc	Pounds/ton	206.6	738	303
Tin	Pounds/ton	1722	3951	3007
Aluminum	Cents/lb	25.90	38.97	37.21[a]

Source: UNCTAD Monthly Bulletin of Commodity Prices, March 1977
[a]April 1976

matter of comparing trend supply and demand. The business cycle upswing that began in the United States early in 1970 (slightly later in Europe and Japan) carried the demand for commodities to be used in the current production process far above trend supply, particularly during 1972. By 1973 a certain normality had begun to appear on the commodity markets, but with the arrival of the oil crisis, an enormous buildup of speculative and transaction inventories took place, and the desire for increased stocks rather than current inputs steered trend demand above trend supply and kept it there until well into 1974.[6] World industrial production continued to increase well into 1973, but the rate of increase began to decline around the end of 1972.

On the supply side, the years 1972-74 were not particularly good if we look at such things as grain harvests in the U.S.S.R. and harvests in general in Southeast Asia. A cotton shortage also began to take shape; certain countries had bad luck with their fishing; and perhaps due to a growing upward pressure on the price of animal feed, the supply of beef cattle was not particularly expansive. Copper was negatively affected by political difficulties in Central Africa and South America.

Given the inelasticity of demand for foodstuffs, we might deduce that shortages of food and other essentials would tend to cause their prices to rise sharply, but would not substantially shift spending away from these items. Instead, spending on nonessentials would tend to fall off. However, along with the rapid increase in international liquidity during this period, incomes in the major industrial countries began to expand at an unprecedented rate, and thus aggregate spending on the whole was maintained throughout the industrial world. In addition, the devaluations and depreciations of the dollar and pound caused the terms of trade of many of the primary commodity exports of the LDCs to decline relative to manufactured goods, since primary commodities generally tend to be priced in these currencies. This means that until the advent of two-digit inflation and unemployment in 1974, most of the ill effects of the commodity price boom and other economic phenomena during this period fell on the Third World, and only during a relatively short period could any of these countries other than the oil producers get a taste of prosperity.

Speculation should also be discussed briefly. Information on inventories shows that speculative and precautionary buying reached a new high just after the October War. To support this we can cite the tremendous expansion in futures trading on the London and New York commodity exchanges. Between the early 1970s and the first half of 1974, futures transactions increased by over 50 percent in lead and tin, 200 percent in zinc and copper, and almost 300 percent in rubber. According to Cooper and Lawrence (1975) it is not possible, either empirically or conceptually, to differentiate between speculation and hedging by traders; but unless there is an explicit change in behavior on the part of these individuals, hedging should increase or decrease with the volume of physical transactions. Under the circumstances, the increase in activity on these exchanges could only have resulted from speculation. Moreover, it seems likely that as the prices of futures contracts were bid up, various traders interpreted these increases as a simple forecast of prices on physical markets, which in turn increased the upward pressure on commodity prices.

Inflation

We have already said a few things about the monetary side of inflation, but another angle deserves to be mentioned. There is no sense in saying that the cause of the worldwide inflation is an excess of money, because excess money does not have a divine origin. Governments used the growing stock of international reserves as an excuse to increase the supply of money, but regardless of the availability (or lack of availability) of these reserves, politicians would have found some means to provide their constituents with more cash.

The crux of the problem is that in modern societies many people actively conspire to consume more than they are prepared to produce. They want more private and more public goods, and because they are voters as well as consumers, can force politicians to commit irrational acts in an attempt to provide them with these things. Looked at another way, most adults no longer believe that unemployment is brought by the stork, and they will not tolerate elected officials who do. They want employment, and those who are highly productive have suddenly become extremely displeased with the prospect of having to wait to be rewarded for their diligence. Unfortunately, however, the counterproductive, including the sizable assemblage occupying well-paid nonjobs, have also become restless, and since they have so little else to do, have become experts in maintaining their share of the pie—a pie that, at least for the time being, seems to have stopped expanding.

As long as this situation prevails, a stable or near-stable price level is impossible. What must be done is to restrain the growth of money incomes and at the same time bring remuneration into line with productivity, if this is still possible. The major dilemma at present, however, is that productivity may decline regardless of how hard or effectively people are willing to work, because productivity also has a technical dimension that is highly vulnerable to increases in the price of energy. Once all this is understood, stagflation—that quaint phenomenon which features inflation, high unemployment, and excess capacity—ceases to be a mystery: excessive compensation together with low productivity means inflation.

A Final Comment on International Monetary Economics

Of late, with the international economy under stresses of a type and magnitude almost unknown in its history, we have been deluged with a flood of academic and quasi-academic literature that purports to point to *the* crucial issue or quandary. This literature has been well surveyed by Russell (1977), who neglects to emphasize two important points. The first is that almost all economists refuse to serve up definitive solutions for international monetary problems, because solutions would not change very much where such things as inflation, employment, and productivity are concerned.[7] Although a great deal of high-level opinion thinks otherwise, the comings and goings on the monetary front are strictly marginal or, as Galbraith (1975) indicates in his brilliant summary of monetary history, a kind of sideshow featuring an inordinate amount of makework for economists. The present discussion is thereby furnished in the interest of completeness, and merely attempts to fill in some gaps in this chapter's previous discussion.

Before the October War, and to a certain extent after, the three big issues in the "reform of the international monetary system" debate were (1) the adequacy of global liquidity, (2) the rules for balance-of-payments adjustment, and (3) confidence in the convertibility of the so-called key currencies—the dollar and the pound. The first of these was tied to import surpluses of the United States and Britain, particularly the former, and of course the question came up of whether these could produce the deficits required by international trade—and if they could, how this would eventually affect confidence in these currencies.

By way of solving these two problems simultaneously, Professor Robert Triffin pleaded for large-scale adoption of a new world reserve asset. Eventually, in 1968, an international fiat money called Special Drawing Rights (SDRs) was established, which could be used for reserve settlement purposes. I think that the SDR is in principle a satisfactory supplement to a genuine monetary unit or gold, while the IMF, which administers SDRs, is on its way to becoming somewhat less than satisfactory, thanks to a bad case of overbureaucratization and overpoliticization.

In considering this matter we invariably find ourselves considering the two arrangements where, conceivably, *no* reserves are needed. The first is the classical gold standard, where payments imbalances result in shipments of gold between countries, increasing the money supply in a surplus country and decreasing it in a country experiencing a deficit. The rest is supposed to be taken care of by price and income movements, with governments standing on the sidelines and watching, but not interfering with the process.

With the exception of Jacques Rueff, the well known French economist, it is now difficult to find anybody who advocates adoption of the classical system and who also understands how the gold standard actually functioned. Various parties vaguely long for more discipline in the system, and in the belief that a gold standard would help restrain the monetary authorities, various amateur economists occasionally come forward with carelessly articulated recommendations for a reconsideration of this standard. For the most part they are not particularly well received.

The other possibility is the antithesis of the classical gold standard: freely fluctuating exchange rates. As with the gold standard, monetary authorities do not interfere in the foreign exchange markets, and a balance-of-payments deficit or surplus is supposed to be eliminated through the automatic depreciation or appreciation of a country's currency. Exchange rates are now probably as flexible as they have ever been during this century, but instead of doing without reserves, or with fewer reserves, it has become necessary to have more reserves than ever—otherwise the monetary authorities would find themselves completely at the mercy of the exchange markets and might have to accept outrageous changes in their exchange rates.

Advocates of freely floating exchange rates are as rare as believers in a return to the fixed rates of the Bretton Woods system. Instead, much effort seems to be going into the creation of mixed systems. Professor Harry Johnson (1973), for example, favors floating rates but accepts the concept of an optimum currency area. This means that regions that are highly integrated in terms of the flows of factors and goods should be linked by fixed exchange rates, while less integrated areas should be linked by floating exchange rates. In addition, or so the theory goes, a small country that sells most of its exports to a single large country should tie its exchange rate to that of the large country. In many cases this has already happened, as can be deduced from table 4-3, which shows exchange rate practices of IMF members.

The adjustment problem can be dealt with summarily. Russell has mentioned that many international economists feel that reserves are quite adequate

Table 4-3
Some Exchange Rate Arrangements

1. Currencies Floating Independently	11
2. Currencies Floating Together	7
3. Currencies Linked to:	
a. U.S. Dollar	54
b. French Franc	13
c. Pound Sterling	10
d. Spanish Peseta	1
e. South African Rand	3
4. Currencies Linked to:	
a. SDR	5
b. Other Currencies	14
5. Currencies likened to a "basket" of other currencies, or to a currency whose value is changed according to a given formula	4

Source: IMF Documents

and that the problem is not to finance deficits but to remove them. Once we use this type of expression, the opprobrium for international monetary disequilibrium tends to fall directly on the deficit nation. At Bretton Woods, however, Lord Keynes and America's chief negotiator, Harry Dexter White, eventually agreed that surplus countries also had some responsibilities in these matters, as indeed they have in normal times.

We are not living in normal times, however, because we cannot see an end to the present crisis. Germany and Japan now tend to be surplus countries, and considerable pressure is being put on them, especially Germany, to expand their economies and thus spare their trading partners the distasteful chore of putting their economies in order. One of Germany's important trading partners is Sweden, which has increased the cost of its manufactured products by record amounts over the past few years, largely on the strength of huge and irresponsible increases in wages and salaries, which are based on a distorted vision of economic reality by politicians, labor leaders, and their incompetent economic advisors. Given that large price increases may be associated with rapid economic expansion in Germany, a more suitable arrangement is for Germany to continue to set an example of economic progress with a low rate of inflation, while countries like Sweden either alter their behavior or learn to live with their mistakes.

The remaining topic was also broached earlier. Although the dollar is still the most important currency, the currencies enjoying the most confidence just now are the West German Mark and the Swiss Franc. There is no question, however, of using these as reserve currencies, since the monetary authorities of West Germany and Switzerland understand perfectly well that the costs of assuming this responsibility outweigh the benefits by colossal amounts. Moreover, even if they felt differently, the capital markets in these countries are apparently too narrow or inefficient to make their currencies acceptable candidates. Of course, as things now stand, the international monetary system can probably function quite satisfactorily indefinitely without an officially designated reserve currency, or without adopting some pretentious but unworkable scheme of the IMF. The deficiencies in the international economic system can be traced to real rather than monetary factors, although a peculiar asymmetry exists here: hardly any conceivable monetary repairs could pull the international economy out of its present doldrums, but further carelessness in the matter of money creation or management could lead to disaster.

Confidence in a currency largely turns on confidence in the country issuing the currency, but other factors are important. C. Fred Bergsten (1975) has argued that the right to adjust exchange rates must be a key United States objective in the future since, according to Dr. Bergsten, this is the least expensive form of adjustment. At the same time, paradoxically enough, he is anxious about the dollar "overhang," because if and when another attractive financial asset becomes available, he says that foreign monetary officials will switch out of dollars and drive down the exchange rate.

Like it or not, many foreign countries are stuck with their overhang of dollars—regardless of their confidence in this asset or its issuers. The governors of some European central banks have done odd things in the past, but we cannot believe that these gentlemen, acting in concert and in cold blood, would drive down the value of a currency they and their countrymen held in such profusion. Naturally, this would no longer be true if they came to believe Dr. Bergsten's judgment, because if it has a chance of obtaining official status, then the correct strategy would be to get out of dollars as soon as possible. Actually, the best advice that Bergsten and people like him can give the United States government is to concentrate on solving the energy problem. Everything else remaining the same, if and when this is done, the exchange rate quandary will resolve itself.

Notes

1. President Eisenhower refused to involve the United States in Vietnam in 1954 because it would have meant an increase in taxes. Naturally, he refused even to consider deficit financing.

2. The issue here reduces the simple banking system multiplier. If we do not explicitly consider the foreign sector, and take G for gold or liabilities of the domestic government, D deposits, R the reserves of the commercial banks, C cash, and L loans, we have the results shown in table 4n-1. We can now assume that $R = rD$ and $C = cD$, where r and c are constants. We define the base of the monetary system as $R + C = B$, which here is equal to G. At the same time money is given its usual definition of $M = C + D$. We now see that $B = rD + cD$, and thus $D = B/(c + r)$. Since $C = cD$, we get:

$$M = \frac{1 + c}{r + c} B$$

We note that $L + R = D$, and since $R = rD$ we have $L = (1 - r)D$. Using $D = B/(c + r)$ we have:

$$L = \frac{(1 - r)}{r + c} B$$

When the foreign sector is brought in, then B is not just gold and the liabilities of the domestic government, but also foreign currencies.

3. Convertibility protects the real value of a currency. If there was inflation in the United States then the dollar could be sold for gold, and the gold either held or used to buy a sounder monetary unit.

4. The assumption here, of course, is that once technicians are trained,

Table 4n-1

	Central Bank		Commercial Banks	
	Debits	Credits	Debits	Credits
	G	C	L	D
		R	R	

some means could be found to give most of them meaningful employment in their home countries. Since 1949 the United States has received as a gift from the LDCs about 50,000 scientists and technicians. If we take a superficial view of this process, (which is the only view possible here) there are two explanations for this brain drain. The first is that the countries playing host to these expatriates want or need them. The money value of immigrant scientists, doctors, and technicians to the United States has been greater than all its foreign aid to LDCs. Then, too, many countries in the Third World have the bad habit of not producing the opportunities for individuals to utilize technical skills. The problem here is the complete lack of other than rhetorical or social skills on the part of many bureaucrats in the LDCs; they are thus unable to allocate or manage technically trained persons.

5. For the story of commodity prices, see Rogers (1976).

6. Cooper and Lawrence (1975) are interested in explaining the percentage deviation of price from its trend by an equation of the type:

$$\frac{p - \bar{p}}{\bar{p}} = h \left[\left(\frac{D^* - \bar{D}}{\bar{D}} \right) - \left(\frac{S^* - \bar{S}}{\bar{S}} \right) \right]$$

where $\bar{D}$ and $\bar{S}$ are trend values of demand and supply; and D^* and S^* are ex ante demand and supply. Difficulties arise when we turn to a "specific variant" of this equation, or $P = aD + (\text{sgn } D)bD^2 + c(dD/D)$, for econometric purposes. Specifically, as Professor Gardner Ackley in his comment on this paper (1975) points out, inventories are useful in explaining short-run prices. Actually, they are not only useful, but essential. On this point see chapter 8.

7. Admittedly, the exchange rate adjustments in the year or two before the October War were probably important, and certainly the economists who encouraged these adjustments performed a valuable service. But all that was part of another age, which may have disappeared forever.

Appendix 4A

The Lewis Model

The discussion of multinational companies will be supplemented here by some concepts associated with the well-known growth model of W.A. Lewis (1954). Since the Lewis model is probably the best known of those treating economic development and less developed regions, we can simply summarize its assumptions and results here. Basically this construction assumes that a less-developed country can be divided into two sectors, a modern (M) sector, and a traditional or agricultural (A) sector. It is then postulated that the A sector contains a manpower reserve that can be transferred, without cost, to the M sector as employment expands in the M sector. ("Without cost" because Lewis assumed that the marginal product in the A sector was zero, and thus when someone left this sector the total product would not fall, and moreover his former consumption or "subsistence bundle" could in principle also be transferred intact.) Development in many low-income countries would be based on the export of primary commodities, which would lead to the import of capital goods, which in turn would lead to the creation of many jobs in the further processing of primary commodities or in the import substitution sector.

To complicate the use of this model, however, the sustained migration from the traditional to the modern sector has been in excess of employment possibilities in the modern sector. Employment in industry, commerce, and public service has often expanded extremely slowly, as has investment in the modern sector, but the physical displacement of persons toward this sector has shown a tendency to speed up. Wages in the M sector have also been negotiated or adjusted up to a point incommensurate with the scarcity wage that should theoretically be paid. This in turn results in a further incentive for people to leave the A sector in order to try their luck in the M sector, which necessitates much nonproductive expenditure on infrastructure in urban areas. On top of this, rising labor costs increase the temptation in the M sector to substitute capital for labor, thereby reducing the demand for labor in the M sector.

Several solutions come to mind here. The first is more productive investment in the M sector to absorb some of the unemployed or partially employed in productive work. If investments of this type could in fact be made as easily as they can be theorized, then there would be no such thing as underdevelopment; they will therefore be considered no further. Another possibility consists of various investments in the A sector to introduce an opportunity or psychic cost to individuals intent upon moving from the A sector: they would find it unreasonable to leave well-fed security for the uncertainties of high-unemployment urban areas. In addition, an exportable agricultural surplus might be created.

Some difficulties immediately present themselves. In certain parts of the world agricultural productivity is extremely low; it would therefore be extremely difficult to convince many politicians that there was any real future in this direction. Evidence suggests, however, that despite present low yields, prospects are in fact considerable. Where then does the problem lie? The problem is that although agriculture can be made very productive, high-yield and high-profit agriculture requires the same systematic inputs of modern technology and organization as does high-yield industry. Agriculture, in other words, also needs more technicians; and these technicians may have to be obtained via the same processes discussed earlier: the involvement of multinational firms.

Vegetables grown in several less developed countries (among them Senegal) are flown daily to Europe. The managements of the agricultural firms producing these products are associated with various European companies. There is clearly a tremendous potential for this type of operation, both at the supply and demand ends. How can this low-yield agriculture supply, at moderate prices, markets thousands of kilometers away? The answer is that some relatively simple innovations and reorganizations were introduced by outsiders to take advantage of what must have been an intrinsically high yield.

As indicated earlier, the Lewis model assumes that the public authorities are instrumental in effecting the transfer of labor between sectors. Many of us who have tried to extend this model have introduced the following line of reasoning: it is too much to hope that, when an individual leaves the countryside and moves into the city, his consumption bundle would be sent to the city every month by his altruistic relatives? Instead the government was seen as stepping in and taxing away at least a part of this bundle and using it to pay wages in the modern sector.

We know better now. In several countries in the Third World, this type of arrangement functions satisfactorily, but for the most part the governments of LDCs have only a limited capacity to obtain revenue from the traditional sector. Moreover, it is no longer certain that government expenditures display the economic rationality that we were inclined to credit them with—although they possess an entirely understandable inner logic. Various political pressures, for example, result in a growing priority for urban infrastructure. The Civil Service must expand to take in school leavers, and traditional education with all its extravagances and lost opportunities must also grow since populations are growing. Wages increase despite an excess supply of employees, and military expenditures grow. All this takes place, of course, at the cost of productive investment and overall economic balance.

We can conclude this discussion by considering the possibility that all labor moving from the traditional or agricultural sector must be paid for. Because there is an oversupply of labor in the economy as a whole and capital is the only scarce factor, then the cost of moving labor can be measured in terms of the capital that can be used in the modern sector, or $\overline{K}$.[a] We can let $s\overline{K}$ be the fraction of capital $\overline{K}$ not used to produce consumption goods in the M sector ($0 \leqslant s \leqslant 1$), and K_a the amount of this capital $s\overline{K}$ that must be allotted to the A-sector to maintain L_m workers in the modern sector. For instance, instead of an individual's subsistence bundle following him, some capital must be sent to the A sector to raise production in that sector so that the food required by the individual while he is in the M sector can be produced. We also see that if no consumption goods are produced in the M sector, then $s = 1$. If we now assume that each employee in the modern sector requires the production of an additional w_a units of A goods, and that the production of one unit of A goods requires v_a units of capital, then L_m units of labor working in the modern sector implies $w_a L_m / v_a$ units of the capital $\overline{K}$ stationed in the A sector. Observe that in this situation the total production of the A sector is that due to traditional capital plus that due to K_a (which in A units is $v_a K_a$).

If we assume a neoclassical production situation in the modern sector (because we want to eliminate the possibility that production can take place with only one factor) we can immediately write the following nonlinear program:

$$\text{Max } F(K_m, L_m) = F(K_m, \frac{v_a K_a}{w_a})$$

$$\text{with: } s\overline{K} = K_m + K_a$$

$$\text{and: } K_m, K_a \geqslant 0$$

We solve this program using the following Lagrangian:

$$L = F(K_m, \frac{v_a K_a}{w_a}) + \lambda(s\overline{K} - K_m - K_a)$$

From this we get:

$$\frac{\partial L}{\partial K_m} = \frac{\partial F}{\partial K_m} - \lambda = 0$$

$$\frac{\partial L}{\partial K_a} = \frac{\partial F}{\partial L_m} \frac{v_a}{w_a} - \lambda = 0$$

$$s\overline{K} - K_m - K_a = 0$$

---

[a]Note here that total capital in this economy is not just $\overline{K}$, but also a block of nonshiftable capital that is located in the A sector, which might be called traditional capital. Essentially, this has been left outside the analysis, and thus the capital that we speak of as being allotted to the A sector might be considered extra or additional capital, and raises the output of this sector above that possible with only traditional capital.

And the first order optimizing condition is:

$$\frac{\partial F/\partial K_m}{\partial F/\partial L_m} = \frac{v_a}{w_a}$$

The Jacobian of the above system is obviously:

$$J = \begin{vmatrix} F_{11} & F_{12} & -1 \\ F_{21} & F_{22} & -1 \\ -1 & -1 & 0 \end{vmatrix}$$

If $J \neq 0$, we can get demand functions for K_m and K_a. More interesting for our purposes, however, is a result we can get from the dual of the above program. With v_a and w_a constant, it should be obvious that we can write $F = F(K_m, K_a)$, and thus the dual would give us:

$$\frac{\partial F/\partial K_m}{\partial F/\partial K_a} = 1$$

Since an increase in the output of the modern sector is possible by increasing K_m or L_m, and L_m increases if we have an increase in K_a, then optimal allocation of capital implies that the marginal unit of capital gives the same increase in output regardless of the sector to which it is allocated.

5 Nonfuel Minerals

It is often pointed out these days that we are gradually moving toward relative resource scarcity instead of the plenitude we have hitherto experienced—and unfortunately have taken for granted. Even some comparatively wealthy countries will have to start paying as much attention to managing deficits as they previously devoted to contemplating surpluses.

Still, these deficits are not going to appear for awhile; right now we should be concerned with a *modus vivendi* that will make their arrival something other than an unmitigated disaster. This will mean changes in both the rate and structure of international economic growth and development, but it certainly does not have to mean a less satisfying existence for anyone. Everything considered, a lower growth rate is merely an obstacle to a higher level of material welfare, not a prerequisite for capsized affluence. Most of the people living in the industrialized world are achieving a material standard disproportional to what even the most optimistic forecasters predicted just thirty or forty years ago, but their level of discontent has reached almost stifling proportions and apparently is still growing. Obviously, what is needed in the future is not a speedup in the old way of doing things, but a New World Economic Order—not the New World Economic Order dreamed up by U.N. rhetoricians lounging in the bars of exclusive hotels, but one based on changing the emphasis of everyday economic life from quantity to quality.

There are, however, no magic formulas for bringing this about. In fact, in the initial stages of the transition to a society oriented toward quality, a higher level of investment than ever may be necessary. Many of the sources of environmental deterioration would have to be eradicated fairly early in such a program, less wasteful energy systems installed, and probably some major surgery on the ecosphere would be in order. Admittedly, over a limited period, fairly large capital costs could not be avoided, and these may in turn necessitate a certain restraint in the aggregate growth rate of consumption. However, regardless of the burdens or pleasures that might accompany a transition to a more rational administration of energy and natural assets, in light of the facts on resource availabilities now becoming available, our Faustian longing for unlimited horizons will eventually have to be restrained.

This chapter will elaborate on some of the topics mentioned above in briefly but comprehensively examining some of the most important aspects of nonfuel minerals. This review is essentially nontechnical, except for the section on pricing, but even that section requires only as much economic theory as is

103

normally taught in the first month or two of an introductory course in economic theory.[1] Finally, to give the reader a chance to consider some of the material from both this and the preceding chapter, a brief survey of the iron and steel industry will be offered.

Ores, Ore Grades, and Exploration

According to Park and MacDiarid (1964), "ores are rocks and minerals that can be recovered at a profit." This definition, while not ideal, is satisfactory for our purposes because it indicates that cost is important in determining what mineral deposits will be exploited when.

Although it is not commonly appreciated, almost any rock contains some of elements appearing in the periodic table, even though only nine elements account for almost 99 percent of the earth's crust. Fortunately, some of the most useful elements belong to this nine. One hundred tons of the usual North American granite or shale contains, on the average, 8.3 tons of aluminum-bearing materials, 4.8 tons of iron, and significant quantities of vanadium, zinc, chromium, nickel, copper, and lead. However, this says nothing about "mineability." According to Govett and Govett (1972), a copper deposit will be mined today only if it contains approximately 100 times the average concentration of copper in the continental crust.

This last figure is at best only a benchmark. Technical change has made it possible to mine increasingly thin veins of minerals, and it is unlikely that this trend will reverse. However, since most technical advances in this field are accompanied by large increases in the use of energy, the immediate future might require a considerable modification of the predictions of just a few years ago.

As shown in figure 1-1 in chapter 1, the real cost of obtaining most minerals is still falling, though perhaps at a decreasing rate. That of copper appears to be turning up, but it is impossible to say now whether this is temporary or permanent. In an important paper Bailly (1976) has stated that for copper in 1970, with an average ore grade of 0.7, the average total energy input per pound processed was 44,300 BTU (about 3.5 pounds of coal per pound of copper). Around the year 2000 this figure will be up to 125,000 BTUs—an energy usage increase of about 3.5 percent a year. By itself this is not excessive, but if we also have a cost increase per unit of at least 10 percent a year, the rate of technical progress must speed up considerably if the decline in real costs is to continue.

We can also ask just what will happen with reserves when the ore grade that can be mined and processed is pressed down below 0.5 percent. This question has led to the formulation of "Lasky's Rule" (which will be discussed later in this section), with its suggestion of indefinite increases in the amount of resources. For instance, Carman (1972) argues that if mineable ore grades were reduced by one-half, reserves would go up by a factor of ten. Unfortunately

Carman's speculations say nothing about the time scale, because even if he is correct we should not expect to have access to this bounty in the short run.

The next topic is exploration. In Canada twenty-five years ago about one in 100 exploration attempts resulted in a metals discovery. Today this ratio is only about one in 1000, despite the increased sophistication of exploration equipment. Moreover, the simple fact of a discovery has nothing to do with whether it is exploitable from an economic point of view: only a minor proportion of strikes are immediately followed up by full-scale extractive operations.

The average cost of a discovery rose from about $2 million in the period 1946-55 to about $15 million by 1976. At the same time the value of an average discovery (in Canada) has gone from $245 million in 1946-54 to $711 million in 1970, and thus the relative cost of finding a dollar's worth of ore has more than doubled. On the other hand, still using Canada as an example, statistics presented by Cranston and Martin (1973) indicate that the cost of finding $115 billion of ore was $1.7 billion. This is about 1.47 percent of the total value of ore discovered, but given that approximately 4 percent of the world's GNP is in the form of mineral products, we may still be far from diminishing returns in exploration.

We must then ask just how much of a given resource we should have on hand. One of the things we notice in scrutinizing reserves is the relative constancy of the ratio of reserves to annual production, even though the ratio may differ considerably between minerals. The thing to remember here is that it is pointless to spend money developing reserves too long in advance of when these reserves will be used. For example, if one dollar is spent today to create a unit of reserves that will not be needed for 20 years, and the discount rate is 10 percent, then the profit from extracting the commodity must be $(1 + 0.10)^{20} = 6.72$ dollars in order to justify the investment. Otherwise a rational investor would have bought a bond or a bank account with his dollar. On the other hand, small ratios of reserves to production may be uneconomical because much of the useful life of the recovery equipment could be wasted if the reserves were used up too soon.

For many of us, it is difficult to observe the increasingly febrile search for minerals without becoming a bit bewildered. It seems that the crust of the earth is being methodically picked clean of its most accessible supplies, and we are putting increasing effort into the location and exploitation of deposits that would have been ignored just fifty or seventy-five years ago. At the same time almost everyone, at least privately, recognizes that the only sensible policy is to start relieving the population pressure on the even less accessible resources that we will be searching for in the next century. Note that the next century is explicitly designated here, since unless a demographic or technological miracle occurs soon, no conceivable rate of resource extraction will be able to boost the standard of living for the majority of the world's inhabitants over the near-subsistence level in the next twenty-five years.

Next we take up some of the mechanics of exploration. To begin, there are the preproject activities: reviewing existing maps and reports, examining air photos, and conducting field inspections to determine the extent of resources that should be applied to exploration. At this stage areas of up to 10,000 square kilometers can be considered. Up to one year is generally spent on these activities.

Then there are the regional reconnaissance surveys, which can take up to two years. Here a project area is systematically screened, employing geological and geochemical sampling and perhaps also airborne geophysical surveys. The purpose here is to discover and discard areas which appear to have a low mineral potential, and to identify for future examination targets believed to possess a high potential.

Next we have detailed exploration surveys, which also take up to two years. Geological, geochemical, and geophysical methods are important at this point, and eventually a certain amount of pitting, trenching, and drilling may be in order. At this stage we notice a growing availability of risk capital, since once fairly detailed probing begins the more attractive targets can often be distinguished from the others easily.

Finally we reach the stage of defining the mineral deposit. Exploration at this point assumes a three-dimensional nature, and generally calls for grid drilling and tunneling to determine orebody configuration, tonnage, grade, beneficiation characteristics, and so on. These investigation could take three years, and while they reduce exploration risks considerably, costs sometimes show a tendency to increase very rapidly. Once a region has been designated a target area, it will almost always remain interesting as far as exploration is concerned. Because of technical change and rising ore prices, marginal deposits may become highly exploitable. For example, many uranium deposits rejected as uneconomic a few years ago are now being reclassified as the global supply and demand picture for energy takes shape.

We now take up some aspects of this topic in the light of recent speculation on how much copper may be present in the upper layer of the earth's crust. At the present time copper is found in three different types of deposits: porphyry copper (67 percent), strata-bound deposits (25 percent), and massive sulphides (5 percent). Porphyry copper deposits are large and three-dimensional, with a comparatively low ore grade. About half of all copper production comes from these deposits, and they are expected to dominate world output over the next thirty years. Most porphyry copper is found along the edges of the countries facing the Pacific Ocean, such as Chile, Peru, Mexico, and British Columbia. Some of the most interesting deposits of this category may soon be found in the Philippines, Indonesia, New Guinea, and the Solomon Islands. These are sometimes called the Pacific Porphyries, and are distinguished by their relatively high content of gold and silver.

Strata-bound deposits are layers that contain a relatively high grade of ore (around 3 to 4 percent). For the most part these are found in Central Africa. Massive sulphides are lenticular and conform to the volcanic and sedimentary rocks which make up eugesinclinal formations. A typical example is the one at Kuroko in Japan which, while important earlier in the century, is of almost no economic significance now. Table 5-1 contains 1973 estimates of world copper supplies. These figures can be compared to estimates published by the United States Bureau of Mines in 1975, which gave reserves as 408 million tons, and total resources as 1,498 million tons. Their estimate of economic underseas reserves came to 363 tons.

This section will be concluded by a comment on what is known as Lasky's Rule.[2] This concept, which has been referred to earlier in connection with the reserves that would become available if thinner deposits could be exploited, deserves a certain amount of attention because, if it is valid, then huge reserves may eventually be made available.

Evidence from the microeconomic level indicates that Lasky's rule is probably not universally applicable. Up to now it has given good results when applied to medium-grade porphyry copper deposits, but even here certain limitations can be noticed. According to Fuller (1976) the rule holds at the outside edge of the giant El Teniente Mine in Chile, but does not appear relevant to the deposit as a whole. This means that as the ore grade of exploitable deposits is lowered, more efficient sifting may not be able to comb out larger amounts of copper, and that to extract larger supplies, more and more material will have to be processed. There seems to be a well-defined limit to the amount of copper that can eventually be obtained from this particular deposit. Even so, as Warren (1973) points out, the time may come when the mining industry can be incorporated into the chemical industry, and minerals obtained by breaking up and processing rocks, or mining seawater. If that actually happened, we would have to begin all over again to estimate the quantities of resources that will ultimately be available.

Reserves, Consumption, and Production

Perhaps the most important fact about mineral resources is the unevenness of their distribution over the earth. Less than 10 percent of the world's population

Table 5-1
World Copper Supplies in 1973

Reserves (Economic Resources)	312 Million Tons
Sub-Economic Resources	346 Million Tons
Hypothetical Resources	363 Million Tons
Speculative Resources	290 Million Tons
	1,311 Million Tons

Source: United States Geological Survey estimates, 1973.

resides in countries producing 50 percent of the global mining output, and less than 25 percent in countries producing 85 percent. The average per capita value of the production of minerals is $42: $31 for the Third World (including China) and $78 for the developed market economies. Thus changes in the price of ores, by themselves, cannot materially increase the incomes of the inhabitants of the producing countries. This would be true even if there were price rises considerably larger than those experienced with oil.

In 1973 the total value of the mining output of the Third World reached the level of the developed market economies, or somewhere around $58 billion. The value of the Third World's share of energy-producing minerals increased from 17 to 40 percent of total world production between 1950 and 1973. Since 1950, world production of non-energy-producing ores has been divided about equally between developed market economies on one hand, and Third World and centrally planned countries on the other. The developed market economies consume about sixteen times as much as the LDCs.

The material that will be presented later shows how five countries—the United States, the U.S.S.R., Canada, Australia, and South Africa—dominate world mineral reserves and production. The United States produces approximately one-fourth of the world supply of minerals, and is a leading producer of the most important minerals entering into world trade. We must emphasize, though, the increasingly important role that imports are playing in the supply of mineral resources to the United States. In the year 1900 the United States produced about one-third of the world supply of the most important minerals, including petroleum, while in 1970 this figure was about one-sixth—even though consumption in the United States during the same period advanced somewhat more rapidly than the world average. Table 5-2 provides some idea of the disparities in consumption.

Several things can be inferred from these data. The most important is that, based on demographics and the very large regional differences in consumption bringing the poorer regions of the world up to the level of even the least-developed countries of Europe would require that gigantic amounts of minerals be produced and processed, which in turn would necessitate astronomical investments in processing facilities, energy transformation and distribution, etc. It therefore seems absurd to continue to ignore the possibility that, except for the few developing countries that can generate more social, political, and moral energies than most poor countries today, sustained economic development could easily remain an impossible dream for much of the Third World.

And this includes the long run! Here, if anything, the situation is even more uncertain. In the long run, population increases could wipe out the short-run gains of even the most fortunate and hard-driving LDCs. Then, too—through no fault of their own—many countries had to delay commencing their development until the price of energy, capital goods, and so on began to escalate. As a result they cannot afford many of the technologies and production factors needed to make their economies take off.

Table 5-2
Mineral Consumption by Region

	World	United States		Japan		West Europe	USSR	Asia	South America	Africa
	PC	PC	P	PC	P	P	P	P	PC	PC
Zinc	1.2	5.9	23		13	30	20	4	0.6	2.4
Lead	1.0	5.7	28		5	31	25	3	1.0	1.5
Copper	2.4	10.8	33	8.8	15	40		2	1.0	0.2
Tin	0.06	0.25	28	0.26	17	30			0.02	0.01
Aluminum	13.5	20.0	47	10.5	12	29		4	0.40	0.20
Petroleum			38		10	30	11			
Steel	250	650		650					50	20

P: Percentage Share (1971)
PC: Per Capita, Kilograms (1973)

The situation of the centrally planned economies is also of some interest. The U.S.S.R. is the world's second-largest producer of minerals, and accounts for about 20 percent of world output. Politicians and geologists in the U.S.S.R. have claimed that the country is self-sufficient in minerals. Although Western Europeans and North Americans tend to be skeptical about these claims, a more realistic attitude might be that the U.S.S.R. has a remarkable supply of resources and, if past history means anything, will soon be able to challenge the United States for the role of leading producer.

China also has enormous mineral potential, ranking first in the world in the production of tungsten and antimony, and just behind the United States and the U.S.S.R. in coal production—although, in coal reserves, China is probably on the same level as these countries. China produces considerable tin and mercury, and sizable amounts of aluminum, iron ore, copper, lead, and zinc. Large quantities of oil are now being produced, and further exploration on the mainland and offshore should add considerably to their inventory of this important mineral.

Before looking at figures, the places of Canada and Australia in the scheme of things should be considered. Canada is the world's leading mineral producer on a per capita basis, but like Russia is hampered in both exploitation and exploration by size and weather. Australia, on the other hand, has had no problem in locating new mineral supplies over the last decade, and exploitation has also gone smoothly: the Australian expansion in bauxite mining has been phenomenal by any standard. Much more than Canada, Australia has professed a desire to limit foreign participation in the production and consumption of domestic resources, although it is not certain what this will mean in practice. Despite this desire and their prosperity, the appetite of the Australians for more consumables appears to be as sharp as ever. Given the way the world economy functions, this almost certainly means a growing export of Australian minerals. We can now go on to table 5-3—an abbreviated listing of world production and reserves, which includes some information on imports and values of production.

The figures in table 5-3 are self-explanatory. The only comment required concerns the small value of production of most nonfuel minerals relative to petroleum—and this data was for the period before the oil price rises. Everything considered, neither the rhetoric nor the reality of nonfuel commodity power amounts to much compared to the financial flows associated with the international oil market.

The Pricing of Nonfuel Minerals

In this section we take a brief detour through some simple economic theory to understand pricing of nonfuel minerals. The discussion below largely follows Banks (1976). To begin we can examine a simple supply-demand model of the type found in elementary textbooks:

$$s = f(p)$$
$$d = h(p)$$
$$s = d$$
$$s = \text{supply}$$
$$d = \text{demand}$$
$$p = \text{price}$$

The variables s, d, and p are termed "endogenous" variables and can usually be solved out of this system of three equations. The units employed here are flow units, in that they are in units per time period. For example, we might have metric tons per year (which are often called tonnes/year). The price is measured in relevant monetary units, such as cents/pound, dollars/ton, etc.

Diagramatically this situation is shown in figure 5-1. Here we also see the equilibrium $(\bar{q}, \bar{p})$, or the price and quantity at which the market is cleared and supply is equal to demand. If we specify that d is strictly current demand, or the amount of the commodity currently being used in the production process, and s is strictly current production, then we have a pure flow model. Most textbooks do not make this specification; instead they take s and d as flows, but also stipulate that d can involve a demand for goods to go into inventory, as well as for current use. Similarly, s represents supplies originating from inventories as well as current production.

However, we need a more sophisticated distinction between the origin and destination of supplies and demands for our work here. This is because changes in inventories or, more specifically, the relationship between changes in inventories and changes in demand plays a key role in determining the change in the market price of most industrial raw materials. Thus the model presented above is not completely adequate for our purposes, although, as the appendix to this chapter shows, it is a comparatively powerful tool of analysis.

Before suggesting an amendment to this model, we can examine price movements on the aluminum market between 1966 and 1976. The pricing of aluminum generally follows a scheme known as producer pricing. Producers—often with the collusion of governments—set what they believe to be a long-run equilibrium price, and make their production decision on the basis of this price. Ideally, this price would enable them to produce exactly the amount required by consumers during the period the price is to prevail. However, for this to happen producers would have to display almost superhuman insight into both present and future market conditions. Since this is not always possible, we find ourselves considering still another price, which is called a "free market," "open market," "dealer," or "merchant" price. If, for example, demand is currently larger than production, then this excess demand will be satisfied by a release of supplies from inventories.

Some of these inventories or stocks are held by producers and consumers, but many of them usually belong to individuals or organizations that are called merchants or dealers. These merchants do not usually sell at the producer price, but at the free market price which, unlike the fairly immobile producer price, is highly responsive to market supply and demand. For instance, when demand is very much larger than production, stocks fall rapidly and inventory holders therefore rapidly increase their prices. Figure 5-2 shows the movement of $d - s$, or excess flow demand; the ratio I/d, where I signifies inventories; and the free market price p on the aluminum market. Note the movement of price in response to movements in I/d.

Movements in I/d depend on excess supply or excess demand. Thus at point A in figure 5-2, excess demand is prevailing and inventories are falling relative to demand. The price responds by rising. The record price increase shown to the right of the diagram were caused by panic over the oil price rises, as well as commodity brokers advising their clients to fly in the face of elementary economic logic and splurge on commodities. We can now extend the simple model given above to include the effects of changes in inventories on prices:

$$s_t = f(p_t)$$

$$d_t = h(p_t)$$

$$p_t - p_{t-1} \equiv \Delta p = g\left(\frac{\Delta I}{\Delta d}\right)$$

$$I_t = I_{t-1} + d_t - s_t$$

Table 5-3
Production and Reserves of Important Nonfuel Minerals
(in percentages) 1 Tonne = 1 Metric Ton

Copper	Production (%) 1962	1972	Reserves	Subeconomic Reserves	Hypothetical Speculative
United States	24.3	22.1	24	20	25
U.S.S.R.	13.1	15.4	10	11	12
Chile	12.9	10.6	17		
Zambia	12.3	10.5	8		
Canada	9.1	10.4	9	6	12
Zaire	6.5	6.0	6		
Philippines	1.2	3.1			
Australia	2.4	2.5			
Total World Production (thousands of tons)	4578	6825			
Value of World Production (billions of dollars)		7.40[b]			
LDC Export Earnings (billions of dollars)		2.430[c]			
Import Dependence			U.S. (6%)	EEC (96%)	Japan (83%)
Bauxite					
Australia		20.7	30		
Jamaica	27.5	19.5			
Surinam	11.8	10.3			
U.S.S.R.		7.1			
Guyana	12.9	5.6			
France	7.9	5.0			
Guinea	5.4	3.9	21		
Greece	4.6	3.6			
Total World Production (millions of tons)	28.0	66.1			
Value of World Production (millions of dollars)		792			
LDC Export Earnings[a]		218			

[a]LDC alumina export earnings 298 million dollars
[b]Refined Product
[c]From ores and processed products

Table 5-3 (cont.)

	Production (%)		Reserves	Subeconomic Reserves	Hypothetical Speculative
	1962	1972			
Import Dependence			U.S. (86%)	EEC (60%)	Japan (100%)
Iron Ore					
U.S.S.R.	35.4	41.3	43	39	
U.S.	13.8	10.4	4	13	
Australia	–	8.26			
Brazil	2.5	6.6			
China	5.7	5.8			
Canada	4.9	5.6	14	16	
Liberia	0.9	5.2			
India	4.2	5.1			
Sweden	4.7	5.0			
France	7.5	3.8			
Venezuela	2.9	2.6			
Total World Production (millions of tons)	288	450			
Value of World Production (billions of dollars)		2.649	(Average: 1970-72)		
LDC Export of Earnings (millions of dollars)		1011			
Import of Dependence			U.S. (20%)	EEC (59%)	Japan (99%)
Tin					
Malaysia	30.5	31.1	14	10	16
Bolivia	11.4	13.1	11	5	
U.S.S.R.	10.2	10.9	5	6	3
China	15.4	9.3	12	19	10
Indonesia	9.0	8.6	13	17	
Thailand	7.7	8.2	32	18	16
Australia	1.4	4.5			
Nigeria	4.2	2.7			
Zaire	3.7	2.6	2	10	
Total World Production (thousands of tons)	195.4	246.5			

cFrom ores and processed products

Table 5-3 (cont.)

	Production (%)		Reserves	Subeconomic Reserves	Hypothetical Speculative
	1962	1972			
Value of World Production (millions of dollars)		750	(Average: 1970-72)		
LDC Export Earnings		653[c]			
Import Dependence			U.S. (87%)	EEC (99%)	Japan (95%)
Manganese					
U.S.S.R.	49.3	43.8	27	39	30
South Africa	8.8	13.6	41	39	20
Brazil	7.8	11.4	5	1	1
Gabon	1.5	9.5	13		1
India	9.5	6.7			
Australia	0.5	4.0			
China	3.6	3.0			
Ghana	2.8	2.2			
Total World Production (thousands of tons)	6581	10064			
Value of World Production (billions of dollars)					
LDC Export of Earnings (millions of dollars)		105.3			
Import Dependence			U.S. (98%)	EEC (99%)	Japan (86%)
Nickel					
Canada	57.4	36.2			
U.S.S.R.	21.8	19.7			
New Caledonia	9.3	15.9			
Cuba	4.5	5.7			
Australia		5.5			
Indonesia	0.1	3.5			
Dominican Republic		2.7			
U.S.	3.4	2.7			
Total World Production (thousands of tons)	366.9	643.4			

Table 5-3 (cont.)

	Production (%)		Reserves	Subeconomic Reserves	Hypothetical Speculative
	1962	1972			
Value of World Production (billions of dollars)					
LDC Export Earnings (millions of dollars)					
Import Dependence			U.S. (72%)	EEC (100%)	Japan (100%)
Lead					
U.S.	8.5	16.2			
U.S.S.R.	13.8	13.3			
Australia	14.8	12.1			
Canada	7.5	10.9			
Peru	6.6	5.2			
Mexico	7.6	4.7			
Yugoslavia	4.0	3.5			
China	3.5	3.1			
Total World Production (thousands of tons)	2542	3665			
Value of World Production (billions of dollars)		1.18[b]			
LDC Export Earnings (millions of dollars)		140			
Import Dependence			U.S. (26%)	EEC (70%)	Japan (70%)
Zinc					
Canada	12.3	22.8			
U.S.S.R.	11.1	11.6			
Australia	9.3	8.8			
U.S.	12.4	7.7			
Peru	5.0	6.2			
Japan	5.2	5.0			
Mexico	6.8	4.8			

[b]Refined Product

Table 5-3 (cont.)

	Production (%)		Reserves	Subeconomic Reserves	Hypothetical Speculative
	1962	1972			
Total World Production (thousands of tons)	3690	5450			
Value of World Production (billions of dollars)		2.16[b]			
LDC Export Earnings (millions of dollars)		178			
Import Dependence			U.S. (63%)	EEC (60%)	Japan (68%)

[b]Refined Product

Kolbe and Timm (1972) have used a model like this to forecast the price of natural rubber; Desai (1966) employs this construction in his examination of the tin market; and Fisher, Cootner, and Baily (1972) and Banks (1974) have used it for copper.

In the United States producer pricing is the rule in the copper market, but there is also an extensive free market. Outside the United States, copper is generally priced using a variant of the free market price. A producer in Zambia or Chile, for example, will sell a certain amount of copper for delivery at some time in the future at the price prevailing on the London Metal Exchange (LME) at or around the time of delivery. The LME price is generally regarded as a free market price. This means delivery of a known quantity at an unknown price—a situation not often treated in the textbooks. We also have the unusual spectacle of an oligopolistic industry behaving in a pronounced nonoligopolistic manner.

The zinc and nickel markets also display this kind of behavior. In Europe, zinc producers simply meet and fix a price; in the United States, producers apply to the Federal Price Commission for permission to charge the desired price. The free market zinc price can be founded on or related to the prices quoted on the London Metal Exchange and the New York Commodities Exchange. Prices quoted on these exchanges are for metals and not ores, but there is a fixed relationship, via costs, between these two prices.

Similarly, primary nickel is sold at prices established by producers. These prices are called posted or producer prices, and refer to certain standard grades sold by the major companies. What could be called the nickel content prices of the various categories of metal differ somewhat; the price of nickel contained in ferronickel is about 5 percent below that of pure nickel or nickel cathodes. In

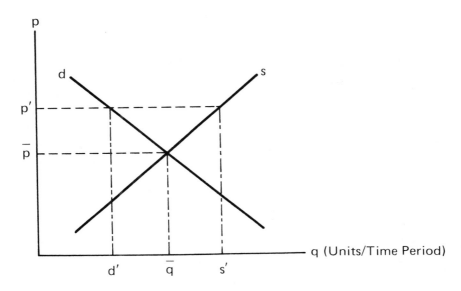

Figure 5-1. Elementary Supply and Demand Model.

addition there is a small open or free market for the sale of both primary and secondary (scrap) nickel. The primary nickel on this free market often originates in the U.S.S.R. or one of the other centrally planned countries, and is purchased by merchants or dealers who resell it at prices dependent upon supply and demand in Western Europe or North America. In 1969-70, after a major strike in the Canadian nickel mines, the British Steel Corporation doubled its purchases from the free market, often paying six or seven times the producer price.

A few major nonfuel minerals do not fall in the above category of pricing behavior. In the market for iron ore the pricing mechanism follows, to a considerable extent, along traditional oligopolistic lines, with the price determined by negotiations between large producers and large buyers. Because of the difference in the quality of ores and the absence of an institution such as the LME where standards are set and monitored, it is impossible to distinguish a representative world market price for iron ore. Perhaps the closest we have is the price of Swedish Kiruna D ore, c.i.f. Rotterdam, which is used by the sales company Malmexport on short-term contracts with European buyers. However, this price is not typical for all iron ore. Similar observations are relevant for such commodities as cobalt, manganese, and tungsten.

Processing

The next step in our exposition is a short review of the processing cycle—the movement of a mineral from ore to refined products to semifabricates and man-

118

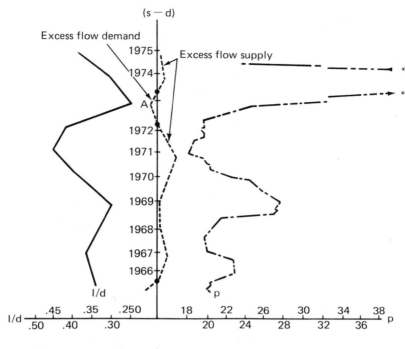

p: Price, U.S. cents/pound   Source: Various publications
I/d: Inventory to Demand ratio
 *:   Price = 51 cents/pound (May, 1973)
(s — d): Excess supply

Figure 5-2. The Demand for and Supply of Aluminum (Non-centrally Planned
Countries) and the Free Market Price of Aluminum.

ufactured goods. In the case of metals we begin with mining, which involves
digging, blasting, separating, and loading. From here we go to the first stage of
processing, which may include crushing, grinding, and concentrating. Then come
the major processing activities of smelting or refining or both. These are
followed by semifabricating, in which the output of the smelter or refinery is
rolled, drawn, and extruded into highly usable shapes such as sheets and rods.
Finally, the particular finished product is fabricated or manufactured.

The discussion in the above paragraph began with ore, and therefore it
concerns *primary* metal. Another important source of industrial raw materials is
scrap, or secondary metal. This comes from the reduction of finished goods
(such as automobiles and transformers) containing the commodity, or from
shavings and rejects that originate somewhere in the processing cycle. In a

normal year about 40 percent of the total copper consumption of the developed market economies originated in scrap. Only a portion of the scrap collected in a given period is "re-refined." Of the 1,178,000 metric tons of copper scrap consumed in the United States in 1965, 403,000 metric tons went to the refinery. The rest, or 75,000 metric tons, was used without refining—mostly as an input for brass mills. Figure 5-3 summarizes this discussion.

For copper, the refining stage is the most interesting, because refined copper is very pure, and comes in only a few shapes. Smelter and concentrator products, on the other hand, are too impure, and semifabricates and manufactured products are too homogeneous. The small diagram in the upper right-hand corner of figure 5-3 shows the supply-demand situation for the refining stage of the United States copper industry in 1966. Two things are important here. In the expression "secondary refined and other," the "other" cannot be identified from existing data. Then, too, some of the scrap used as a feedstock for the refining stage will itself be transformed to scrap. The figure 1377 is thus a net figure, and is an output from the refining stage rather than an input.

In a less-developed country the pattern of movement in and out of the various stages of transformation would probably be very different. Figure 5-4 shows the arrangement for Peruvian copper in 1968. The thing to be noticed in particular is the large export of partially processed copper as compared to refined copper. Copper concentrates contain only about 32 percent copper, and while blister is 99 percent pure copper, it still requires considerable processing before it is ready for the semifabricators. One of the perpetual and justifiable complaints of LDCs is that the world market often forces them to export raw materials they are perfectly capable of refining further, which means that they lose important factor incomes as well as even more valuable industrial training.

The inventory figures shown in figure 5-4 are net, and it is easy to see that more of an item could come out of stock than goes in. Then, too, ore production is shown here as 212,537 metric tons. This is copper content, and means that with the ore grade in Peru averaging out as 1 percent, it is necessary to mine and treat $212,537/0.01 = 21,253,700$ metric tons of material to obtain 212,537 tons of copper.

A Brief Survey of the World Iron and Steel Industry

The iron and steel industry is the object of this survey because: (1) It produces an extremely important input at a relatively low cost. (2) In a developed economy, the value of its production is a significant portion of GNP, generally from 3 to 5 percent. In a country with a high growth rate, this could come to 6 to 10 percent. (3) It is a highly capital-intensive industry, requiring very large investments. At present the creation of a ton of steel capacity calls for an investment approaching $1000. (4) Its technology is changing rapidly, and (5) It

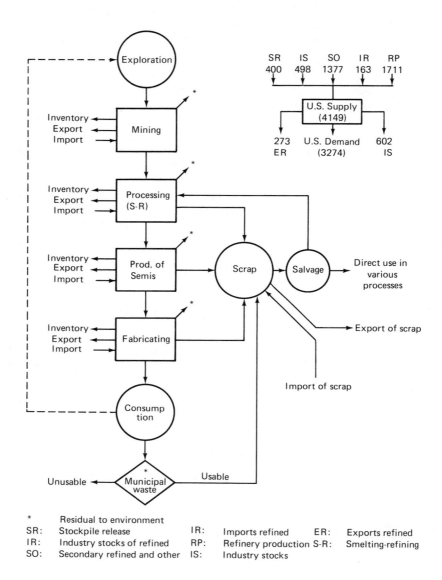

Figure 5-3. Processing Cycle for a Typical Metal, and Supply-Demand Relation-ship for Refined Copper in the United States (1966).

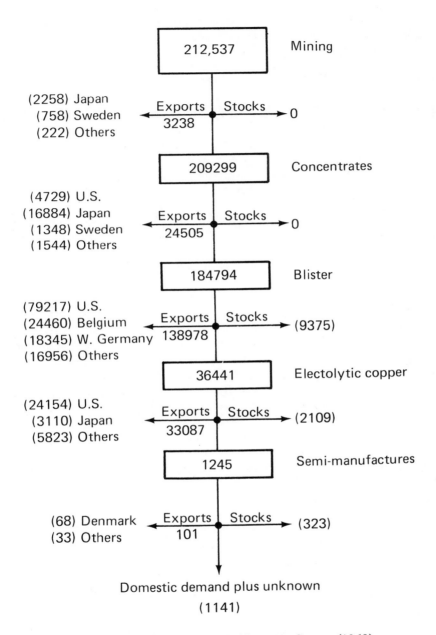

Figure 5-4. The Disposition of Peruvian Copper (1968).

generates a large volume of trade in its own products and about one-half of all manufactured goods traded contain some steel.

Semifabricated steel products take the form of plate, sheet, bars, rods, wire, heavy and light sections, tubing, and so on. These are used in all types of industries and construction work. In addition, some of the by-products of the steel industry are very important. Pig iron is needed for cast iron foundries; coke by-products are used in the chemical industry; and slag is an input in the production of cement. In 1973 the total world production of steel ingots, or raw steel, was 694 million tons, while 550 million tons of finished steel products (such as plate, sheet, and bars) were manufactured. The average price of this material was about $350/ton, as compared to an average price of $150/ton between 1969 and 1972. Worldwide steel production was distributed as shown in table 5-4.

The international trade in iron ore, pellets, coking coal, semifinished and finished steel products involved transporting about 1.1 billion tons per year of various inputs and products, with a value of approximately $70 billion. About three tons of ore, coking coal, scrap, and fluxes are needed to produce one ton of steel; for the world steel industry to function normally, about two billion tons of inputs and 700 million tons of outputs must be handled per year. Direct and indirect energy inputs into the iron and steel industry come to almost 12 percent of the total world energy production.

Figure 5-5 shows the processing cycle from iron ore to finished product. According to this diagram direct inputs into the world steel industry amounted to 1760 million tons (Iron Ore + Coking Coal + Scrap + Fluxes). Two hundred million tons of scrap was purchased from external sources, and the remainder (345 − 200 = 145) was generated within the industry itself, and is called "home" and "prompt" scrap. The cost of these inputs was $50 billion, which can be broken down as follows: 16.2 percent iron ore, 38.3 percent coking coal, 40.8 percent scrap, and 4.59 percent fluxes. We see here that coking coal requirements have become extremely large, and because good coking coals are not available everywhere, the procurement of this input could raise serious problems for some countries in the coming years.

In steelmaking the principal innovation since World War II has been the adoption of the basic oxygen furnace (BOF)—sometimes called the Linz-Donnitz (LD) process—the electric arc furnace, and the gradual phasing out of the conventional open hearth furnace. This improvement in technology has meant that the Japanese, who began to install their capacity en masse in the middle 1950s, were able to avail themselves of the wave of the future in the present, and therefore eventually took the absolute technical leadership in world steel.

Why did American producers, who have always prided themselves on their innovative dynamism, not begin abandoning their older equipment earlier? The return on equity in the United States steel industry did not begin to sag until the early 1960s, and until that time was around 11 percent—the average for the

Table 5-4
The Production of Raw Steel, 1973
(in millions of tons)

	Production
Europe	
EEC	150
Centrally Planned Econ. (Except U.S.S.R.)	49.5
U.S.S.R.	131.5
Other	26.1
Asia	
Japan	119.3
China	24.00
India	6.924
Other[a]	4.975
Americas	
U.S.	137.5
Canada	13.4
Brazil	7.2
Mexico	4.7
Other	4.7
Africa	
South Africa (Republic)	5.7
Egypt	0.3
Rhodesia	0.3
Other	0.34
Oceania	
Australia	7.5
New Zealand	0.2
World Total	694.5

[a]Includes Israel

United States manufacturing industry over the past 25 years; thus the financial markets were not inclined to withhold their favors from the producers of steel. However a simple cost-benefit calculation undoubtedly would have shown that, given the steady world increase in demand for steel and the acquisition costs of new technology, there was no point in retiring older facilities quickly, assuming that the Japanese would not display an exceptional precocity in utilizing the advantages of their new equipment.

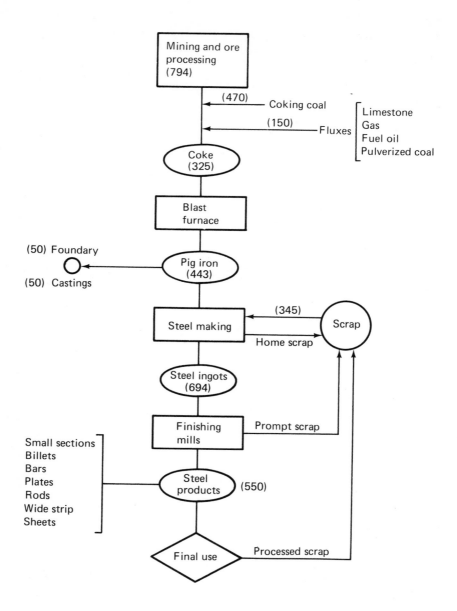

Figure 5-5. The Processing of Iron Ore into Steel.

As bad luck would have it, this is exactly what happened. Aided by the increasing returns to scale that seem to characterize BOF installations, productivity in the Japanese steel industry rose extremely rapidly as it did in all Japanese industrial operations. Japan became the world's largest exporter of steel, and by employing a price and profit policy that was tantamount to dumping, forced its way into decisive positions in all the important markets. This matter is now being discussed extensively, and competitors of the Japanese may arrange some type of tariff and quota scheme that can temporarily check the next attack on the steel markets of Europe and North America. Regardless of the outcome of these exertions—and fundamentally, in the long run, they can be classified as nonsense—what cannot be done is to match the productivity growth in the Japanese steel industry that results from scale economies, an extremely rapid diffusion throughout the industry of various innovations, and the diligence and competence of workers and technicians. The productivity of the main steel producers has developed as shown in figure 5-6.

In 1976 the Japanese steel industry was working at about 80 percent of capacity; in early 1977, at slightly less. However, investment has only been stretched out slightly, and the Japanese intend to have 140 million metric tons of capacity ready by 1978. Assuming that the world demand for steel continues to expand by about 4.5 percent (the long-term trend rate), the Japanese will be

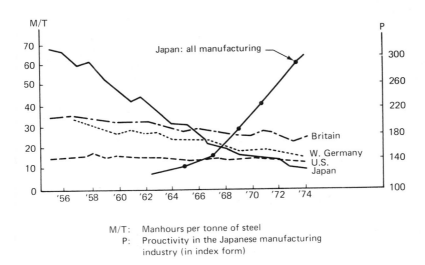

M/T: Manhours per tonne of steel
P: Prouctivity in the Japanese manufacturing industry (in index form)

Figure 5-6. Some Productivities in the Steel Industry.

ready to service both old and new customers with a stock of the most productive steelmaking plant in the world.

Although the long-term demand for steel has been increasing at about 4.5 percent a year, steel consumption grew by 5.6 percent a year from 1960 to 1973 and is expected to grow by 3.5 to 4 percent a year up to the early 1980s. This, incidentally, says something about general economic growth over this period: it cannot possibly regain the levels of the last decade or so. Energy price increases should, by themselves, raise the cost of steel at least 10 percent (assuming that the energy price itself increases about 10 percent a year). The competitive position of plastics (a substitute for steel) has worsened considerably, thanks to the large input of oil in plastics. This is also true of plastics vis-à-vis copper. On the other hand, the competitive position of aluminum relative to steel will probably remain unchanged, although aluminum producers are somewhat more vulnerable to increases in the price of bauxite than steelmakers are with the price of iron ore.

Iron Ore

The demand for iron ore is derived from the demand for steel, and the relationship is almost purely input-output.[3] On the supply side, planning for new capacity turns on the estimate of future demand and price. Confirmed expansion plans now call for new mining facilities coming on stream at a rate of about 4 percent a year up to 1980-81.

More than one-third of the world trade in iron ore takes place under long-term contracts that specify both prices and quantities. These contracts are, however, occasionally renegotiated, particularly when there have been major price movements on the "free" market. In the latter market, the price is generally negotiated once a year; this bears little or no resemblance to pricing arrangements in other so-called free markets. About 32 percent of the trade in iron ore is carried on in this manner.

The remainder of the iron ore traded on the world market originates in captive mines, which are owned by the steel companies they supply. In 1968 captive mines provided 96 percent of United States requirements, and 31 percent of those of the United Kingdom and European Economic Community (EEC). Nationalization and nationalism have made considerable inroads into the enthusiasm of the large steel companies and their governments for this type of arrangement, and the time seems to be coming when long-term contracts rather than ownership will link buyer and supplier. The free market could conceivably gain in importance, but much of the financing for mining enterprises in the LDCs will continue to originate with or be influenced by ore buyers in the developed countries, who like to know the price of ore over a fairly long period. In addition, long-term contracts could create some problems for a cartel of exporting countries attempting to administer a coordinated price policy.

As with oil, copper, and aluminum, the iron ore-exporting countries have formed a producers organization, which they call IOEC. Their ultimate goal cannot yet be discerned, but they profess a desire to reduce the competition for investment funds that characterizes this industry; should discussions begin on regulating the price of iron ore, they stand ready to act as an intermediary. The IOEC also claims innocence of any intention to place ore buyers under the kind of pressures that oil buyers have begun to experience, and given the large amount of iron ore reserves located outside the Third World, there is no reason to think otherwise.

Iron ore mining capacity is projected to expand by 200 million tons in developed countries and 90 million tons in LDCs over the next eight years or so. Assuming no serious economic downturn, the major additions to capacity will take place in Australia, Brazil, Canada, and the United States, and big projects are also under way in Liberia and the Ivory Coast. Interestingly enough, present investments indicate that North America may become almost self-sufficient in iron ore in 1980, although there is no estimate of how long this condition could last. Finally, because such a large proportion of new facilities are being constructed in developed countries, where costs have a high correlation with inflation, the price of iron ore should not be expected to decrease, even though there may occasionally be some excess supply.

Japan and Some Further Problems

The first question we will ask here concerns the possibility of beating back the Japanese incursion into the steel market with conventional means (but not tariffs, quotas, or general economic retaliation). There is no such possibility. Figure 5-6 shows that the steel industry in the United States, for example, has experienced almost none of the productivity gains over the past few years that we might have expected from the introduction of new equipment and modernization. The reasons for this should be clear, but in case they are not the following summary should be of some help to the reader.

Since the dawn of the industrial revolution, the social status of manual workers has steadily declined. In some countries this decline is becoming a torrent, and has fallen most heavily on the least glamorous industries, such as the steel industry. Wage movements in these industries are largely explained by their growing unattractiveness relative to other occupations; but given the general advance in the standard of living, and particularly the possibility of making a reasonable living without having to perform work that demands excessive strength or concentration, high wages no longer buy high productivity, or even not-so-high reliability.

This problem exists everywhere, and although the Japanese solution may not be absolutely ideal, it at least enables them to stay ahead of their competitors. The Japanese wage structure gives most categories of employees a sense of advancing materially as they grow older, and not asymptotically approaching a limit fairly early in their working lives. In the steel industry the shop floor is considered the logical place for innovations to originate, and workers, technicians, and engineers that participate in this process are liberally rewarded. In many firms, immediately after the first oil price rises, management and higher administrative personnel voluntarily accepted salary decreases, thus setting an example for other employees. But most important, neither the wage-setting mechanism, the media, nor society as such deliberately encourages the impression that white-collar workers performing trivial or economically marginal activities are more important than members of the industrial work force.

Needless to say, disaffection with productive and socially useful work has spread to all occupational categories in most countries. Until recently American steel manufacturers have experienced some difficulties in recruiting engineers, and a pertinent question might be just where this and other American industries expect to be once the microcomputer revolution moves into high gear. The Japanese, of course, expect to take the lead in this sweepstakes, and to keep up the momentum of their productivity advances over the last twenty years. Earlier in this section we noted that supplies of first-rate coking coal are far from inexhaustible. The Japanese, however, are already making plans to use inferior coking coals or, in the long run, even other types of coal. Obviously, this may have to be done someday; if necessity demands, they are prepared to advance that day substantially.

We can close this section by saying something about where steel is likely to be produced during the rest of this century. Despite the wishful thinking of the United Nations Industrial Development Organization (UNIDO) and other superfluous creations of the United Nations, any large shift in steel production toward the LDCs is unlikely in the near future. To begin, there are only a few success stories on the economic horizon in the Third World, and most of these are in Latin America, in countries possessing cultural and other advantages that make them—or at least regions within them—part of the developed world in all except name and ideological affiliation.

Moreover, although steelmaking is a fairly simple proposition, as compared with the science-based industries, it presents both direct and indirect technical problems that the available engineering and administrative talent in many LDCs are not particularly anxious to solve. If steel could be manufactured with rhetoric, then the goals of the so-called Lima Declaration, which called for the location of 25 percent of the world's steelmaking (and other manufacturing) capacity to be located in the LDCs by the year 2000—might be realizable. But under the circumstances, the next twenty-five years should see little change in who manufactures or consumes this valuable product.

Notes

1. Chapter 4 of the well-known textbook by Paul Samuelson (1973) provides all the background necessary to follow the present exposition. Another excellent elementary book is Dorfman's (1964). The author also strongly recommends the introductory textbooks of Clower and Due (1972) and Alchian and Allen (1964). The question of stocks and flows is taken up in chapter 8 below, as are some other topics that are important for doing empirical work in this field.

2. This rule is named after S. Lasky of the United States Bureau of Mines. Algebraically it can be expressed as Ore Grade $= K_1 - K_2$ Log Tonnage. If this expression is rearranged we see that a decrease in ore grade implies an increase in the tonnage that can be extracted.

3. As an example, the following regression results can be cited:

$$C_s = -54{,}224 + 287.75 \text{ GNP} \qquad \bar{R}^2 = 0.978 \quad DW = 1.98$$
$$(27.2)$$

In this equation C_s is steel consumption (raw) in thousands of metric tons, and GNP is the gross national product of the OECD countries deflated to 1963 dollars. Then:

$$Q_i = 1.09\, C_s + 2600\, P_i \qquad \bar{R}^2 = 0.949 \quad DW = 2.10$$
$$(37.3) \qquad (6.0)$$

Here Q_i is world iron ore production in thousands of metric tons, and C_s is as above. The t ratios are in parentheses. World Bank sources indicate that world income elasticities of demand are about 0.9 for steel, and the econometricians of this organization also feel that this figure is higher for countries for a low GNP per capita. This seems to agree with the tendency for rapidly growing countries to attribute a larger portion of GNP to the iron and steel industry than more mature economies do. In the case of price elasticities, a reasonable figure for the United States would seem to be about -0.6, but this may be lower. The demand elasticity for iron ore ranges between -0.1 and -0.2. For an interesting report on the thinking of the steel industry in the United States in regard to the development of costs, as well as a summary of some prognoses, the reader can refer to the work of the well-known iron and steel industry consultant Jack Robert Miller (1974).

Appendix 5A

This appendix contains an exercise dealing with steel pricing. It follows, in general, an instructive article of Weston and Rice (1976). The intention here is to show the reader some of the uses of linear approximations in combination with partial equilibrium analysis. The overall purpose of this appendix, however, is pedagogical, and deals only with techniques.

As Weston and Rice pointed out, the steel industry in the United States had a good year in 1974, shipping 100 tons and realizing a 14 percent rate of return on net worth. But between the third quarter of 1974 and the second quarter of 1975, the gross national product declined 10 percent and steel shipments went down by 20 percent. Assuming a linear demand curve for steel, we have the arrangement shown in figure 5A-1(a).

The price of steel in 1974 was 275 dollars per ton. As the figure shows, the shift of the demand curve is parallel; but the flow demand for steel—or the demand for current use—is almost price elastic, as shown in figure 5A-1(b). Thus the slope of the demand curve is accounted for by speculative and precautionary buying. We might therefore expect that in a business cycle downturn, the demand curve would not only shift to the left, but also twist as illustrated in figure 5A-1(b). This twist is related to a change in the behavior of inventory holders during a business cycle downturn.

Weston and Rice say the elasticity of demand for steel is normally between -0.4 and -0.6. What we want now is the elasticity of demand after the parallel

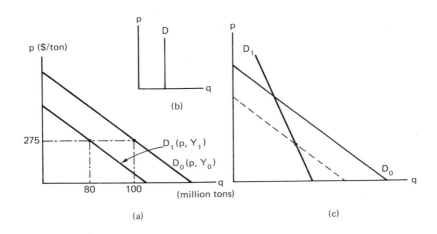

Figure 5A-1. Demand Curves for Steel.

131

shift. Using the subscript 0 to denote the situation before the shift, and 1 after the shift we have:

$$\left(\frac{\Delta q}{\Delta p}\right)_0 \frac{p_0}{q_0} = e_0$$

and:

$$\left(\frac{\Delta q}{\Delta p}\right)_1 \frac{p_1}{q_1} = e_1$$

but:

$$\left(\frac{\Delta q}{\Delta p}\right)_0 = \left(\frac{\Delta q}{\Delta p}\right)_1 \qquad \text{(Parallel Shift)}$$

so:

$$e_1 = \frac{q_0}{q_1} \cdot e_0$$

We have q_0 = 100, and with a twenty percent decrease in shipments, q_1 = 80. If we take e_0 = −0.6 we get e_1 = −0.75. If we assumed that the demand curve twisted then this value would be higher (since $[\Delta_q/\Delta_p]$ would be smaller). We can now tabulate our data and question what happens when we try various price strategies. These strategies will be labeled option 1 and option 2. Option 1 involves no steel price increase, but because of a 10 percent increase in the general price level this is equivalent to a 10 percent decrease in the steel price. With a price elasticity of −0.75, this would call for a 7.5 percent increase in steel consumption, or from 80 million tons to 86 million. On the other hand, if we take option 2 and raise the price of steel by $15/ton—which was the actual increase—the 10 percent increase in the general price level would mean that the steel price fell by 4.54 percent. ($15 is approximately 5.45 percent if we begin with $275. Subtracting this from 10 percent gives 4.54.) Again, with an elasticity of −0.75, this would mean an increase in steel consumption of 3.402 percent, or from 80 to 82.73 million tons.

We now come to the cost side. The variable cost of producing 100 tons of steel was $19 billion. A 10 percent inflation rate would make this $20.9 billion, but assuming linearity, a fall in production to 86 million tons would make the variable cost (86/100) × 20.9 = 17.974; and if production were 82.73, then the variable cost would be 17.29. Taking fixed cost as $5 billion and the net worth of the United States steel industry as approximately $12 billion, we get table 5A-1.

We have attempted to show here that, on the basis of the given data, and employing simple linear approximations, it could be argued that a profit-maximizing steel industry would have raised its price in 1975. This is an ex ante

Table 5A-1
Two Options for Pricing Steel in 1975

		Option 1	Option 2
		1974	1975	1975
1.	Year	1974	1975	1975
2.	General Price Index	1.00	1.10	1.10
3.	Price Elasticity	−0.60	−0.75	−0.75
4.	Tons Shipped (Million Tons)	100	86	82.73
5.	Nominal Price (Dollars/Ton)	275.0	275.0	290.0
6.	Total Revenue (Billions of Dollars)	27.5	23.65	23.99
7.	Variable Cost (Billions of Dollars)	19.0	17.97	17.29
8.	Fixed Cost (Billions of Dollars)	5.0	5.0	5.0
9.	Total Cost (Billions of Dollars)	24.0	22.97	22.29
10.	Earnings (6 − 9)	3.5	0.68	1.7
11.	Interest (Billions of Dollars)	0.60	0.60	0.60
12.	Profit before Tax	2.9	0.08	1.1
13.	Tax (0.40 Profit)	1.2	0.032	0.44
14.	Net Profit	1.7	0.048	0.66
12.	Net Worth (Billions of Dollars)	12.0	12.0	12.0
13.	Return on Net Worth (Percent)	14.1	0.4	5.5

calculation and essentially uses no cost data other than that available for 1974. For this reason, among others, the results do not conform exactly to those of Weston and Rice.

But there is still a question: why stop with a price increase of $15 per ton? In the present example there is no reason to do so, since as long as the price elasticity of demand is greater than minus unity, the correct strategy is to continue to raise the price. Weston and Rice evaded this problem by assuming a price elasticity of −1.2, or what they call an extreme value. It could be correctly argued that as we increase price, we move up the demand curve and increase the elasticity; but whether we could justify a price elasticity of less than minus unity cannot be taken up here.

Environment, Population, and Food

It has been suggested that the deterioration of the environment can mainly be attributed to nonconsumption, in the sense that many goods do not disappear a short time after they are purchased, but are discharged into the environment in some form. This may well be, but until recently the environment was quite capable of absorbing this litter. The problem today is that there are so many people polluting their surroundings that the natural absorptive capacity of the environment is often exceeded.

The attack on environmental decay must therefore proceed in a number of directions. First and foremost, everything possible must be done to check the rate of increase in world population. At the ostentatious charade called the Conference on the Environment, held in Stockholm in 1972, it was often suggested that poverty was the greatest pollutant, and that the cure was an accelerated transfer of resources from the rich to the developing nations. Many of us share this opinion of poverty, but certainly nobody could passively accept this cure. The so-called rich nations are rapidly—though not rapidly enough—nearing zero population growth, while in many LDCs the slightest increase in per capita income increases the population growth rate and the general misery.

Of course, simply pointing out that population growth must be brought under control will not cause it to happen. Worse than that, it may be impossible. It has been suggested, in fact, that the population problem may not have a technical solution. (Another such problem is said to be the arms race, where as both sides increase their military power they apparently decrease their national security.) In a celebrated article Hardin (1972) has looked at this matter in light of a Benthamite welfare calculus, where the goal is the greatest good for the greatest number, and has concluded that with population, the greatest number means less than the greatest good, but the logic of population dynamics leads to the greatest number anyway.

Hardin's analysis of the dangers implicit in overbreeding turns on the externalities paradigm, which deals with uncompensated effects, third-party effects, or simply nonmarket effects. Economic situations invariably involve costs and benefits, and in most elementary textbook examples the individual paying the costs receives the benefits. But things do not have to work this way. If someone builds a sandpile in his backyard for his children, the neighbors' children usually end up playing there also. They and their parents therefore receive a benefit without a cost, or an external economy.

Hardin is more concerned with external diseconomies, and the following

135

simple numerical example illustrates the main issue. Suppose that 100 sheep owned by 100 men are grazing on a plot of 100 square meters that provides 100 cubic meters of fodder. Each sheep can consume up to one cubic meter of fodder, and if it does consume one cubic feet of fodder it can be sold for one dollar. Unfortunately, in this situation private profitability calculations lead directly to overgrazing, and what Hardin repeatedly refers to as ruin.

The individual who has one sheep asks himself if it will pay to have two. Two sheep owned by one person, and one owned by all the others, means a total of 101 sheep. Assuming linearity, this reduces the amount of fodder available for each sheep to 100/101 cubic meters and reduces the market value per sheep correspondingly. Maintaining our assumption of linearity, each sheep now sells for 100/101 dollars. The person with two sheep can sell them for 200/101, and the increase in his income as he goes from 1 sheep to 2 is $(200/101) - 1$. The loss to each of the other sheep owners is $1 - (100/101)$, and the total loss to the other ninety-nine is $[1 - (100/101)]99$. We now see that the net gain for the sheep-owning community, assuming no cost for adding the extra sheep, is $[2(100/101) - 1] - [99(1 - (100/101))]$, and this is equal to zero[1] (which is the same thing as saying that the net loss is zero).

Under the circumstances, everyone has an incentive to add an extra sheep. The individual adding the sheep increases his gain, and although each of the other sheep herders takes a small loss, our linearity assumptions lead us to the convenient result that the community as a whole does not suffer a loss. The logic here is that as long as we suppose a zero acquisition cost for sheep, each herder should increase his herd to infinity, although the amount of fodder is finite. Clearly, no good can come from this arrangement in the long run.

Some Basic Environmental Economics

By way of continuing the above discussion, a very brief introduction to the economics of the environment is in order. Our analysis commences with a partial equilibrium model of the type made famous by Marshall (1898) and further refined for the purposes of welfare economics by Pigou (1932). The basic issue is essentially as follows. Suppose a firm, while producing product A, generates a spillover or externality, such as pollution, that adversely affects product B. In summing up the cost of this situation, we say that this spillover causes the marginal private cost of producing A to differ from the marginal social cost, in that the marginal social cost includes not only the direct cost of producing an extra unit of A, but also the additional cost of producing and selling B due to spillovers from A. This situation has undesirable consequences for resource allocation in a market economy.

In the usual example of external diseconomy spillovers, a paper mill upstream emits waste that deleteriously affects fisheries downstream. (This exercise took on a special relevance in Germany in 1969, when the discharge of wastes from a single factory killed all the fish in the Rhine.) The difficulty here is that the water of the stream presents itself as a free good to the mill, which responds by using the water for waste disposal. Now in a market economy, prices are supposed to be proportional to production costs, and thus the prices of the products of the mill will be understated, while those of the fisheries will be higher than they would have been without the mill. Because demand is a function of price, we end up with too many mill products and too few fish. In a sense, consumers of fish are subsidizing consumers of mill products.

The two most important methods of controlling pollution in this situation appear to be tax subsidy programs and legal restraints. Looking at the tax aspect of the first of these, we find that its purpose is to force a polluter to internalize the costs associated with polluting—costs that would, without a tax, be placed on others. Ideally it amounts to putting a tax on each unit of untreated waste; if the tax is high enough, the polluter would presumably be forced to reduce the amount of waste. Since this might also entail a reduction in output and employment, tax subsidy policy has its shortcomings. In addition, some individuals think of pollution taxes as equivalent to purchasing a license to pollute.[2]

Another arrangement is for the community to subsidize pollution suppression. This policy makes particular sense for facilities already established, since most steel mills, refineries, and the like were constructed before the dangers of pollution were recognized, and it hardly makes economic or legal sense to make them the object of some kind of retrospective tax. Instead pollution control standards can be established for new equipment, and the cost of cleaning up the mess caused by the older equipment can fall on the people who will benefit from a reduction in emissions, and who in fact have already benefited from the spread of pollution in that it is a by-product of economic progress. We are speaking, of course, of the general public.

Another possibility is to divide pollution control charges between the polluter and the taxpayer. The trouble here is that when it comes down to figuring out how much each must pay, there seem to be as many solutions as there are economists making the calculation. In order to avoid complicated and perhaps insuperable computations, it has been suggested that the best way to come to grips with pollution is just to forbid it over a certain level—that is, to establish some kind of limit on the amount of pollution that an industrial installation can produce, and to punish anyone overstepping this boundary by fines or incarceration. This way out is not without costs, however, because if the limit is too low it will increase unemployment.

The problem of funding pollution control will be attacked indirectly, mainly by discussing some of the possible consequences of letting environmental deterioration run rampant. We can begin by commenting on an issue raised by Gordon R. Taylor (1970). Taylor just wants to know just how insane the world can get, given that so-called rational men insist upon setting up conditions in which their food and water is constantly polluted, their children subjected to all sorts of dangers, and their whole environment made more obnoxious, not through their failures, but as a by-product of what is known as progress.

In truth, it is not insanity that has led to this sorry state of affairs, but a simple conspiracy of silence on the part of those organs whose ostensible function is to inform the citizenry of present and palpable danger, the media and the government. More simply, people just don't know what they are up against. The dangers to human health associated with such things as smoking, overeating, and air pollution are so serious that it would be natural for governments to assail this problem with the same kind of propaganda campaigns they used during World War II. But even in a country highly aware of these problems, such as sweden, the media, apparently with the good wishes of the government, prefer to entertain their audience with the exploits of vagabonds on the rim of the Sahara than with issues that could mean life or death to future generations.

Among the most important recent investigations of the damage that may be associated with pollution is that of Lave and Seskin (1970, 1971, 1975). Much of their research is incomplete, since the dull blade of multiple regression analysis tends to leave as many questions unanswered as it purports to illumine, but no one who values his or her health can afford to overlook the issues they have raised.

The position of Lave and Seskin is that there is a significant correlation between air pollution and such things as emphysema, bronchitis, lung cancer, heart disease, and infant mortality. These economists may have overstated their case, which indicated in a study of pollution by region that if all pollution was reduced to the level of the cleanest region, the death rate from bronchitis would drop by as much as 70 percent; but during the first part of 1974, when the consumption of fossil fuels decreased considerably, the incidence of chronic lung diseases decreased in cities such as San Francisco and Alameda, California.

Unfortunately, extensive research will be necessary to check the figures offered by investigators such as Lave and Seskin and to clarify other problem areas. This is not just to satisfy scientific curiosity, but because with today's technology large reductions in atmospheric impurities are relatively very expensive. Such things as stack gas scrubbers for coal-burning power plants can absorb as much as 10 percent of a power plant's energy output, and may also create other dangerous pollution in the form of residues. Many of us who imagined that a major cleanup of the atmosphere and water would be cheap were wrong; we must now begin to consider abatement programs that could cost as much as education or defense.

This leads us back to our earlier discussion of how pollution suppression should be financed. Given the connection between environmental deterioration and human health, the greater part of the burden belongs on the taxpayer, who should be glad to accept it. Despite the expert opinions of Archie Bunker and his free-thinking associates, a pollution control program financed by taxes could be the very opposite of a welfare program, as the higher gains would very likely attach themselves to the higher incomes.[3] I doubt that any member of the television audience enjoys thinking about men in Rolex watches being treated for emphysema, and certainly the Girl Who Has Everything doesn't need chronic bronchitis. On the other hand, air and water pollution are the least of the problems that lower-income groups enjoy contemplating; but they would prefer a tax to fewer employment opportunities, which could result if all the burden for pollution suppression was placed on the firms with which the pollution originates.

Two Problems in Environmental Economics

One of the most important uses of economics is to ask and answer questions via simple models that involve a few variables of interest. Problems begin to arise when the model becomes so complex that meaningful questions cannot be treated unless quantitative information about the parameters is available. As often happens, once data is applied to these models, both questions and answers turn out to be nonsense.

A simple but suggestive model is that of Strotz (1968), which takes up the possibility of measuring some of the benefits of pollution abatement programs through changes in land values. Strotz's work indicates that this possibility cannot be excluded. The model is based on a closed city—one where new renters cannot enter and bid up land rents—that is divided into two equal parts. The first part is polluted, and sites there rent for $100; the second is unpolluted and rents are $200. If a government program eliminates pollution, so that all the sites in the city are essentially identical, changes in the demand for sites by city residents may cause a change in land values. He goes on to assume that this happens, and the new uniform land value is $150.

We can now look at some of the benefits and costs of this situation. The people who rented unpolluted land at $200 gain $50, since they now pay $150 for this land. Those who previously paid $100 end up somewhere between a loss of 50 or a gain of zero, depending upon the value they set on a clean environment. For instance, if someone wanted one of the pollution free sites but was only willing to pay $25 for it, he lost $25 as a result of the change in property values. Thus total benefits are positive if anyone living on a polluted site was willing to pay for a pollution-free site.

What about losses? The landlords at the original pollution-free sites lose $50 per site; those who had polluted sites to begin with gain $50 per site. Assuming that the numbers of polluted and unpolluted sites were equal to begin with, money losses (or gains) for landlords sum to zero, and the only cost is the cost of the program. This should be compared to the benefits mentioned above, and if the benefit/cost ratio is satisfactory, then it could be argued that the pollution abatement program should be undertaken. It should also be observed that under certain circumstances the abatement program could have a one-time cost, but that benefits would be realized repeatedly.

The fact that this model specifies a closed city is an obvious deficiency, although introducing openness would hardly change the conclusions. We know, for instance, that in many United States cities, when the authorities have cleared slums adjacent to the city's center and replaced them by middle- and upper-income housing, many suburban dwellers abandoned their commuter idylls and returned to the splendors of urban life. However, it would be hard to find evidence anywhere that land values in any area were depressed by this shift: rents in the rehabilitated areas were increased enormously, while the comparatively small-scale displacements of suburbanites to the new areas, and former residents of the new areas to other parts of the inner city, would hardly change suburban or inner-city rents significantly. In our previous example, openness probably increases the money value of total benefits and diminishes the money value of individual losses, except for those associated with the abatement program.

This model, though simple, suggests many relevant questions. Similarly, it may be possible some day to construct general equilibrium models that can more thoroughly describe the actions of landlords and consumers. Some suggestions of what questions these models would ask and attempt to answer can be found in the magnificent survey of Fisher and Petersen (1975). Now, however, the most fruitful approach to environmental problems can be found in the articles of Baumol, Bradford, and Oates, and in the textbooks of Baumol and Oates (1975) and Pearce (1976).[4]

It is a short step from conceptualizing the effect of pollution abatement on land values to examining its influence on wage rates. Hoch (1972) and Tolley (1974) have suggested that higher wages are required to compensate employees for various disamenities, one of which is pollution. For example, everything else being equal, if Cicero, Illinois, has more pollution than Aberdeen, Washington, then real wages should tend to be higher in Aberdeen. Nordhaus and Tobin (1973) have used multiple regression to examine this problem, and they conclude that urban disamenities amount to about 5 percent of the GNP. Some doubt can, of course, be expressed about the ability of various statistical techniques to measure, even approximately, the impact of environment on our most conventional welfare indicators; but Nordhaus and Tobin seem to be on the right track. People *are* willing to pay for improvements in the quality of life and, everything else being equal, the individual living in a less polluted milieu is palpably better off than someone submerged in noise and smog.

Option Value

The final topic of this section is somewhat abstract, but it is important, and we need not go into great detail. Option value is very often considered as the value of scenery or the effect of spillovers from industrial or commercial operations on scenery and wildlife. One example involves the damming of a large river, which would cause certain things to disappear forever. A problem here is that no market price can be put on the preservation of an amenity such as scenery. Moreover, even if a private owner is involved, such large diseconomies occur that resource allocation would be severely distorted if market prices were not adjusted. For example, the mayor of Paris could not just stand by and sing the praises of the market mechanism if Notre Dame were in private hands and its owner decided to tear it down and erect a hamburger stand. Obviously subsidies or bribes would be in order—either for Monsieur Le Propriétaire or his potential customers.

In examining this issue we will pose an example like the ones Krutilla has used in much of his published and unpublished work. Assume that a gentlemen living in New York or California believes that he will someday be interested in visiting the South Pole. He may therefore be willing to pay something to ensure the future availability of the South Pole in the condition he imagines it to be in today. In other words, he would like to have the option of finding it in its present condition, which he may not have if there is a large oil strike in the district. Once the situation is expressed in these terms, it is a short step to conceptualizing a market where such options are sold, and the proceeds of these sales used either to purchase land near the South Pole, or to bribe oil companies not to drill in this area until after our tourist and similar individuals have made their trips.

If such a market were to come into existence, the dilemma facing any person buying such an option is that, when he or she got around to making the trip, he or she might be surrounded by people who had not made any contribution to preserving the Pole. The reader who has some background in welfare economics immediately realizes that we have no way at present to resolve this dilemma. From another perspective, although someone might desire to visit the South Pole some day, and nominally might be willing to turn this desire into the demand for an option, the knowledge that others were paying for options could easily change his mind. He might want to let others do the paying while, when the opportunity presents itself, he does the visiting. In other words, he might become a free rider.

Another aspect of this topic has to do with reversibility and irreversibility. Krutilla was interested in the use of natural valleys for reservoirs, particularly the Hell's Canyon region of Idaho. This natural site is one of a kind; if used for power production and irrigation, it could never regain its scenic value. Regardless of the value of the electricity that might be generated at Hell's Canyon, someday the money demand for scenery might be much greater. Moreover, if this happened, the mistake of having built the dam could not be rectified. Obviously, an extremely sophisticated analysis is necessary to clear up this riddle, and as yet no definitive explanation is available.

Krutilla's own approach, as described by Barkley and Sekler (1972) in an elementary—but valuable—exposition, is based on the benefits and costs of exploiting Hell's Canyon. The cost of scenery can be taken as the profit given up by not generating or providing irrigation facilities. Assuming that there would be no cost for viewing the scenery, the benefits would be equal to the total area under a demand curve for scenery (assuming that the curve sloped downward and intersected the the horizontal axis). Unfortunately this is not an easy calculation, for a number of factors might influence both costs and benefits over time. Monte Carlo and Biarritz might come back into style, and there might not be any interest in watching the sun go down over the canyon. Similarly, safe and highly economical minibreeders might be developed some day, which could decrease the demand for power from expensive hydroelectric installations.

As things turned out, Krutilla's analysis demonstrated that the value of Hell's Canyon as scenery exceeded its commercial value; and although it was nip and tuck with the power interests for a while, eventually they understood that they would have to find somewhere else to put their dam.

Food and Population

In his well-known essay "Economic Crisis in World Agriculture" (1965), T.W. Schultz has postulated a juncture in economic development when stagnant agriculture causes a crisis for countries who have singlemindedly concentrated on industrialization. According to Schultz, industrialization by itself is not enough to optimize the growth rate.

The important term here is not "crisis" but "optimize," which in some sense must be tied to consumption per head. As a first approximation, an optimum rate of growth probably means increasing consumption per head together with a high rate of investment in the industrial sector. (Higher-order approximations would explicitly consider environmental deterioration, the existing level of consumption, etc.) Unfortunately, consumption per head may react negatively to increases in consumption because increases in consumption cause faster population growth. This is the Malthusian impasse, and it means that in the context of the less-developed world, any discussion of optimum growth must somehow take up population growth.[5]

Earlier in this book we speculated on how many people the world will eventually end up supporting. A distinguished Swedish professor of economics recently created quite a stir by suggesting that 20 billion might fit comfortably into spaceship earth, although it is doubtful that he would offer a Nobel Prize to anyone attempting to fit them into his part. Dr. Herman Kahn (1975) has also estimated between twenty and thirty billion, with many of them enjoying a nice standard of bourgeois comfort. However, the record for this variety of psychopathic prognostication seems to belong to Professor Colin Clark (1963), who ventures that with a proper administration of resources, the earth can support 45 billion. U.N. demographers seem to be aiming at a figure of six to seven billion by the end of the century—at which time, presumably, people will be either intelligent or aware enough to understand the dangers of unrestricted breeding, and take steps to see that the figure does not go too much higher. But a leading authority in this field, Professor Joseph Spengler (1976), sees the population leveling off at around 15 billion if the Third World fertility pattern follows that of Western Europe, and somewhere around 22 to 25 billion if the present trend continues.

Regardless of what the final figure turns out to be, it will be too many. We have already been warned by impeccable sources that a world of cheap, abundant food may now be history, and already only a few areas of the world show a long-run capacity to supply all their food requirements. As pointed out by Spengler, in 1976 every region of the world except North America, Australia, and New Zealand was importing grains from these regions; just a few years earlier, in 1974, the principal underdeveloped regions were importing between 16 and 33 percent of their food requirements. Table 6-1 shows the situation for 1970.

Not everybody, of course, is capable of looking on the dark side of these matters. At the recent U.N. conference on food, which was held in Rome— commonly referred to as the "pigs conference," since many delegates busied themselves with breaking most of the existing world records for gluttony—the general theme was that everything would come out all right in the end if the rich countries did their duty and divested themselves of their property for the benefit of the poor, including the pasta-proud representatives of the poor countries filling the better restaurants of the Eternal City. Similarly, at the U.N. conference on population, held at Bucharest in 1974, many delegates openly

Table 6-1
The World Trade in Grain, 1970
(In millions of dollars f.o.b.)

Export From	Export to			
	Developed Market Economies	Less Developed Market Economies	Centrally Planned Economies	Total
Developed Market Economies	2193	1577	441	4211
Underdevel. Market Econ.	557[a]	490	99	1146
Central. Planned Economies	108	190	422	720
Total	2858	2257	962	6077
Balance	1353	−1111	−242	

Source: Herin and Wijkman (Den Internationella Bakgrunden, Långtidsutredningen, 1975)

[a]Of which Argentina accounted for 80 percent

insisted that population control was not necessary, and that advocates of slowing down the high rate of population growth in the Third World were conspiring to retain their present large share of the world's food and raw materials.

Under the circumstances, it was only a matter of time until these attitudes provoked a reaction. Some official and semiofficial circles in the industrial world believe that development assistance and the sale of food by the developed world to the less-developed world must be linked to family planning policies in the latter. First contraceptives, and then victuals, is the general line of reasoning.[6] This amounts to an OPEC in food, except that it could be argued that the energy problem is probably much easier for the industrial countries acting as a group to solve than the food problem would be for the Third World. During the post-World War II period, almost all the food donated or sold at favorable terms to the Third World has been grown in North America; and although a number of theoretically attractive solutions would permit LDCs to increase their agricultural production considerably, these are rapidly growing too expensive. Moreover, as Brown (1973) and Ehrlich and Holdren (1973) point out, many of these solutions—which call for modification of techniques developed and employed in the developed regions of the world—carry sociological and psychological costs which may turn out to be too high.

Since World War II, the world production of food increased about three-quarters of one percent annually between 1954 and 1972. Total food production increased at approximately the same rate in both the developed and less-developed worlds, but the rapid rate of population growth in the LDCs reduced the per capita increase in production to an average of less than one-half of one percent annually, while the developed regions achieved an annual per capita increase of about one and one-half percent.

The total production of grain over the past twenty years or so, increased more than 60 percent in the developed countries, while the cultivated area remained constant at slightly under 300 million hectares. The total grain production of LDCs increased even more, by 75 percent, but this required a one-third increase in crop area, since yields were only rising one-half as fast as in the developed countries. Average grain yields in the LDCs are roughly 60 percent of those in the developed countries. While this in itself is not particularly discouraging, it is disastrous when the population factor and such things as the low marginal yield are thrown in. It means that probably one-fourth of the population of the Third World has an insufficient diet, and there is not much chance that things will get better in the near future.

Table 6-2 summarizes some figures relevant to the present discussion. The size of the world food supply is determined by biological, climatic, and economic factors; the latter are apparently assuming increasing importance. In Spengler's opinion, the main obstacles to increased global agricultural production are the price disincentives to which agriculturists are exposed. In the underdeveloped world he singles out price and export controls, restrictions on

Table 6-2
Some Demographic and Agricultural Data

	Population (millions) (1973)	Annual Growth Rate	Density (persons/ km²)	Land Suitable for Crops (mil. ha.)	Land Used for Crops (mil. ha.)	Acres of Cultivated Land per person
World	3860	2.1	28			
Africa	374	2.8	12			1.3
Africa South of Sahara				304	152	
North West Africa				19	19	
America	545	2.2	13			
North America	236	1.3	11			2.3
South America	309	2.9	15	570	130	1.0
Asia	2204	2.3	80	252	211	0.7
Mainland East Asia	806	1.7	72			
Japan	107	1.2	290			
South Asia	1225	2.9	77			
Middle South Asia	828	2.8	122			
Europe	472	0.7	96	0.43[a]	0.38[a]	0.9
Oceania	21	2.2	2	0.38[a]	0.04[a]	2.9
USSR	250	1.0	11	0.88[a]	0.56[a]	2.4

[a]In billions of acres

credit, outmoded land tenure customs, nonoptimal farm sizes, and so on. The World Bank also seems to follow this line. Incompetence, corruption, and general cultural backwardness were not named, although they should have been named first, for it is principally these factors that explain the failure to effect a more rapid transfer of agricultural practices from the developed to the less-developed world, as well as the senseless persistence which characterized the destructive agricultural practices that led to the Sahelian calamities.

As table 6-2 indicates, about one fourth of the world's land area is suitable for crops. Roughly 7.8 billion acres of land can be used to grow crops or for livestock; however, multiple cropping could increase this to the equivalent of 16.3 billion acres. Of this additional 8.5 billion, all but 2 billion would be dependent on irrigation, and considerable fertilizer and weed and insect control would be required. At present, however, fertilizers are showing the same explosive price development as oil, thanks to the use of fertilizer-intensive miracle grains, a lag in the construction of new production facilities (because of their sharply rising cost), and reductions in petroleum-based fertilizer production because of the oil price rise.

The agricultural situation varies significantly by region. In Asia it will not be easy to increase the total amount of land under cultivation, although in parts of South Asia there is considerable room for increasing the efficiency of irrigation. Groundwater potential is large throughout most of the region, and in relation to many other parts of the underdeveloped world, it could be exploited at a fairly moderate cost. Of late, agricultural expansion in Thailand has featured the increased production of maize, but usable land for this crop is almost exhausted. Malaysia still has considerable land suitable for the production of rubber, palm oil, and other tree crops. In Indonesia, the cultivated acreage in the outer islands has increased, and further expansion is envisaged; but it is impossible to predict its profitability.

On the other hand, there is as yet no nominal scarcity of agricultural land in Latin America. Fertility, however, falls off as we go from currently cultivated land to new land. To make future agricultural investments profitable will require huge investments in infrastructure, but countries such as Brazil and Venezuela may be willing to make these commitments, either now or in the near future. Sub-Saharan Africa also has much land that is suitable for agriculture, but here the constraint on increased production is technical and organizational ability.

Almost all these regions will probably increase their agricultural output in the coming years, but it is doubtful whether this increase will match the increase in consumption in these regions *and* the major oil-exporting countries. In the latter, consumption is still fairly low in relation to per capita income and will almost certainly increase sharply as the benefits derived from the increase in oil prices are diffused throughout these economies. The overall result, at least in the near future, can only be stagnation in per capita consumption in the non-oil-producing countries. According to the World Bank, the grain surplus countries—particularly North America—should be able to make up the deficit experienced by the others, but the lower-income countries might be unable to pay for the food they import, and other importers will find themselves paying more than they reckoned. In addition, the World Bank has expressed concern over the ability of the centrally planned economies to feed themselves, although the evidence now seems to indicate that this problem will decrease.

Finally, something should be said about the weather. Like industry, modern agriculture has prospered by substituting large amounts of mechanical energy for human or animal energy. Sophisticated machine-based systems are very productive as long as weather patterns are favorable, but may be less efficient when the weather goes bad. This happened in the United States in 1972, when considerable heavy equipment was immobilized by a very heavy rainfall.

The last three or four decades have been characterized by fairly good climatic conditions in the major food-producing regions; it has been suggested that the present margin of food reserves is the result of good luck with the weather in recent years. But there is no statistical reason to believe that weather will continue to be so favorable; given that the trend in reserve stocks of food seems to be unequivocally downward, this can only mean that the next few years will be more perilous than ever.

Conclusion

The pollution part of this chapter does not require much summing up. In relation to the rest of the book, it means that we not only need a technology that enables us to do more with less, but one that will enable future prosperity without bad smells, exploding noise levels, foul water, and higher levels of lead in the bloodstream. We are worthy of such a technology—at least most of us are—but like so many things we think we deserve, this may not be enough to bring it into existence. The trouble is that it must be paid for—perhaps out of present consumption.

The adequacy of future food supplies will depend largely on the development of population. Since population in the LDCs can be expected to increase by 1.5 to 2.5 percent per year, the food supply must grow by 2.5 to 3.5 percent to permit a per capita growth of one percent. Again citing Spengler, growth rate in this range has not, on the average, been achieved by the less developed countries over the past twenty-five years. Instead, per capita growth has been about one-third of one percent; and since much of the growth of the food supply was accounted for by almost-developed countries like Argentina, there has been almost no per capita growth in food production over much of the Third World.

This means that there can be no significant improvement in the per capita food supply of the world unless population growth rates drop sharply. Unfortunately, nobody seems to know exactly how this can be achieved. It is said that when the standard of living increases in the LDCs, fewer children will be needed to provide for the security of parents; some evidence may support this opinion. For instance, a drop in reproduction rates can be observed when moving between the poorer and better off districts of India. However, I have not detected this difference in moving between countries. Instead, based on an elementary statistical analysis, the richest and most confident countries in the Third World seem to have the highest rates of population growth. Of course, this could be a short-run phenomenon, but the problem exists in the short run. As Keynes has so graciously reminded us, in the long run we are all dead.

Notes

1. In the example take $100/101 = a/b$, and thus $99 = a - 1$. Taking G for gain we get:

$$G = \left[2\left(\frac{a}{b}\right) - 1 \right] - \left[(1 - \frac{a}{b})(a - 1) \right] = \frac{a}{b}(1 + a) - a$$

but $b = (1 + a)$, and so $G = 0$. Since Gain = − (Loss), we also have Loss = 0.

2. If we take *FC* and *VC* as fixed and variable cost, T_p as a pollution tax which is directly proportional to pollution, or $T_p = t\alpha q$, where pollution αq is a simple linear function of production, we have Cost $= FC + VC(q) + t\alpha q$, and thus

$$MC = \frac{dC}{dq} = VC'(q) + \alpha t = \bar{p} \qquad \bar{p} = \text{constant price}$$

thus:
$$\frac{\partial VC'}{\partial q} \frac{dq}{dt} + \alpha = 0 \qquad \text{(or)} \qquad \frac{dq}{dt} = -\frac{\alpha}{\partial VC'/\partial q}$$

If, as is normal, α and $\partial VC'/\partial q$ are positive, production falls as the tax rate t increases.

3. Mr. Bunker never thinks about pollution because, as he puts it, he has become used to it.

4. The work of Scarf (1973) and Shoven and Whalley (1972) on general equilibrium models may well be among the most important in modern economic theory. On the other hand, it might be best for all concerned if some of the outwardly impressive but essentially empty constructions based on control and neoclassical growth theory could be forgotten as soon as possible.

5. If we signify population by N, and consumption per head by I, then we have:

$$\frac{1}{N}\frac{dN}{dt} = f(I) \quad \text{and} \quad I = g(N)$$

Here we would expect $f' > 0$ and $g' < 0$. We can now write:

$$\frac{1}{N}\frac{dN}{dt} = f(g(N)) = h(N) \quad \text{and} \quad h' = f'g' < 0$$

We can now draw a phase diagram for N, and from this note that we have a kind of steady-state value for I $(= I^*)$, which could be very low. Moreover, from the slope of the phase diagram in figure 6n-1, we can infer stability for these steady-state values. We can also mention that according to Malthus, food supplies would increase at an arithmetic rate $(2,4,6,8, \dots)$, while population would increase geometrically $(2,4,8,16,32, \dots)$.

6. This may be the correct reaction. It hardly makes sense, as usual, for leading scholars to maintain—both privately and publicly—that the population issue is the most crucial of our time, and then fill articles and books with textbook solutions based on irrelevant and high-flown concepts of social justice.

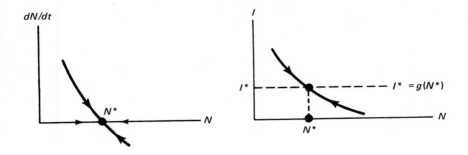

Figure 6n-1.

7

Some Comments on the "Antidoomsday" Models

The doomsday models of Forrester (1971) and Meadows and Meadows (1972) might best be described as substance without form. However, because of the seriousness of the topic, form may well be irrelevant. As Professor Paul A. Samuelson made clear in an interview with Dorothy Crook (1974), the prophets of doom, (to include the Club of Rome) have made the world aware of a genuine danger, even though they have oversold their case in order to give it maximum impact and distribution.

Given Samuelson's enormous prestige and insight, it might be appropriate to inquire into the reason for the howls of rage that greeted successive elaborations of the doomsday models, particularly the clamor emanating from some of the most skilled practitioners of mathematical economics and econometrics. The principal reason is money. Like Rome, these models were not built in a day. Their construction took a fairly long time, and the model builders, who for the most part were not economists, were well rewarded for their work. But if the reader stops to think about it, this situation was inevitable. The successes of the natural sciences stretch as far as the senses can register, while people like Paul Samuelson and Professor Barbara Bergman have on occasion referred to the precious advice of economists as crank, moonshine, and snake oil.

Once terminology of this nature comes into widespread use, (and in addition questions are continually raised as to the competence of the economics section of the Nobel Academy, as well as its ability to distinguish gossip from economic science) the demand for high-level economists to construct models dealing with fact rather than elegant fantasy shrinks considerably. This is not to say that economists do not have anything to offer in interpreting reality; at this point we have as much to offer as physicists—probably more. The trouble is that we seldom deliver.

To see this the reader has only to regard some of the most advertised criticism of the doomsday models. Professor Wilfred Beckerman's work is probably the most widely known outside academia, but his insistent and completely illogical refusal to recognize the validity of the law of compound interest has been a source of increasing embarassment to economists inclined to cite his research, and his decision to leave resource economics to devote his talents to income distribution has not therefore engendered a wave of protests from other "growthmen." Similarly, Professors Kay and Mirrlees (1975) can hardly have raised the credibility of economic theory when, in the course of a long algebraic demonstration designed to expose the frailty of the doomsday

151

models, they made the startling announcement that current rates of depletion of natural resources may be too low.

Rather than continue with examples of this type—of which there are too many—some attention will be paid to the two most recurrent criticisms of the Forrester and Meadows and Meadows models, namely, that they do not consider prices, and that they do not allow for substitution. As many of us are aware, the price mechanism is a marvelous device; this should be immediately clear to anyone who thinks through the classic example of the provisioning of cities like Paris and New York via its functioning. But it has its limitations. Anybody who spent a few minutes a day reading German newspapers from 1935 on should have known that Germany was going to war; this must have been even more apparent to various diplomats and businessmen in Central Europe at that time. Even so, this information was not transmitted into price movements on the Paris stock exchange, nor for that matter through any channel to the armament industries of France, Czechoslovakia, Poland, Belgium, Holland, Norway, and so on. It is also doubtful that the price mechanism is making United States cities more pleasant or healthier places to live; nor does it seem to be promising any imminent relief for the 15 million unemployed of North America and Western Europe.

Moreover, while the literature of economics has become one of the most extensive of any academic discipline, no growth models or econometric models in existence or under construction apply prices actively and significantly. On the contrary, much of the theoretical literature on the economics of information and externalities indicates that price systems cannot be constructed to deal with doomsday situations, or even with less drastic emergencies. This is what T. Bradshaw was essentially saying in the Fortune article cited earlier. If a resource is becoming scarce, its price would normally tend to rise very rapidly, choking off further demand and providing the incentive for increased exploration. But what about the users of this resource, who only a few years earlier, armed with first rate information about resource availability and aggregate demand, purchased expensive equipment that could not function without the resource? In addition, a price rise may not succeed in securing more of the resource because there may not be any left. The OPEC price increases, for example, are largely motivated by the desire to be paid enough for a wasting asset so that it can be replaced by other types of assets. They are only marginally concerned with increasing the production from existing facilities, or with making a search for additional oil profitable.

We can next go to the problem of substitution, beginning with an example. Suppose that a platoon of pioneers from the 24th Infantry Regiment, equipped with hatchets, is waiting for a platoon of tanks to come along. Their orders are to build a log bridge across a stream twenty meters wide, so they cut down some trees and arrange the logs across the stream. The tanks can pass, and the colonel will not be upset when he comes up to examine the situation.

Further on there is another stream of exactly the same width, and when the platoon arrives at this stream it will have to repeat its performance. However, at the first stream the trees they cut down were actually twice the thickness necessary to bear the weight of the tanks. Were it possible to slice the logs in half along their longitudinal axis, no tree cutting would be necessary at the second stream; but in fact the hatchets cannot do that. Thus, instead of using x cubic feet of logs to bridge the two streams, the platoon used $2x$ cubic feet.

Now suppose that in place of their hatchets, our platoon had some portable, battery-driven electric saws. Then they could have sliced the logs in half and built two bridges using the material that, without this capital equipment (the saws), would only have sufficed for one. Here we have substituted capital (and perhaps some extra labor to carry the logs forward) for raw materials—in this case the logs that would have been necessary at the second stream. Note, however, that substitutions of this nature have limits. Even if the pioneers could slice and notch the wood in a way that augmented its strength, so that even less than x cubic feet was needed for the bridges, some wood is necessary to build a bridge across a stream.

Next we can look at the way *production functions* (describing the relationship between inputs and outputs) have been constructed in the literature of economics. These production functions usually deal only with capital and labor inputs or factors of production; land, labor, and capital are designated primary factors. Many production functions feature unlimited substitutability among the primary factors, but input-output or perfectly complementary production functions are also occasionally used, in which we have no substitutability, and we think in terms of limiting factors. For instance, if it takes one unit of capital and two units of labor to produce one unit of output, and if we have 2000 units of labor and 100 units of capital available, then we can produce the minimum of 2000/2 = 1000 or 100/1 = 100 units of output. In other words, we can produce 100 units of output, and capital is the limiting factor. The available labor is more than enough to cooperate with given amount of capital: to get 100 units of output we need only 200 units of labor; the other 1800 units of labor are superfluous because we cannot substitute them for capital. Raw materials were nowhere to be found in these production functions.

The latter situation changed when models criticizing the doomsday models appeared. Raw materials not only began to appear in production functions, but were considered as primary factors—which is usually completely wrong. In other words, they were not employed as intermediate goods, and potentially a limiting factor, but were used to give the impression that if raw materials began running out, other factors of production could substitute for them. To use the example with which we opened this discussion, these models—taken at face value—suggest that a tank could cross a stream on a splinter of wood not as wide as the stream. Put another way, it is theoretically possible to move oil from one end of Alaska to the other by satellite, pipeline, or in the hollowed-out platform shoes of mannequins; but it would be impossible if there was no oil. This means that substitution between raw materials and other production factors should not be accepted or even considered as a long-run antidote to natural resource depletion.

We can now consider substitution between different raw materials. In the first chapter and earlier in this chapter, we referred to the effect of compound interest that caused a huge supply of raw materials to disappear in a comparatively short time if their use grew exponentially. Some materials, particularly aluminum and iron ore, have such huge supplies that they seem almost infinite; moreover great possibilities exist to substitute these minerals for many others. But exploiting these possibilities would entail social and economic costs that would be unthinkable to almost any government. Huge amounts of energy would have to be made available, and a number of unorthodox changes in living patterns would probably have to be introduced relatively quickly. As was made quite clear in West Germany a few years ago, it would have been much easier for the government to solve their energy problem by recruiting armies and crossing borders than by decreasing the speed limit on the autobahns ten miles per hour.

Moreover, if Spengler (1976) is correct about where world population is heading, no supply of raw materials can be considered huge. Harold E. Goeller and Alvin M. Weinberg of the Oak Ridge Energy Laboratory have presented a scenario for moving into what they call an "Age of Substitutability," based on recycling, biological resources (such as wood), and minerals they regard as "unlimited," but which I think are limited. They see this age of substitutability as being several hundred years away, but they don't address how the world is going to traverse an intermediate stage, when traditional energy sources will be in full decline, some of the more familiar nonferrous metals may be extremely scarce, and, most important, world population levels could be much higher than those currently projected—with poor and rich alike more insistent than ever on having their share of the good things in life. Goeller and Weinberg only say that to reach this state without immense disruption will require unprecedented foresight and planning. Those are precisely the qualities which, in the light of today's preferences, seem to be in shorter supply than ever.

Appendix 7A

Nordhaus (1973) has made an interesting analysis of the World Dynamics model, employing conventional economic concepts and terminology. He effectively reduces one of its subsystems to the following equations:

$$\frac{\dot{C}}{C} = BiF - \theta \qquad\qquad (7A.1)$$

$$\frac{\dot{F}}{F} = -\phi BC \qquad\qquad (7A.2)$$

C is capital, F exhaustible resources, i investment per capita (a parameter), and B, θ, and ϕ complicated coefficients that Nordhaus has shown to be positive. In examining equations 7A.1 and 7A.2, we see that this system has no place to go: with a given F capital expansion must eventually stop, at which time the depreciation coefficient θ takes over, and existing capital begins to decompose. We note from equations 7A.1 and 7A.2 that $\partial \dot{F}/\partial C = -\phi BF$ (<0) and $\partial \dot{C}/\partial F = BiC$ (>0). We can thus go directly to the sample phase diagram in figure 7A-1.

This diagram indicates that we eventually end up with no capital or natural resources. If we want this in mathematical form we can begin by writing the system as $\dot{C} = f(C,F) = (Bif - \theta)C$ and $\dot{F} = g(C,F) = (-\phi BC)F$. Stability of this system implies that the following conditions, first postulated by Olech (1963), are satisfied:

	1. $f_C + g_F < 0$	everywhere
And:	2. $f_C g_F - f_F g_C > 0$	everywhere
And either:	3. $f_C g_F \neq 0$	everywhere
Or:	4. $f_F g_C \neq 0$	everywhere

We see that we have $f_C = BiF$, $g_F = -\phi BC$, $f_F = BiC$, and $g_C = -\phi BF$. If we use these results in equations 7A.1 and 7A.2, we see immediately that the equation 7A.1 is not satisfied at point Z in figure 7A-1. To see this, observe that $f_C + g_F = BiF - \phi BC$, and at point Z, $\phi BC = 0$ and BiF is positive. The system asymptotically approaches the origin.

155

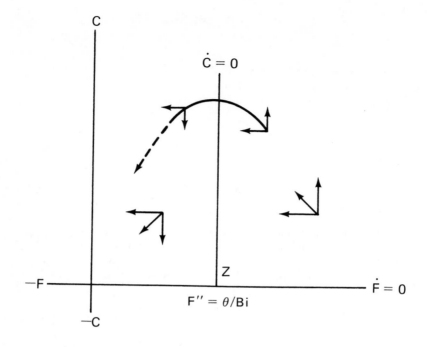

Figure 7A-1. Phase Diagram for C and F.

8

The Econometrics of
Primary Commodities:
An Introduction

This chapter will consider the econometrics of primary commodities, extensively discussing demand, supply, and price equations, and their theoretical basis.

I must assume that the reader is familiar with basic econometrics, since it would be impossible to provide even a superficial introduction to this topic in a single chapter. Moreover, many superior introductory texts in econometrics are now available, such as Wonnacott and Wonnacott (1970), Kelejian and Oates (1974), Koutsoyiannis (1973), and Wallis (1972). The reader who wishes to delve deeper into commodity econometrics should examine the work of Professors Franklin Fisher (and associates) and F. Gerard Adams (and associates), as well as the commodity economists of the World Bank, UNCTAD, the HWWA Institute for Economic Research at Hamburg, and (most recently) Professor Robert Pindyck (1976).

Dynamic Analysis

The type of analysis that will interest us in this chapter falls under the heading of dynamic analysis, because the observation of such things as demand and price take place over time rather than at any specific point. As Wallis (1972) points out, a system becomes dynamic as soon as dated variables relate different time periods, or link the past to the present and future through trends, time lags, rates of change variables, and expectations hypotheses or adjustment processes. Most of this should become clear in the sequel.

One of the principal purposes of dynamic analysis is to study the time path of variables that are passing from one equilibrium to another, and which were displaced from the original equilibrium because of the shift in a parameter or exogenous variable. Consider, for example, a simple demand curve for coffee. Demand is clearly a function of price, but it is also dependent on income: if income increases so does the demand for coffee at every price. This means that an increase in income shifts the demand curve for coffee to the right. Here income is an *exogenous* variable in coffee consumption, because—except in the coffee-producing countries—it influences the consumption (and price) of coffee without being influenced itself. On the other hand, price and quantity are *endogenous* variables, because they are determined in the model on the basis of behavioral relationships and assumptions about market clearing. A model of this type might take on the following appearance:

157

$$s_t = \beta_0 + \beta_1 p_{t-1} \tag{8.1}$$

$$d_t = \alpha_0 + \alpha_1 p_t + \alpha_2 y_t \tag{8.2}$$

$$s_t = d_t \tag{8.3}$$

Through simple manipulation we get:

$$\alpha_1 p_t - \beta_1 p_{t-1} = \beta_0 - \alpha_0 - \alpha_2 y_t \tag{8.4}$$

This is a first-order difference equation; it took this form because we assumed that supply is a lagged function of price, that is, that suppliers react to the market price attained in the previous period. To examine equation 8.4, we can begin by inquiring into the nature of the equilibrium. In particular we want to know the value of the equilibrium and, if attained, whether it will be maintained over time. We must recognize here that in our most common form of equilibrium, as in physics, we have stationarity. In the present situation this means that we have $p_{t-1} = p_t = p_{t+1} = p_{t+2} = \ldots$ which means that we can call the equilibrium price $\bar{p}(= p_{t-1} = p_t)$. Substituting this into equation 8.4 gives us:

$$\bar{p} = \frac{\beta_0 - (\alpha_0 + \alpha_2 y_t)}{\alpha_1 - \alpha_2} \tag{8.5}$$

In dynamic economics we usually concern ourselves with the train of events from one equilibrium to another. If we assume that the α's and β's in the above equations are constant, then disturbances which cause a movement from one equilibrium to another originate in changes in y_t. For the moment, consider a situation where we have a value of $y = y'$, which at time t_0 goes to y''. Taking $\bar{p}'$ as the initial equilibrium, we can immediately establish the new equilibrium $\bar{p}''$ from equation 8.5, but until we solve equation 8.4, the difference equation, we do not know how or if we attain the new equilibrium. Figures 8-1(b) and 8-1(c) demonstrate two possible situations. Following a change in y we shown an asymptotic movement to the new equilibrium, in figure 8-1(b), and an oscillatory movement which goes past the new equilibrium.

Difference Equation

Solving the first-order difference equation 8.4 is simple. We already have our steady-state solution, as given in equation 8.5, and what we need now is a "complementary" solution. This solution has to do with the movement of the

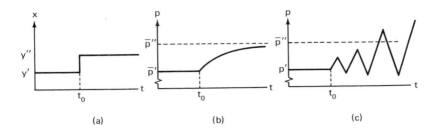

Figure 8-1. Price Movements Following a Change in x.

variable around the equilibrium, or its "damping" properties. To obtain this solution we deal only with the homogeneous part of equation 8.4, or:

$$\alpha_1 p_t' - \beta_1 p_{t-1}' = 0 \tag{8.6}$$

This could be solved through simple iteration, taking $p_{t-1}' = p_0$, and thus $p_t' = (\beta_1/\alpha_1)p_0$, $p_{t+1}' = (\beta_1/\alpha_1)p_t' = (\beta_1/\alpha_1)^2 p_0$, $p_{t+2}' = (\beta_1/\alpha_1)^3 p_0$ and so on. We thus see that if we take as a solution $p_t' = (\beta_1/\alpha_1)^t p_0$ and substitute this into equation 8.6, we get $\alpha_1(\beta_1/\alpha_1)^t p_0 - \beta_1(\beta_1/\alpha_1)^{t-1} p_0$, which equals zero. Our problem is, however, that we are solving equation 8.4, not just equation 8.6, and so we must have a solution that will also satisfy 8.4.

This solution has two parts: the steady-state solution plus the complementary solution, or $p_t = \bar{p} + p_t'$. Unfortunately the solution to equation 8.6 will not work as a solution to 8.4 as it now stands, but it can be easily modified. Take as a solution to equation 8.6, $p_t' = A(\beta_1/\alpha_1)^t$, which the reader can easily show to satisfy 8.6 by direct substitution. Now put this in $p_t = \bar{p} + p_t'$, which yields:

$$p_t = \bar{p} + p_t' = \bar{p} + A\left(\frac{\beta_1}{\alpha_1}\right)^t \tag{8.7}$$

We now need a value for the unspecified constant A. If we take $p_t = p_0$ when $t = 0$ (where $t = 0$ is the beginning time) we get from equation 8.7, $\bar{p}_0 = p + A$, or $A = p_0 - \bar{p}$. Our solution is then:

$$p_t = \bar{p} + (p_0 - \bar{p})\left(\frac{\beta_1}{\alpha_1}\right)^t \tag{8.8}$$

Using equation 8.8 and the value of $\bar{p}$ from equation 8.5, we can show by direct substitution that this is a solution for equation 8.4. We should also notice that if $0 < (\beta_1/\alpha_1) < 1$ we have a movement from one equilibrium to another, like the one shown in figure 8-1(b). In this case the initial equilibrium is at p_0, and the new equilibrium at $\overline{p}$.

Above we have dealt with a first-order difference equation with constant coefficients. Second-order (linear) difference equations are only slightly more complicated, and readers who want a thorough insight into their intricacies are referred to Baumol (1970). However, difference equations of higher than second order or nonlinear difference equations present a number of difficulties, which is why they are studiously avoided. Thus within certain branches of economics— such as dynamic inflation theory—we very seldom find a higher-order difference equation, although we have no a priori reason to believe that first- and second-order linear difference equations were specifically ordained to describe the real world.

A Simple Stock-Flow Model

We shall continue our discussion by reminding the reader of the difference between a flow and a stock. A flow designates a quantity per unit time at a point in time; a stock is a quantity at a point in time. In the markets for many primary commodities we have a demand for a stock to be held for speculative and precautionary purposes, and we also have a demand for these materials for flow purposes—that is, as current inputs in the production process. We can infer directly from actual markets that as the ratio of the inventory of an item to its current consumption increases, its price falls. We therefore found model A, shown in table 8-1, unsuitable and proposed model B instead.

In model A, s and p represent supply and price, while x could be income, industrial production, or even a vector of similar variables. On the other hand, d is the demand for a commodity to be used in the current production process *and* as a stock. In model B, $I_t - I_{t-1}$ $(=\Delta I_t)$ is the change in stocks, while d is strictly a flow demand.

Table 8-1
Simple Supply-Demand Models

	Model A	Model B
	$s_t = f(p_t)$	$s_t = f(p_t)$
	$d_t = g(p_t, x)$	$d_t = g(p_t, x)$
	$s_t = d_t$	$s_t - d_t = I_t - I_{t-1}$
	$s_t = d_t$	$p_t = p_{t-1} + h(\Delta I_t/\Delta d_t)$

We can now go to a stock demand and stock supply curve. Stock supply is a datum. It is simply the amount of an item at a given point in time, and therefore it is not a function of price. In contrast, stock demand would normally be a function of present price. This may be true because at any given time we have certain expectations about the future price of a commodity. If the present price falls, the spread between present and future price increases, so it is more profitable to acquire a larger inventory. We might also expect a relationship between stock demand and such things as the interest rate, expected future price, and even flow demand. Normally, if the interest rate were to fall, the cost of financing a given amount of inventory would decrease, and thus the stock demand (demand for stock) would tend to increase; if the present price was constant, an increase in the expected future price would cause the expected profit from each unit held in inventory to increase, and stock demand would therefore increase. Finally, it seems that the larger the amount of a commodity used for current production, the larger the amount held in inventory. Typical stock supply and demand curves are shown as $\overline{S}'$ and D in figure 8-2(a).

The stock supply curve is simply designated $S = \overline{S}'$, while the equation for the stock demand curve is written $D = D(p_t; p_t^e, r_t)$. Here p_t is the price in period t, p_t^e is the price expected in some future period, where the time at which we consider the expectation is t; and r_t is the interest rate prevailing at time t. Obviously, many other variables could fit into the argument of this function. As for flow supply and demand, these are shown in figure 8-2(b), and are algebraically designated $s_t = s_t(p_t)$ and $d_i = d_i(p_t)$.[1]

Now notice the situation at A and A'. Here we have a full stationary equilibrium, with flow supply equal to flow demand, and stock supply equal to stock demand. In each period q_0 is produced, and this is consumed in the current production process. The stock of the item is constant at $\overline{S}'$, and the price is also constant and equal to $\overline{p}'$. Next assume that the expected future price

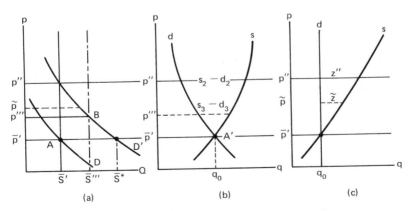

Figure 8-2. Stock and Flow Demand and Supply Curves.

increases. We show this by shifting the stock demand curve to the right: at every value of the present price, more of the item is demanded by profit-conscious holders. This increase in stock demand causes an increase in price, which leads to an augmentation in the stock of the commodity. This works in the following way.

With an increase in price, flow supply becomes larger than flow demand. As shown in the diagram, the price increase caused the present consumption of the commodity to fall, while profit-maximizing producers increased production. We now face a situation where in every period the stock is increasing, since as long as price is greater than $\bar{p}'$, we have an excess of production over present consumption. As shown in the diagram, price initially goes up to p'' where the excess of production over consumption is shown by $s_2 - d_2$. Given the model, this amount would be added to stocks during the first period if the price stayed at p''; but remember that as various consumers obtain their stocks, the pressure on the market decreases and the price falls. The assumption here is that by the end of the period price has fallen to p''', and the addition to stocks is some amount between $s_2 - d_2$ and $s_3 - d_3$. For figure 8-2(a) the exact amount is equal to $\bar{S}''' - \bar{S}'$. The thing the reader should pay particular attention to just now is that the vagueness with which the flow supply and demand curves describe the exact amount of the stock increase is not particularly important. Rather, note that the excess flow supply represented by $s - d > 0$ causes the stock supply curve to move to the right.

The beginning of the next period finds us at point B, and we go through the same sequence as above: excess flow supply, increase in stocks, and a decreasing price. Eventually, on the basis of both the present and the expected price, stocks have reached the desired level, which for figure 8-2(a) means that the stock supply curve asymptotically approaches the new equilibrium value $\bar{S}^*$. The price has again returned to the full equilibrium value $\bar{p}'$, where flow demand is once again equal to flow supply, and all production goes to current use. In other words, we again have stationarity on all markets, with flow demand equal to flow supply, and stock demand equal to stock supply. Even though we do not have a full equilibrium at prices above $\bar{p}'$, we may have some market equilibriums, because in some periods producers are producing exactly the amounts that buyers desire for current consumption and for additions to inventories.

Equations which describe the above situation are not easy to come by or to use. But to simplify things, suppose that instead of the falling flow demand curve shown in figure 8-2(b), we have a vertical flow demand curve of the type shown in figure 8-3(c). This type of flow demand curve is certainly appropriate for copper, aluminum, iron ore, etc., because in the short run we would not expect changes in price to influence the use of the item. We can then postulate two equilibrium situations. The first is a market equilibrium. The relevant equations are given under A in table 8-2. The second is also a market equilibrium, but at the same time it is a full equilibrium, with flow demand

Table 8-2
Simple Stock-Flow Model

	A		B
(a)	$s_t = s_t(p_t)$	(a')	$s_t = s_t(p_t)$
(b)	$d_t = \bar{d}_t + i_t$	(b')	$\bar{d}_t = d_t = s_t$
(c)	$i_t = k(D_t - S_t) = kZ_t$	(c')	$D_t = D_t(p_t; p_t^e)$
(d)	$D_t = D_t(p_t; p_t^e)$	(d')	$S_t = D_t$
(e)	$S_{t+1} = S_t + i_t$		
(f)	$s_t = d_t$		

equal to flow supply, and stock demand equal to stock supply. This system is designated B in table 8-2.

Although in principle this chapter is not supposed to avoid mathematical manipulations, no attempt will be made to solve system A; but the key issues involved in obtaining a solution must be reviewed. To begin, the reader must look at equation (c) in table 8-2, which is an equation for the investment demand (i_t). To grasp this, we can begin again with a full equilibrium, and $S_t = D_t$. Now assume that an increase in the expected price causes the stock demand curve to shift to the right.

This means that initially, before the price increases, we have an excess stock demand that, in figure 8-2(a), is equal to $\bar{S}^* - \bar{S} = \bar{Z}$. If the price were to remain at $\bar{p}'$, would we want all of $\bar{Z}$ immediately after the shift in the demand curve, or all of $\bar{Z}$ later, or a portion of $\bar{Z}$ right away and the rest later on? Taking the first case, is our investment demand equal to our excess stock demand in the initial period? If it is, then k in equation (c) is equal to unity. However, we may only want a portion of $\bar{Z}$ in the initial period, in which event k would be somewhere between unity and zero.

Thus, regardless of price, whenever we have excess stock demand we must determine investment demand. Investment demand rather than excess stock demand is the relevant demand in a given period. But once investment demand takes over, it may be impossible to handle the situation with simple diagrammatics or mathematics. As should be obvious, investment demand determines how fast price rises and how far. Algebraically this situation could not be classified as intractable, but we may not be able to use our previous diagram as it was presented, as we can easily see from the following simple example.

Assume an excess stock demand is the beginning of period t. Also assume that investment demand functions so that buyers do not want any of the commodity in period t. This is the same as saying that there will not be any investment demand in period t: the excess stock demand will only begin to make itself felt as an investment demand in later periods. Thus, although we would show a shift in the stock demand curve in figure 8-2(a), we could not justify an increase in price in period t. To repeat: we have an increase in the excess stock demand in period t but no increase in price in that period, so the arrangement shown in figure 8-2(a) is inapplicable. This is a special situation, but it is certainly conceivable. Note, however, that this situation is not covered by equation c, because with k constant and not equal to zero, there is a positive investment demand in every period that we have an excess stock demand.

We can now start over and get another insight into how complicated the dynamics of these equations can be. Assume that $k = 1$ in equation c, which means that investment demand is equal to excess stock demand. Now assume at time t an increase in the expected price of a commodity, leading to an increase in the stock demand and the excess stock demand. In the very small interval immediately after this change in the expected price, the present price is still $\bar{p}'$, and we have an excess stock demand equal to $\bar{S}^* - \bar{S}$ in figure 8-2(a). Then the effect of this stock excess demand hits the market, and the price goes up very rapidly to p''.

Observe that the demand for *existing* stocks initially increases. In the very short run there is no possibility of increasing production, so those individuals who are sure that prices will increase buy from those who are less sure; those who think that prices will go very high buy from those who think that the price will only increase by a small amount, and so on and so forth. Observe also in figure 8-2(a) that the price eventually increases enough to choke off excess stock demand. As shown, this price is equal to p''.

Producers may take this price as a signal that considerable production is warranted. If they increase production by the amount z'' and attempt to sell it at price p'', they may not find any buyers. But if the price is slightly less than p'', say $p'' - e$, then an amount can be sold equal to the difference between the stock demand and supply curve at price $p'' - e$. Continuing in this fashion, we can imagine an excess flow supply $\tilde{z}$ which, at price $\tilde{p}$, is equal to the excess stock demand at that price. This price, excess stock demand (given that $k = 1$), and excess flow demand constitute a market equilibrium, but not stationarity or a full equilibrium. Instead, the stock supply curve displaces to the right by the amount $\tilde{z}$, and we begin our sequence all over again. If things continue in this fashion, the price eventually approaches $\bar{p}'$, and stocks approach $\bar{S}^*$. In other words, we approach a full equilibrium, with all production being used as a current input. In the present example the sequence of price and stock movements shown in figure 8-3 might be considered normal.

We can close this section by considering a simple variation on the above theme. Remember that the initial price signal to producers, following the increase in stock demand, was p''; but at this price it was postulated that excess

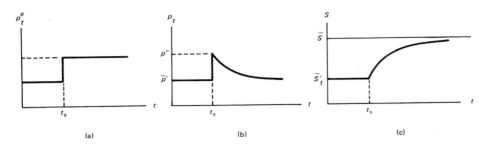

Figure 8-3. Price and Stock Movements Following an Increase in the Expected Price.

stock demand had been eliminated. But consider a situation where it is possible to increase production very rapidly, and so very shortly after the appearance of this price, production is increased by z''. A mistake has thus been made: based on an assumption that price will be p'', production has been raised by an amount which, had the price actually turned out to be p'', could have been sold without producers taking a loss. But now, to sell all or part of z'' in the present period, the price will have to be reduced below p'', and with the given flow supply curve, producers regard this as unsatisfactory. Alternatively, this increased production could be stored and sold the next period, but such an arrangement involves inventory and other costs in addition to production costs. This simple variation is actually quite intricate. It has led us into a situation with frustrated expectations, undesired producer stocks, and various disequilibria that probably can only be treated verbally case by case. Facile generalizations carried out with the aid of simple algebra and elegant diagrams are out of the question.

Distributed Lags

The issue in this section is the reaction of one variable to the value of another taken at different periods of time rather than at a given instant. For instance, demand in period t might be a function of income in that period as well as in a number of previous periods. We would then write $d_t = f(y_t, y_{t-1}, y_{t-2}, \ldots)$ of, if this relationship was linear and did not have an intercept term:

$$d_t = \alpha_0 y_t + \alpha_1 y_{t-1} + \alpha_2 y_{t-2} + \ldots = \sum_{i=0}^{\infty} \alpha_i y_{t-i} \tag{8.9}$$

Obviously it would be extremely difficult to work with this kind of equation. Fortunately, however, Koyck (1954) was able to prescribe a general form for the behavior of the αs: he assumed that they declined geometrically. The logic here seems reasonable: with demand and income, a consumer planning his consumption would almost certainly be more influenced by his recent income than by his income fifteen or twenty years earlier. This means that as i becomes very large, we would expect α_i to get very close to zero. Analytically we have:

$$\alpha_i = \lambda^i \alpha \quad i = 0,1,2,\ldots \quad \text{and} \quad 0 < \lambda < 1$$

Here α is a constant. We can now look at our previous equation, where we obtain by simple substitution:

$$d_t = \alpha(y_t + \lambda y_{t-1} + \lambda^2 y_{t-2} + \ldots) \tag{8.10}$$

Now we lag this equation by one period, and multiply both sides by λ. Thus we obtain:

$$\lambda d_{t-1} = \lambda \alpha(y_{t-1} + \lambda y_{t-2} + \lambda^2 y_{t-3} + \ldots)$$

If we subtract this equation from equation 8.10 we get:

$$d_t = \lambda d_{t-1} + \alpha y_t \tag{8.11}$$

Observe that the infinite series we started with in equation 8.9 has been replaced by two simple expressions. The econometric problem that we will take up later uses observations on d and y to estimate λ and α. We can also point out that having an intercept in our original expression does not change very much. Then we begin with:

$$d_t = \bar{\alpha} + \sum_{i=0}^{\alpha} \alpha_i y_{t-i}$$

As before, we make the substitution $\alpha_i = \lambda^i \alpha$, which gives us:

$$d_t = \bar{\alpha} + \alpha \sum_{i=0}^{\alpha} \lambda^i y_{t-i} \tag{8.12}$$

If we lag this by one period and multiply by λ we get:

$$\lambda d_{t-1} = \lambda \bar{\alpha} + \lambda \alpha \sum_{i=1}^{\alpha} \lambda^{i-1} y_{t-i} \tag{8.13}$$

Subtracting 8.13 from equation 8.12 gives us:

$$d_t - \lambda d_{t-1} = \bar{\alpha} - \lambda \bar{\alpha} + \alpha y_t$$

or:

$$d_t = (1 - \lambda)\bar{\alpha} + \lambda d_{t-1} + \alpha y_t \qquad (8.14)$$

We shall be making the acquaintance of this type of equation in the sequel, but its dynamic properties can be mentioned here. This is a first-order difference equation with an equilibrium value of $\bar{\alpha} + \alpha y_t/(1 - \lambda)$. Thus changes in y unleash the dynamic process. As the reader can easily verify, with values of λ between unity and zero, we have an asymptotic movement from one equilibrium to another.[2]

A few other things are relevant here. The αs in the above equations are weights that we attach to past values of the independent variable. It could be argued that the time form of the lag should be constrained so that we have $\alpha_0 + \alpha_1 + \alpha_2 + \ldots = 1$. Technically, this makes d (in an expression such as equation 8.9) a proper average of the y terms, if there is no systematic trend. This arrangement obviously makes sense when we have output related to demand via a distributed lag, or $q_t = \alpha_0 d_t + \alpha_1 d_{t-1} + \alpha_2 d_{t-2} + \ldots$, and all past demands are equal to the current level, or $q_t = (\alpha_0 + \alpha_1 + \alpha_2 + \ldots)d_t$. In this case we would expect output to equal demand in the limit, or $q_t = d_t$, and thus $\alpha_0 + \alpha_1 + \alpha_2 + \ldots = 1$. Similar circumstances prevail if we relate the completion of investment projects to their starting dates in this way: $j_t = \alpha_0 x_t + \alpha_1 x_{t-1} + \ldots$. Imposing $\Sigma \alpha_i = 1$ explicitly requires that investment projects are completed once they are started. Using the Koyck simplification on the αs means that the above yields:

$$\alpha_0 + \alpha_1 + \alpha_2 + \ldots = \alpha(1 + \lambda + \lambda^2 + \ldots) = \frac{\alpha}{1 - \lambda} = 1$$

We thus obtain $\alpha = 1 - \lambda$. If we used this result in equation 8.11, we would get $d_t = \lambda d_{t-1} + (1 - \lambda)y_t$, or $d_t - d_{t-1} = (1 - \lambda)(y_t - d_{t-1})$. Expressions of this nature are quite common in macroeconomics, especially in matters having to do with permanent income.

Another Stock-Flow Model

We can conclude this section by examining figure 8-4.

The thick line shows the movement of product from supply s to flow demand d and inventories. These inventories are labeled AI to signify actual physical inventories as opposed to desired inventories. These desired inventories, DI, are a function of such things as the present price, the expected price in one or more future periods, the interest rate, and so on. This is indicated in the

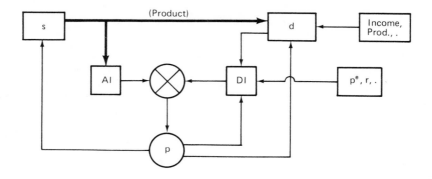

Figure 8-4. Supply-Demand System Showing the Interaction of Desired and Actual Inventories.

figure. In line with the discussion in the previous section we expect that if $AI = DI$, then $p_{t+1} = p_t$; and, for example, if $DI > AI$, then $p_{t+1} > p_t$. In general we can postulate a relationship between price and excess stock demand of the type $p_{t+1} = p_t + \theta'(DI_t - AI_t)$, where $\theta' > 0$.

Similarly, if we are interested in the movement of inventories then we might postulate $AI_{t+1} = AI_t + $ (the change in inventories) $= AI_t + \theta(DI_t - AI_t)$, with $0 < \theta \leqslant 1$. The reader should note that θ is not generally equal to θ. θ' translates an excess stock demand into an increase in price, while θ is an adjustment coefficient related to the behavior of inventory holders and the way they regulate stocks in response to a gap between desired and actual inventories. We can now rewrite this last expression to give $AI_{t+1} = (1-\theta)AI_t + \theta DI_t$. This relationship is analogous to $d_t = \lambda d_{t-1} + (1-\lambda)y_t$, and suggests that the discussion preceding the latter equation is applicable to an inventory model of the type introduced here.

One important reminder. Distributed lags can cause considerable problems in econometric work. For a thorough and not very difficult discussion of these matters see Miller and Rao (1976).

Partial and Stock Adjustment Hypotheses

As indicated above, the demand for a given commodity turns largely on the demand for a stock. The problem is to work this concept into some kind of usable mechanism. We end up with the type of demand curve found in basic economics textbooks, but with a more complicated movement from one equilibrium to another. This can be explained by the fact that the consumption or demand variable d_t involves both current input and stocks; for example, a decrease in the price of a typical primary commodity may not increase demand for the commodity as a current input, but may call for an increase in inventories. On the basis of the previous discussion, we know that this could be expected to take place gradually rather than instantaneously. A diagrammatic presentation of this adjustment process is shown in figure 8-5.

In this figure the original price is p_0, and the long-run demand curve is d^*. If demand adjusted immediately to a fall in price to $\bar{p}$, we would move to d. Instead, in the very short run, with price $\bar{p}$, demand becomes only slightly larger than d_0. Later it arrives at d_1', still later at d_2', and as time goes by we get an asymptotic movement to $\bar{d}$. Another typical intermediate demand curve is d_2 (with d_2' an intermediate consumption), and as the reader can easily verify, it is possible to draw many such curves either to the right or left of d_2.

The law of adjustment for this model is $d_t = d_{t-1} + \lambda(d_t^* - d_{t-1})$, where d^* is an equilibrium level of demand, and $0 < \lambda < 1$. When $d_t = d_t^*$, or the actual value of demand at time t is equal to what is perceived as the equilibrium or desired value at time t, our system is stationary. In figure 8-5(a) we relate long-run demand to price by $d^* = a + bp_t$, and put this into the adjustment equation. We then get $d_t = \lambda a + (1 - \lambda)d_{t-1} + \lambda bp_t$. When $d_t = d_{t-1} = d^*$, we have an equilibrium; this can be verified by putting this condition into the previous equation. This takes us back to the long-run demand

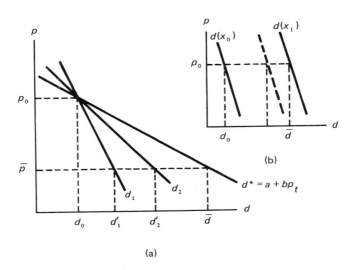

(a)

(b)

Figure 8-5. Demand Adjustment Following a Change in (a) Price and (b) an Aggregate Variable such as Income or Industrial Production.

curve $d_t^* = a + bp_t$, which functions conceptually as an equilibrium demand curve.

This is an example of the partial adjustment or stock adjustment hypothesis. In general we have a desired level of some variable, z_t^*, that depends on an explanatory variable x_t in a relationship such as $z_t^* = \phi_0 + \phi_1 x_t$. Frictions, delays, the inertia of habit, or cold calculation may make it impossible or undesirable to reach the new equilibrium in a single period, and so the actual change in z_t from the level of the previous period, or $z_t - z_{t-1}$, is made some fraction of the change needed to achieve the difference $z_t^* - z_{t-1}$. If we take λ to be this fraction, with $0 < \lambda < 1$, then the partial adjustment hypothesis can be written:

$$z_t - z_{t-1} = \lambda(z_t^* - z_{t-1})$$

or:

$$z_t = (1 - \lambda)z_{t-1} + \lambda z_t^* \tag{8.15}$$

We can now substitute the expression $z_t^* = \phi_0 + \phi_1 x_t$ into the adjustment equation. The result is $z_t = \phi_0 \lambda + (1 - \lambda)z_{t-1} + \lambda \phi_1 x_t$, which is a perfect analogue of the earlier equation.

The Adaptive Expectations Hypothesis

We began the previous discussion with a change in price, without explaining how this change could have come about. Assuming the demand relationship shown in figure 8-5(a), one explanation might be an increase in supply. Of course, for a typical raw material such as copper or aluminum, prices can be adjusted administratively, in response to market or nonmarket forces. We must also consider a possible change in demand in response to a change in industrial production. If this variable increases, then our entire demand curve shifts to the right. In such a situation we may be increasing demand because a larger production requires a larger input of a primary commodity; but because of this larger *flow* demand, stock demand could also increase, because it may be desirable to maintain a fixed relationship between the use of a primary commodity in the current production process and the amount held in inventory.

We will not try to distinguish between these two forces; instead we will simply postulate an increase in some variable x from x_0 to x_1, which shifts our demand curve to the right. This is shown in figure 8-5(b). The assumption will also be some kind of elastic supply, so that price is constant. Once again we can observe a gradual displacement from d_0 to $\bar{d}$, where we have a partial adjustment situation such as we have already discussed. The only difference is that now consumption is related to industrial production (or a similar variable) and price is a parameter. If the relationship were linear we would have $d_t^* = h + wx_t$. Putting this in an adjustment equation of the previous type, with $d_t - d_{t-1} = \lambda(d^* - d_{t-1})$, we get $d_t = h\lambda + (1 - \lambda)d_{t-1} + w\lambda x_t$, as expected.

A similar approach to this type of problem begins with an expected change in a variable such as price, and relates the demand for a commodity to this expected value. We can begin by taking $d_t = h + wp_{t+1}^e$. Our problem now centers on how expectations are formed, and we will assume that we have adaptive expectations, or $p_{t+1}^e = p_t^e + \lambda(p_t - p_t^e)$. Using this in the previous equation gives $d_t = h + w[p_t^e + \lambda(p_t - p_t^e)]$. Next we lag $d_t = h + wp_{t+1}^e$ by one period, multiply the result by $(1 - \lambda)$, and subtract it from $d_t = h + w[p_t^e + \lambda(p_t - p_t^e)]$. As a result we get $d_t = h\lambda + (1 - \lambda)d_{t-1} + w\lambda p_t$. This is the same equation that we obtained using the adjustment hypothesis. The identification of this duality is largely due to Nerlove (1958). Although the econometric exploitation of these results takes place in the next section, if we fit a regression equation that provides a satisfactory explanation of d_t, we cannot say whether adjustment or expectations is at work. In some situations, however, economic theory may be able to provide an answer.

Some Econometrics of Consumption

If, in the analysis directly above, we had begun with a stochastic equation $d_t = \alpha + \theta p_{t+1}^e + u_t$, and then carried out the same manipulations, we would have ended up with:

$$d_t = \alpha\lambda + (1 - \lambda)d_{t-1} + \theta\lambda p_t + [u_t - (1 - \lambda)u_{t-1}] \qquad (8.16)$$

u_t and u_{t-1} are stochastic variables, and the estimating equation is:

$$d_t = \beta_0 + \beta_1 d_{t-1} + \beta_2 p_t + (\quad)$$

Thus we get $\lambda = 1 - \beta_1, \alpha = \beta_0/(1 - \beta_1)$, and $\theta = \beta_2/(1 - \beta_1)$. The βs are obtained from the regression. A problem is raised by the stochastic term, however. One of the criteria placed on this term when ordinary least squares are used is no serial correlation, or $E(\epsilon_t, \epsilon_{t-1}) = 0$, where this expression is one of the off diagonal terms of the variance-covariance matrix. In the present analysis $E(\epsilon_t, \epsilon_{t-1}) = E[u_t - (1 - \lambda)u_{t-1}][u_{t-1} - (1 - \lambda)u_{t-2}]$, and if we assume no serial correlation among individual disturbances we get $E(u_t u_{t-1}) = E(u_t u_{t-2}) = E(u_{t-1}u_{t-2}) 0$; but $E[-(1 - \lambda)u_{t-1}u_{t-1}] = (1 - \lambda)\text{var } u_{t-1}$, and since var $u_{t-1} \neq 0$, the composite stochastic term displays serial correlation. This means that least square estimates of α, θ, and λ are not consistent.

By way of completeness, two other demand equations should be referred to. Instead of adaptive expectations we could imagine a situation where extrapolative expectations prevailed, and thus we have $p_t^e = p_{t-1} + \phi \Delta p_{t-x}$. A simple lag structure might give $p_t^e = p_{t-1} + \phi \Delta p_{t-1} = p_{t-1} + \phi(p_{t-1} - p_{t-1})$. If consumption is a function of expected price we get right away $d_t = \alpha + \theta p_t^e = \alpha + \theta p_{t-1} + \theta \phi \Delta p_{t-1}$. The estimating equation for this case is $d_t = \beta_0 + \beta_1 p_{t-1} + \beta_2 \Delta p_{t-1}$ and so $\alpha = \beta_0$, $\theta = \beta_1$, and $\phi = \beta_2/\beta_1$. As above, the βs are estimated using a suitable regression technique.

In an interesting and important contribution, Witherell (1967) seems to have attempted to combine adjustment and extrapolative expectations, ending up with a consumption equation in the following form: $d_t = \lambda \alpha + (1 - \lambda)d_{t-1} + \lambda \theta p_{t-1} + \phi \lambda \theta \Delta p_{t-1}$. The estimating equation here is $d_t = \beta_0 + \beta_1 d_{t-1} + \beta_2 p_{t-1} + \beta_3 \Delta p_{t-1}$. From these two equations we get $\lambda = 1 - \beta$, $\alpha = \beta_0/(1 - \beta_1)$, $\theta = \beta_2/(1 - \beta_1)$, $\phi = \beta_3/\beta_2$. Some questions could be raised about the theoretical soundness of this type of equation, but it is useful because it often gives good "fits."

Before looking at several econometric equations, we can say something about elasticities. A price elasticity, for example, is defined as

$$\epsilon_p = \frac{\partial q}{\partial p} \frac{p}{q}$$

If we use regression results, we get $\partial q/\partial p$ from the regression equation, and for p and q we use the mean of the observations on price and quantity, or $\bar{p}$ and $\bar{q}$. This elasticity would normally be negative; but if demand is a function of the present price and expected price—for example, the price expected to prevail in the next period—we might have:

$$d_t = d_t(p_t, p_{t+1}^e) = a_0 + a_1 p_t + a_2 p_{t+1}^e \quad a_1 < 0, a_2 > 0$$

Let us now take expectations as extrapolative, which means that we have $p_{t+1}^e = p_t + \phi(p_t - p_{t-1})$. Taking $\phi \neq 0$, and putting this expression in the above equation gives:

$$d_t = a_0 + [a_1 + a_2(1 + \phi)]p_t - a_2 p_{t-1}$$

As is easy to show, we could have $[a_1 + a_2(1 + \phi)] \lesseqgtr 0$; everything depends on the magnitudes of a_1, a_2, and ϕ. Speculative effects could thus cause the relation between d_t and p_t to be positive instead of negative, which would mean a positive price elasticity. In any event, speculation based on conjectured future prices may play an important role in modifying elasticities. Cooper and Lawrence (1976) seem to have considered this possibility when dealing with certain primary commodity elasticities.

Then, too, we must distinguish between long and short term elasticities when we have dynamic equations. With an equation such as $d_t = \eta_0 + \eta_1 d_{t-1} + \eta_2 p_t$ we have a (long-run) equilibrium when $d_t = d_{t-1}$, and thus we get:

$$d_t = \frac{\eta_0}{1 - \eta_1} + \frac{\eta_2}{1 - \eta_1} p_t$$

Accordingly, the long-run elasticity is:

$$\epsilon_L = \frac{\partial d_t}{\partial p_t} \frac{\bar{p}_t}{\bar{d}_t} = \frac{\eta_2}{1 - \eta_1} \frac{\bar{p}_t}{\bar{d}_t} \tag{8.17}$$

On the other hand, the short-run elasticity is taken directly from $d_t = \eta_0 + \eta_1 d_{t-1} + \eta_2 p_t$, and is:

$$\epsilon_S = \frac{\partial d_t}{\partial p_t} \frac{\bar{p}_t}{\bar{d}_t} = \eta_2 \frac{\bar{p}_t}{\bar{d}_t} \tag{8.18}$$

In line with the theory we have discussed earlier, we expect the short-run elasticity to be smaller than the long-run: in the short run a price change changes demand slightly, but in the long run we may get a fairly large change in demand. This story is illustrated in figure 8-5. As pointed out above, η_2 should be negative if we do not have any unseemly speculative effects; and we should also have $0 < \eta_1 < 1$. If η_1 was in fact larger than unity, this would signify satiation on the part of buyers.

We can now present a few consumption equations that seem to follow from the above theory. Taking the case of tin in the United States we have:

$$d_t = 54.56 + \underset{(0.186)}{0.563} \, d_{t-1} - \underset{(0.057)}{0.13246} \, p_{t-1} + \underset{(0.014)}{0.050} \, \Delta g + \underset{(4.279)}{9.97} \, D$$

$$\bar{R}^2 = 0.667 \qquad \epsilon_{PS} = -0.550 \qquad \epsilon_{PL} = -1.262$$

Here Δg is the change in inventories of durable goods in the United States, taken as an index, with 1963 = 100. D is a dummy variable equal to unity for 1953 (and zero elsewhere), while standard errors are in parentheses. Next we present an equation for refined zinc in the United States:

$$d_t = 242.17 + \underset{(2.49)}{0.48998} \, d_{t-1} + \underset{(1.31)}{2.171} \, x_t + \underset{(3.46)}{12.736} \, \Delta x_t + \underset{(1.14)}{44.66} \, D$$

$$\bar{R}^2 = 0.991 \qquad \epsilon_{XS} = 0.230 \qquad \epsilon_{XL} = 0.403$$

In this equation the dummy D is equal to unity for 1963-65, and is zero elsewhere). The t ratios are in parentheses; x_t is an index of industrial production, and elasticities are taken with reference to this variable. (These elasticities, like income elasticities, are positive.) Finally, we take the case of the demand for primary copper in France. (Again, t ratios are in parentheses.)

$$d_t = 57.99 + \underset{(2.19)}{0.400\, d_{t-1}} - \underset{(2.53)}{0.310\, p_t} + \underset{(3.04)}{1.10\, x_t}$$

$$\bar{R}^2 = 0.925 \qquad \epsilon_{PS} = -0.253 \qquad \epsilon_{PL} = -0.421 \qquad \epsilon_{XS} = 0.540 \qquad \epsilon_{XL} = 0.900$$

Here we have both price elasticities and elasticities with respect to the variable x_t, which is the index of industrial production (1963 = 100). The logic of the deflation of the price by the wholesale price index has been examined at great length by Herfindahl (1959), among others. This deflation relates the cost of copper as an input to the price of the output in which it is used, thus saying something about its desirability relative to other inputs: if the price of the output, the input in question, and relative substitutes for the input doubled, we would expect no decline in the demand for the input per unit of output.

Just as the above elasticities were computed for individual countries, it would have been equally simple, in theory, to compute them for blocs of countries. The matter of projections will not be discussed here, but the above estimates are of interest primarily because they shed light on the general size of the elasticities for primary commodities: in line with our suspicions and intuition, these elasticities are quite low. The table 8-3 presents price and income elasticities for the most important commodity groups; the values in this table are weighted averages of the elasticities for individual products.

The significance of elasticities for such things as cartel forming has been referred to earlier in this book; for more on this matter, see the work of Marian Radetzki and Herin and Wijkman (1976).

Table 8-3
Price and Income Elasticities for Major Commodity Groups

	Food	Metals and Minerals	Fuels
Price Elasticity			
Low	−0.370	−0.140	−0.250
High	−0.540	−0.390	−0.250
Income Elasticity			
Low	0.401	0.669	0.900
High	0.490	0.891	0.900

The Econometrics of Supply

Next we turn our attention to supply. The groundwork for this topic was carried out in the beginning of the previous section, and we obtain a dynamic equation for supply in the same way that we obtained one for consumption. First we relate equilibrium supply to price by $s^* = \beta + \pi p_t$; then we postulate an adjustment equation $s_t = s_{t-1} + \phi(s^* - s_{t-1})$, and by the usual manipulations we obtain $s_t = \phi\beta + \phi\pi p_t + (1 - \phi)s_{t-1}$. The adjustment hypothesis may make more sense for supply than for consumption, because changes in production invariably take time.

Another advantage of this type of equation, as we have seen, is that it permits us to regard supply as a function of a weighted average of present and former prices, which we might occasionally find useful. This can be shown simply by lagging the equation for s_t, and using it to replace s_{t-1} in the same equation. This gives us:

$$s_t = \phi\beta + (1 - \phi) [\phi\beta + (1 - \phi)s_{t-2} + \phi\pi p_{t-2}] + \phi\pi p_{t-1}$$

Repeated application of this procedure results in:

$$s_t = \beta + \phi\pi \Sigma (1 - \phi)^i p_{t-i} \tag{8.19}$$

We have seen many expressions of this type earlier; in addition, the supply equation is, like its consumption analogue, a simple first-order difference equation. A device associated with multiplier theory will be used to clarify the dynamics of this equation. Our assumption is that we begin with an equilibrium (s_0, p_0), and that we have an increase in the price to p_1. Supply begins moving toward s_1, but in line with the adjustment hypothesis, we assume that this takes time. The supply curve in its usual form is shown in figure 8-6(a), with the initial equilibrium at point A. The new equilibrium, which is on the long-run supply curve $s^* = \beta + \pi p_t$, is at (s_1, p_1).

This situation can also be studied with the aid of our supply difference equation. The beginning of our sequence is at point A' in figure 8-6(b), where we have an equilibrium with $s_{t-1} = s_t = s_0$. The slope of FF is the coefficient of s_{t-1}, and is equal to $(1 - \phi)$. The intercept of FF is a function of the price, and so at the initial equilibrium it is a function of p_0. Next the price increases to p_1, and as a result FF shifts upward to $F'F'$. This arrangement is shown in figure 8-7(a). The new equilibrium is s_1, but this is only reached asymptotically. In the first period the increase in production is TT', while in the second period it is $T'A$, etc. We thus have a multiplier sequence consisting of:

$$\phi\pi(p_1 - p_0) [1 + (1 - \phi) + (1 - \phi)^2 + \ldots] = \frac{\phi\pi(p_1 - p_0)}{1 - (1 - \phi)} = \pi(p_1 - p_0)$$

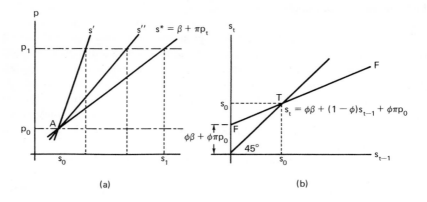

(a)   (b)

Figure 8-6. (a) Supply Changes Given an Increase in Price and (b) the Initial Equilibrium in a Dynamic Supply Model.

This expression shows that $\phi\pi(p_1 - p_0)$ is equal to TT'; $\phi(1 - \phi)\pi(p_1 - p_0)$ is equal to $T'A$; and so on. The asymptotic movement to the new equilibrium is also shown in figure 8-7(b).

It could be argued from figure 8-7(a) that if producers were willing to supply the increase in demand $\Delta s = s_1 - s_0$ by reducing inventories, as well as from current production, inventory reduction would be $T'T''$ in the first period,

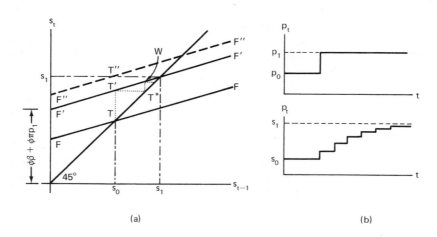

(a)   (b)

Figure 8-7. Movement to the New Equilibrium.

$T'T'' - T^*W$ in the second period, and so on—assuming the full amount of Δs is supplied in each period, either from current production or from stocks.

We could also postulate that production could be increased by TT'' (to s_1) in the first period if consumers were willing to pay a price corresponding to the intercept F''. The reasoning here is that with $\phi\pi$ constant, every value of the intercept corresponds to a price. The initial intercept corresponded to p_0; the increase in price to p_1 is associated with the intercept of $F'F'$ (and an increase in production of $FF' = TT'$ in the first period), and so there should be some price greater than p_1 which would cause producers to increase—or to attempt to increase—production by more than FF' in the first period.

Some Econometric Estimates

We shall now provide some supply equations for newly mined copper. The estimating equation corresponding to $s_t = \phi\beta + (1 - \phi)s_{t-1} + \phi\pi p_t$ is given by $s_t = \psi_0 + \psi_1 s_{t-1} + \psi_2 p_t + u_t$, where u_t is the error term. We thus see that $\phi = 1 - \psi_1$, $\beta = \psi_0/(1 - \psi_1)$, $\pi = \psi_2/(1 - \psi_1)$. If the lagging procedure used at the beginning of this section is applied to the estimating equation, we obtain a composite error term $v_t = u_t + \psi_1 u_{t-1} + \psi_1^2 u_{t-2} + \ldots$, but this expression can be lagged one period, multiplied by ψ_1, and subtracted from v_t to yield $u_t = v_t - \psi_1 v_{t-1}$. This indicates serially correlated error terms that the estimating procedure must take into account.

The logarithmic form of the estimating equation was chosen simply because it gave better "fits" than other types of estimating equations. This also simplifies the matter of obtaining supply elasticities, since if we have $\log s_t = \psi_0 + \psi_1 \log s_{t-1} + \psi_2 \log p_t$, our short-run elasticity is $\epsilon_{SS} = \psi_2$, and the long-run elasticity (obtained employing the criterion that $\log s_t = \log s_{t-1}$) is $\epsilon_{SL} = \psi_2/(1 - \psi_1)$. The supply being examined here is the supply of newly mined copper in thousands of metric tons (copper content), expressed as an index with 1963 as the base year. The prices used here are the price of refined copper on the London Metal Exchange, p_t, and the American copper price, which is called p_{ut}. (This American copper price is actually an average of several prices.) Both prices are in index form.

In the equations shown in table 8-4, we have t ratios in parentheses, and D is a dummy variable that equals unity for the years given, and zero otherwise. The basic data are annual observations over the period 1948-67. The reader may also question the absence of time trend variables in the above estimates, particularly since this book argued earlier that for less-developed countries there is a secular expansion of raw material production that has nothing to do with price. However, using time trend variables introduced an unacceptable amount of multicollinearity into the estimating equations.

Estimates of supply elasticities usually depend on who is doing the

Table 8-4
Supply Equations for Primary Copper in Canada, Chile, and Zaire

Canada	$\log s_t = 0.21511 + 0.7949 \log s_{t-1} + 0.2365 \log p_{ut}$
	$ (6.876) \phantom{\log s_{t-1} + } (2.245)$
	$\bar{R}^2 = 0.8114 \qquad \epsilon_{SS} = 0.2365 \qquad \epsilon_{SL} = 1.16$
Chile	$\log s_t = 0.1236 + 0.7694 \log s_{t-1} + 0.2890 \log p_{t-1}$
	$ (8.412) \phantom{\log s_{t-1} + } (2.670)$
	$\bar{R}^2 = 0.920 \qquad \epsilon_{SS} = 0.2890 \qquad \epsilon_{SL} = 1.22$
Zaire	$\log s_t = 0.4144 + 0.7204 \log s_{t-1} + 0.1726 \log p_t + 0.031 D$
	$ (8.854) \phantom{\log s_{t-1} + } (3.120) (2.869)$
	$\bar{R}^2 = 0.947 \qquad \epsilon_{SS} = 0.1726 \qquad \epsilon_{SL} = 0.625 \qquad D: 1959\text{-}62$

estimating; table 8-5 shows estimates by United States Bureau of Mines of the supply elasticities for several of the most important minerals. Other organizations that are involved in determining supply elasticities for primary commodities are UNCTAD and the World Bank, and the interested reader should examine their publications.

Exhaustible Resources

At this point we question whether our econometric results might or should be modified because we are, for the most part, dealing with nonrenewable resources. (However, the techniques being discussed in this chapter also apply to such things as natural rubber, tea, wheat, and probably timber.) We need a rule

Table 8-5
Supply Elasticities for Metals

	Price Range	Elasticity
Aluminum	27-37	1.15
Copper	52-75	0.77
Nickel	128-200	2.03
Lead	14-20	1.84
Zinc	16-25	1.75

Source: U.S. Bureau of Mines estimates

for the optimal extraction of a nonrenewable resource. Hotelling (1931), of course, derived such a rule many years ago, and Solow (1974) and Banks (1974), among others, provided further elaboration and discussion.

The rule goes roughly as follows. A mineral should be extracted so long as the prevailing rate of interest is larger than the rate of profit appreciation of the mineral if it were left in the ground. Take a simple example, where the profit from extracting a mineral now is $100, and the expected profit from extracting it in the next period is $105. This is a profit appreciation of 5 percent. Assume an interest rate of 10 percent. If the mineral were extracted now and the profit put in a bank, it would give $110 in the next period—or a rate appreciation of 10 percent. Thus it should be extracted now.

We can now formalize this beginning with a continuous version of the analysis in Banks (1974). First write the profit in each period as $B = R - C$, or profit equals revenue (pq) minus cost (cq), where p is unit price, c unit cost, and q quantity. Generally, p and c are functions of q. We can then write for our intertemporal discounted profit function (or objective function):

$$B^* = \int_0^T [p(q)q - c(q)q]e^{-rt}dt = \int_0^T B(q)e^{-rt}dt \qquad (8.20)$$

The amount of the resource at the arbitrary time t is K, which is taken as the state variable. The control variable is the amount removed at time t, and this is q. We thus have $q = \dot{K}$, and with extraction the sign of q is negative. The Hamiltonian is thus:

$$H = B(q)e^{-rt} + \lambda \dot{K} = B(q)e^{-rt} + \lambda(-q) \qquad (8.21)$$

Assuming the transversality conditions are satisfied[3], and intertemporal optimization requires:

$$\frac{\partial H}{\partial q} = B'(q)e^{-rt} - \lambda = 0 \qquad (8.22)$$

$$\frac{\partial H}{\partial K} = 0 = -\frac{\partial \lambda}{\partial t} \qquad (8.23)$$

Using the second of these results leads to:

$$-\frac{\partial \lambda}{\partial t} = -rB'(q)e^{-rt} + e^{-rt}\frac{dB'(q)}{dt} = 0$$

or:

$$r = \frac{1}{B'} \frac{dB'}{dt}$$
(8.24)

This is the algebraic form of the simple rule discussed above. A graphic presentation may also be useful to the reader, but first a further comment on and interpretation of the above is necessary. The expression $B'(q)$ is obviously equal to $MR(q) - MC(q)$, where MR is marginal revenue and MC marginal cost. Accordingly $B'e^{-rt}$ is discounted marginal profit, and in equilibrium this is equal to λ. However λ is the shadow price or opportunity cost of the exhaustible resource, and so our optimal condition is also equivalent to $\overline{MR} = \overline{MC} + \lambda$, where $\overline{MR}$ and $\overline{MC}$ are discounted values. Note that in equilibrium, marginal revenue must exceed marginal cost by λ in order to allow for profits that might have been realized in the future had the resource not been extracted. λ functions as a royalty, and thus this situation departs from the Marginal Revenue = Marginal Cost rule that is so important in elementary economic theory.

We can now ask what happens when λ exceeds $B'e^{-rt}$. This means that the value of the resource is increasing faster in the ground than the profit from selling this resource would in a bank—and so it should be left in the ground. Of course, because of the way the problem is set up, we can resort to Kuhn-Tucker theory right away, which tells us that if $\lambda_t > B'(q_t)$, then production in period t is zero, or $q_t = 0$. We also know that if we have $K > \Sigma q_t$, then $\lambda = 0$, and the shadow price or scarcity value of the resource is zero. In this situation we do not have to worry about scarcity or the future value of a resource, and thus we are back to our $MR = MC$ profit-maximizing criterion.

We can now examine figure 8-8, which shows values of the discounted marginal profit $\overline{B}'(q) = \overline{MR}(q) - \overline{MC}(q)$ for each period within our time horizon T. These curves, of course, are based on predicted values for prices and costs over the time horizon, and thus it would hardly make sense to stretch this horizon out to infinity. Ideally, we make up our intertemporal production plan at the beginning of the initial period, and as we receive new information on predicted prices and costs, the amount of the resource, the desired time horizon, etc., we alter the program. Unfortunately, one of the shortcomings of this diagram is that to get an interesting solution, we have to make sure that our time horizon is long enough to give us a condition of scarcity, or $\lambda \neq 0$; but if we do that, then we can use this diagram to discuss such things as changes in λ given changes in K, the effect of "backstop technologies," etc. Also note that in principle this problem could have been approached by way of the Lagrangian:

$$L = \int_0^T [p(q) - c(q)] q e^{-rt} + \lambda \left[\int_0^T q \, dt - \overline{K} \right]$$

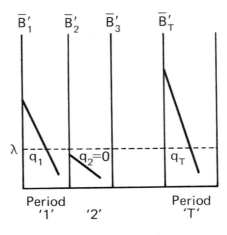

Figure 8-8. Intertemporal Extractive Program for an Exhaustible Resource.

This Lagrangian shows that we actually have only one value of λ (because we have only one resource $\bar{K}$). Therefore, because of the discrete form our diagram takes, we must explicitly point out that $\lambda_t = \lambda_{t+1} = \lambda_{t+2}$ and so on. This means, in figure 8-8, that if the resource has a greater discounted scarcity value in one period than in another, then units are transferred into that period until we get an equality across periods. This arrangement is patently Ricardian; however, Fisher (1977) has taken particular notice of the intertemporal nature of the analysis by differentiating between what he calls Hotelling rents and conventional Ricardian rents.

Can the above discussion be incorporated into our econometric investigations? To begin, we might postulate a different type of supply function—one that takes explicit consideration of the amount of the exhaustible resource we have. Then we have:

$$s = \phi_0 + \phi_1 K + \phi_2 p \qquad (8.25)$$

In this equation K is the stock of the natural resource—for instance, it could be the known amount of economical reserves of a mineral. If we differentiate this equation we get:

$$\frac{ds}{dt} = \phi_1 \frac{dK}{dt} + \phi_2 \frac{dp}{dt} \qquad (8.26)$$

But it must also be the case that:

$$s = -\frac{dK}{dt}$$

If we put this expression in equation 8.26 we get:

$$\frac{ds}{dt} = -\phi_1 s + \phi_2 \frac{dp}{dt} \tag{8.27}$$

A discrete approximation of this equation is:

$$s_t = s_{t-1}(1 - \phi_1) + \phi_2 \Delta p \tag{8.28}$$

My attempts to turn this equation into a valuable econometric property were not very successful, but most minerals may now be so far from exhaustion that producers are not inclined to consider exhaustion effects. (For instance, until recently the real price of oil has been falling—despite a clear-cut recognition by all parties that if the traditional growth rate in the consumption of oil is not broken, the world's oil supplies will be exhausted in half a century or so. However, given normal social discount rates, a half century is an extremely long time.)

But when the day does come when exhaustion looms for certain minerals, let us hope that economic theorists remember that price must not only cover conventional costs, but also a scarcity rent; and even if, for example, these conventional costs remain constant until the exhaustion of the resource, the royalty that will have to be added to the (marginal) cost to take growing scarcity into account will increase, and so will the price of the commodity.

The Econometrics of Short-Run Prices

The background for this section is to be found in the material on stocks and flows. There we related price changes to the difference between desired and actual inventories. Rather than take levels of inventories, we can relate price changes to changes in desired and actual inventories. In doing this we might postulate the following equation:

$$\Delta p = p_t - p_{t-1} = \lambda(k\Delta d_{t-1} - I_{t-1})$$

In this expression d is demand and I stocks. The estimating equation takes the form $\Delta p = \beta_0 + \beta_1 \Delta d_{t-1} + \beta_2 I_{t-1}$, from which we get $\lambda = -\beta_2, \beta_1 = \lambda k$, and so $k = \beta_2/\beta_1$. We also expect $\beta_2 < 0$ and $\beta_1 > 0$. This construction will now be used to estimate a price equation for refined zinc in the United States. The flow variable here is actually disappearance, and thus represents zinc being used as a current input and for inventories. Theoretically, this situation is not ideal. We use annual data for the period 1953, and t ratios are in parentheses.

$$\Delta p = -0.885 + 0.0403\ \Delta d_t - 0.195\ \Delta I_{t-1}$$
$$\qquad\qquad (1.476) \qquad\ (3.13)$$

$$\bar{R}^2 = 0.5339 \qquad D.W. = 1.74$$

This equation is not particularly impressive, although it might be possible to improve it. Rather than speculate on its shortcomings, we can present a variant of this type of equation:

$$p = 74.46 + 4.55\ \frac{d_{t-1}}{I_{t-1}} + 0.348\ \frac{\Delta d_t}{\Delta I_t} + 5.24\ D$$
$$\qquad\qquad (4.70) \qquad\quad (1.95) \qquad\quad (1.00)$$

$$\bar{R}^2 = 0.754 \qquad D.W. = 1.89$$

The dummy here is unity for 1967 and 1968 (during and after the severe strikes in the United States) and zero otherwise. One of the largest zinc companies in the world has used an equation like this for rough price forecasting and, at least until a few years ago, seemed quite satisfied.

Estimation and Some Other Problems

The estimation of commodity models has not presented as many problems as has the estimation of macroeconomic models, since for the most part—with commodity models—there are only a limited number of relevant variables, and these either result in satisfactory equations or don't. In macroeconomics, on the contrary, there are so many variables available that, in principle, any type of equation can be estimated and any desired result can be obtained. Of course, irrelevant variables have been introduced in certain commodity models, but for the most part these frauds are so flagrant that even amatuer econometric sleuths are capable of detecting them.

Then, too, ordinary least squares or some version of the Cochrane-Orcutt technique will handle most commodity problems; and limited-information and full-information methods (as embodied in the TROLL system) should suffice for almost any conceivable estimating problem. However, a great deal of the concern shown by econometricians for simultaneous equation bias and the like is wasted on commodity models; I am convinced that single equation estimates can do virtually everything that needs to be done in this area.

The Future of Commodity Econometrics

The matter of forecasting with economic commodity models can be settled quickly. Many corporations, government agencies, and international organizations spend a large amount of money on expensive econometricians and computing facilities, when they would be better off with a gypsy and crystal ball. In my book *The World Copper Market*, I made one of the few usable price forecasts of recent years, with the help of the elasticities computed in the book, some simple time trends of copper consumption borrowed from various sources, income and industrial production projections made by the World Bank, and investment activity in the world copper industry as compiled by the *Engineering and Mining Journal*. Essentially the same equipment was being used, although much less successfully, by a well-known consulting firm in the commodity field, although its director—in his public pronouncements—enjoyed giving the impression of being in command of a full-scale econometric masterpiece capable of predicting prices down to the pence or sou over several months.

At the same time another consulting organization was busy constructing a forecasting model for an international organization. This model, which cost several hundred thousand dollars, reduced to a straight line. It may well have forecasted effectively over a few hundred or perhaps a few thousand years, but it was quite hopeless for investigating the events on the world copper market for the next decade or so. Rather than continue with anecdotes like this, I would like to assure the reader that models for forecasting commodity prices belong, for the most part, in the classroom—though not in a reputable classroom.

On the other hand, econometric commodity models may help us to understand the functioning of commodity markets. I have already cited the work of Pindyck, and the serious reader should consider it. Some spectral techniques described by Labys and Granger are undoubtedly valuable in studying commodity cycles, and may be useful in future forecasting arsenals, but things seem to be moving rather slowly in this field right now. The present author is also convinced that Box-Jenkins methods have an important role to play in the study of industries such as iron and steel, and lead, where conventional regression techniques seem unable to produce interesting results.

Commodity-oriented development models probably qualify as an elegant fraud, though not so much as commodity link models and the enterprise from which they were derived. Spatial equilibrium models, recursive programming models, and linear (and nonlinear) models probably have a great deal to offer in theory, but not much in practice. The difficulty here, however, is the shortage of economists that are properly trained in these techniques. By way of summation, the following seems appropriate: in commodity econometrics, as in econometrics generally, the key word will continue to be quantity rather than quality. This is so because the sponsors and purchasers of these models do not demand quality. As long as hundreds of thousands of dollars are available to purchase pseudoscientific rubbish served up on printouts and in expensive brochures, it will continue to be produced at an increasing rate.

Notes

1. Flow supply is our usual supply curve, showing the amount a producer would produce in a given period on the basis of a given price. Flow demand is almost the usual demand, but shows only the amount demanded for current consumption.

2. This demonstration can also be put in continuous form. Here the relationship between d and y takes the following form (instead of as in equation 8.10):

$$d(t) = \int_0^\infty \alpha(\tau)y(t - \tau)d\tau \quad \text{with} \quad \alpha = \int_0^\infty \alpha(\tau)d\tau$$

Taking the case of exponential weights, or $\alpha(\tau) = ae^{-\lambda\tau}$, then:

$$\alpha = \int_0^\infty ae^{-\lambda\tau} d\tau = \frac{a}{\lambda}e^{-\lambda\tau}\Big|_0^\infty = \frac{a}{\lambda}$$

This gives us $a = \alpha\lambda$. We now have

$$d(t) = \int_0^\infty \alpha\lambda e^{-\lambda\tau}y(t - \tau)d\tau$$

Taking $x = t - \tau$ we get $dx = -d\tau$, and thus:

$$d(t) = \alpha\lambda e^{-\lambda t} \int_t^{-\infty} y(x)(-dx)$$

This can be rewritten to give:

$$d(t)e^{\lambda t} = \alpha\lambda \int_\infty^t e^{\lambda x}y(x)dx$$

When differentiated this yields:

$$\dot{d} = \frac{dd(t)}{dt} = \lambda(\alpha y - d)$$

The rate of change of d with respect to time depends on the difference between the desired value of d, which is y, and the actual value, which is d. What we have here is a kind of adjustment equation.

3. I have always treated the transversality conditions rather lightly, and encouraged my students to do the same. But in a recent meeting of the Higher Seminar for Economic Analysis at the University of Stockholm, Harvey E. Lapan demonstrated that these conditions are crucial when dealing with problems of exhaustible resources.

A Note on the Literature

The reader who plans to delve deeper into the subjects treated in this book will find a great deal of both elementary and specialized literature at his or her disposal. All students, economists, engineers, and laymen interested in natural resources and energy should get acquainted with the journals *Resources Policy* and *Energy Policy*, both from the IPC Science and Technology Press, London. This organization also publishes *Food Policy* and *Marine Policy*. The *Engineering and Mining Journal*, based in New York, is very good for industrial raw materials, and provides indispensible information on investment. Of the scholarly journals, primary commodities are best treated in the *Journal of World Trade Law*, which has its origin in Geneva. The publications of the commodities division of UNCTAD and the World Bank are also useful, and the reader should watch for the work of John Cuddy and M.J. Colebrook of UNCTAD, and Kenji Takeuchi, Jos de Vries, F. Pinto, and P. Pollak of the World Bank. I also strongly recommend the American periodicals *Fortune* and *Business Week*; the English weekly *New Scientist*; and the daily *London Financial Times*. For energy matters the *Bulletin of the Atomic Scientist* is important, as is the *Scientific American* and *Science*. Also, for commodities, *Intereconomics* is important.

On environmental problems I recommend the books of Pearce (1976), Baumol and Oates (1975), and the excellent survey of Anthony Fisher and F.M. Petersen (1975). For books on natural resources, refer to the book edited by D.W. Pearce (1975) and my own book on the economics of natural resources (1976). Interesting and important material on these matters is also to be found in Rogers (1976).

Books on energy have just started to arrive, and the work of the Ford Foundation Energy Project deserves to be singled out. In particular I would like to mention the contributions of Dale Jorgenson and Edward Hudson. Other important work in this field has been done by George Perry of the Brookings Institution and Thomas Willet of the United States Treasury. As a counterweight to some of the material in the *Bulletin of the Atomic Scientists*, I can refer to an article by R.E. Lapp in Fortune Magazine (1975).

The politics of oil is well surveyed by Blair (1977) and Rustow and Mugno (1976). P.G. Bradley (1967) provides an important introduction to petroleum economics; I attempt to build on these analyses in a forthcoming book. No economist can afford to miss Corden's article on the macroeconomics of oil in the book edited by Rybczynski (1976) and the paper by Tumlir in the same book is quite informative. Professors Robert Mundell and Harry Johnson seem to have covered all the key international monetary matters, but R.Z. Aliber, Richard Cooper, Michael Connelly, Herbert Grubel, Robert Stern, and Joseph Finger have done or are doing work that is relevant to both international monetary economics and the economics of primary commodities.

On the economic theory of energy and resources, the basic writings still seem to be Solow (1974,1975) and Nordhaus (1973,1974). Solow in particular has published several papers on the economics of natural resources that are "must" reading for specialists. On the economics of specific commodities, the reader can examine Desai (1966), Franklin Fisher et al. (1972), Banks (1974), and Witherell (1967). Professor F. Gerard Adams has also published considerable econometric work dealing with industrial raw materials. The elementary economic background for tackling much of the literature in this appendix can be found in Samuelson (1975), Alchian and Allen (1964), and Clower and Due (1974); readers who want to go deeper into the pure economics needed to handle resource problems should refer to the assorted contributions of Robert Dorfman, Paul Samuelson, Robert Solow, Edmond Malinvaud, Franklin Fisher, Lars Svensson, and Robert Clower. In addition, topics dealing with uncertainty are going to be extremely important in coming to grips with natural and energy resources, and in this context I can refer to the work of Professors Kenneth Arrow and James Meade.

Cartels have received exemplary treatment at the hands of Kenji Takeuchi and Marian Radetzki. John Cuddy and Jos de Vries have done important work on commodity agreements. The economists of the German Development Institute at Berlin have produced useful material on commodities, particularly Dieter Weiss and Klaus Billerbeck. The comments of Hildegard Harlander of the German Research Institute at Munich were important for me in preparing chapter 7 of this book; and significant research on raw materials is being carried out by Heikki Lehtimäki of the Research Institute of the Finnish Economy.

Finally, as far as I am concerned, the best economics library in the world is still to be found at the Institute of World Economics (kiel).

References

Adelman, Maurice. "The World Oil Cartel: Scarcity, Economics, and Politics," *Quarterly Review of Business and Economics*, Summer 1976.

Alchian, A., and W. Allen. *Exchange and Production Theory in Use* (Belmont, Cal.: Wadsworth Publishing Company, 1964).

Arrow, Kenneth. *Information and Economic Theory* (Stockholm: Federation of Swedish Industries, 1975).

Bailly, P.A. "The Problems of Converting Resources to Reserves," *Mining Engineering*, 1976.

Banks, Ferdinand E. "An Econometric Note on the Demand for Refined Zinc," *Zeitschrift fü Nationalekonomi*, 1971.

_____. "The Economics of Exhaustible Resources: A Note," *Ekonomiska Samfundets Tidskrift*, 1971.

_____. "An Econometric Model of the World Tin Economy: A Comment," *Econometrica*, July 1972.

_____. "A Note on Some Theoretical Issues of Resource Depletion," *The Journal of Economic Theory*, October 1974.

_____. *The World Copper Market: An Economic Analysis*, Boston: Ballinger Publishing Company, 1974.

_____. "Multinational Firms and African Economic Development," *Journal of World Trade Law*, May/June 1975.

_____. "The Economics and Politics of Primary Commodities," *Journal of World Trade Law*, November/December 1976.

_____. *The Economics of Natural Resources* (New York: Plenum Publishing Company, 1976).

_____. "Natural Resource Availability: Some Economic Aspects," *Resources Policy*, March 1977.

Basevi, G., and A. Steinherr. "The 1974 Increase in Oil Prices: Optimum Tariff or Transfer Problem," *Weltwirtschaftliches Archiv*, August 1976.

Baumol, William J. "Economic Dynamics: An Introduction," 3rd ed. (New York: The Macmillan Company, 1970).

_____, and W.E. Oates. *The Theory of Environmental Policy* (Englewood Cliffs, N.J.: Prentice-Hall, 1975).

_____, and D.F. Bradford. "Detrimental Externalities and Non-Convexity of the Production Set," *Economica*, May 1972.

Beckerman, Wilfred. "Economists, Scientists, and Environmental Catastrophe," *Oxford Economic Papers*, November 1972.

Berg, Helge. "En Ny Ekonomisk Världsordning?" *Ekonomisk Revy*, March 1977.

Bergsten, C. Fred. *The Dilemmas of the Dollar: The Economics and Politics of United States International Monetary Policy* (New York: New York University Press for the Council on Foreign Relations, 1975).

189

Bergsten, C. Fred. "A New OPEC in Bauxite," *Challenge*, July/August 1976.

Billerbeck, K. "On Negotiating a New World Order of the World Copper Market," *Occasional Paper of the German Development Institute*, No. 33, 1975.

Blair, John M. *The Control of Oil* (London: The MacMillan Press, 1976).

Bradley, Paul G. *The Economics of Crude Petroleum Production* (Amsterdam: North Holland Publishing Company, 1967).

Bradshaw, T. "My Case for National Planning," *Fortune*, February 1977.

Brookes, L.G. "The Nuclear Power Implications of OPEC Prices," *Energy Policy*, June 1975.

Brown, Lester. "Rich Countries and Poor in a Finite Interdependent World," in *The No Growth Society*, edited by Mancur Olson and Hans H. Landsberg (New York: W.H. Norton and Company, 1973).

Carman, J. "Comments on the Report Entitled 'The Limits to Growth.'" Address at the University of New Brunswick, 1972.

Clark, Colin. "Agricultural Productivity in Relation to Population," in *Man and His Future*, edited by G. Wolstenholze (Boston: Harvard University Press 1963).

Clower, R.W. "An Investigation into the Dynamics of Investment," *American Economic Review*, 1954.

———, and J.F. Due. *Microeconomics* (Homewood Ill.: Irwin Publishing Company, 1972).

Cochran, Neal P. "Oil and Gas From Coal," *Scientific American*, May 1976.

Connelly, Phillip, and R. Perlman. *The Politics of Scarcity* (London: Oxford University Press, 1975).

Cook, C. Sharp. "Don't Say We Weren't Warned," *Bulletin of the Atomic Scientists*, September 1976.

Cooper, Richard and R.Z. Lawrence. "The 1972-75 Commodity Boom," *Brookings Papers on Economic Activity*, no. 3, 1975.

Corden, W.M. "Framework for Analysing the Implications of the Rise in Oil Prices," in *The Economics of the Oil Crisis*, edited by T.M. Rybczynski (London: The Macmillan Press, 1976).

Cranston, D.A. and H.C. Martin. "Are Ore Discovery Costs Increasing?" *Canadian Mining Journal*, 1973.

Davis, R.F. "La Inversión Extranjera en la América Latina," *El Trimestre Económica* (Mexico), January/March 1973.

Desai, M. "An Econometric Model of the World Tin Economy, 1948-61," *Econometrica*, 1966.

———. "An Econometric Model of the World Tin Economy: A Reply to Mr. Banks," *Econometrica*, 1972.

Dorfman, Robert; Paul A. Samuelson; and Robert Solow. *Linear Programming and Economic Analysis* (New York: McGraw-Hill, 1958).

Ehrlich, J.R. and J.P. Holdren. *Human Ecology: Problems and Solutions* (San Francisco: W.H. Freeman and Company, 1973).

Ertek, Tumay. "The World Demand for Copper, 1948-63: An Econometric Study," Ph.D. dissertation, University of Wisconsin, 1967.

Finger, J.M. and M. Kreinin. "A Critical Survey of the New International Economic Order," *Journal of World Trade Law*, November/December 1976.

Fisher, Anthony C. "On Measures of Natural Resources Scarcity," *International Institute for Applied Systems Analysis*, February 1977.

_____, and F.M. Petersen. "Natural Resources and the Environment in Economics," University of Maryland, 1974. Mimeographed.

Fisher, Franklin M. *The Identification Problem in Econometrics* (New York: McGraw-Hill, 1966).

_____, P.H. Cootner, and M.N. Baily. "An Econometric Model of the World Copper Industry," *Bell Journal of Economics and Management Science*, Autumn 1972.

Fisher, John C. *Energy Crisis in Perspective* (New York: John Wiley and Sons, 1974).

Forrester, Jay W. *World Dynamics* (Cambridge, Mass.: Wright-Allen Press, 1971).

Fox, William A. *The Working of a Tin Agreement* (London: Longmans, 1974).

Fuller, Carlos R. "The Future Development of World Copper Mining," *CIPEC Quarterly Review*, July/September, 1976.

Galbraith, J.K. *Money: Whence It Came, Where It Went* (London: Andre Deutsch, 1974).

Govett, M.H. "Geographic Concentration of World Mineral Supplies, Production, and Consumption," in *World Mineral Supplies: Assessment and Perspective*, edited by G.J.S. Govett and M.H. Govett (New York: Elsevier Scientific Publishing Company, 1976).

_____, and G.J.S. Govett. "Defining and Measuring World Mineral Supplies," in *World Mineral Supplies: Assessment and Perspective*, edited by G.J.S. Govett and M.H. Govett (New York: Elsevier, 1976).

Grillo, H. "The Importance of Scrap," *The Metal Bulletin*, special issue on copper, 1965.

Harlinger, Hildegard. "Neue Modelle für die Zukunft der Menschheit," IFO-Institut für Wirtschaftsforschung, February 1975.

Heller, Robert. "International Reserves and World Inflation," Staff Papers, March 1976.

Herin, Jan, and Per M. Wijkman. *Den Internationella Bakgrunden* (Stockholm: Institut für Internationella Ekonomi, 1976).

Herfindahl, O.C. *Copper Costs and Prices: 1879-1957* (Baltimore: Johns Hopkins Press, 1959).

Hippel, Frank Von, and Robert Williams. "Solar Technologies," *Bulletin of the Atomic Scientists*, November 1975.

Hoch, I. "Urban Scale and Environmental Quality," in *Population, Resources, and the Environment*, edited by R.G. Ridker. Volume 3 of Research Reports of the United States Commission on Population Growth and the American Future (Washington: Government Printing Office, 1972).

Hotelling, Harold. "The Economics of Exhaustible Resources," *Journal of Political Economy*, April 1931.

Johnson, Harry. *Further Essays in Monetary Economics* (Cambridge: Harvard University Press, 1973).

_____. "Commodities: Less Developed Countries' Demands and Developed Countries' Response," unpublished manuscript, 1976.

Jorgenson, Dale, and Edward Hudson. "Economic Analysis of Alternative Energy Growth Patterns, 1975-2000," in *A Time to Choose*, edited by D. Freeman et al. (Cambridge, Mass: Ballinger Publishing Company, 1974).

Kapitza, Peter. "Physics and the Energy Problem," *New Scientist*, October 1976.

Kay, J.A., and J. Mirrlees. "The Desirability of Natural Resource Depletion," in *The Economics of Natural Resource Depletion*, edited by D.W. Pearce (London: The Macmillan Press, 1975).

Kelejian, Harry, and Wallace Oates, *Introduction to Econometrics*, (New York: Harper and Row, 1974).

Kolbe, H., and H.J. Timm. "Die Bestimmungsfaktorn der Preisentwicklung auf dem Weltmarkt für Naturkautschuk—Eine Ökonometrische Modellanalyse," no. 10, HWWA Inst. für Wirtschaftsforschung, Hamburg, 1972.

Koutsoyiannis, A. *Theory of Econometrics* (London: The Macmillan Press, 1973).

Koyck, L.M. *Distributed Lags and Investment Analysis* (Amsterdam: North Holland Publishing Company, 1954).

Krutilla, J.V. "Conservation Reconsidered," *American Economic Review*, September 1967.

Labys, Walter C., and C.W. Granger. *Speculation, Hedging, and Commodity Price Forecasts* (Lexington, Mass.: D.C. Heath, 1970).

_____, W.C. Rees, and C.M. Elliott. "Copper Price Behavior and the London Metal Exchange," *Applied Economics*, 1971.

Lapp, R.E. "We May Find Ourselves Short of Uranium Too," *Fortune*, October 1975.

Lave, L.B., and E.P. Seskin. "Air Pollution and Human Health," *Science*, August 1970.

Lave, L.B., and E.P. Seskin. "Health and Air Pollution," *Swedish Journal of Economics*, March 1971.

Lave, L.B., and E.P. Seskin. "Acute Relationships among Daily Mortality, Air Pollution, and Climate," in *Economic Analysis of Environmental Problems*, edited by E.S. Mills, 1975.

Lecomber, Richard. *Economic Growth vs. The Environment* (London: The Macmillan Company, 1975).

Lovins, Amory. "Energy Strategy: The Road Not Taken," *Foreign Affairs*, October 1976.

Malinvaud, E. *Lectures on Microeconomic Theory* (Amsterdam: North Holland Publishing Company, 1972).

McCulloch, Rachel. "Commodity Power and the International Community." Harvard Institute of Economic Research, Discussion Paper no. 440, October 1975.

Meade, J.E. *The Controlled Economy* (London: Unwin Books, 1971).

Meadows, Donella H. and Dennis Meadows. *The Limits to Growth* (New York: Universe Books, 1972).

Mikdashi, Zuhayr. *The International Politics of Natural Resources* (Ithaca, N.Y.: Cornell University Press, 1976).

Miller, J.R. "Iron, Steelmaking Metallics Supply Seen Meeting World Demand Forecast for '75-'85," *Engineering and Mining Journal*, September 1974.

Miller, R.L., and Potluri Rao. *Applied Econometrics* (Belmont, Cal.: Wadsworth Publishing Company, 1971).

Mundell, Robert. "The New Inflation and Flexible Exchange Rates," in *The New Inflation and Monetary Policy*, edited by Mario Monti (London: The MacMillan Press, 1976).

Nordhaus, W.D. "The Allocation of Energy Resources," Brookings Institution Papers, 1973.

_____, and J. Tobin. "Is Growth Obsolete?" in *The Measurement of Economic and Social Performance*, edited by M. Moss. Volume 38, Studies in Income and Wealth (New York: Bureau of Economic Research, 1973).

_____. "World Dynamics: Measurement Without Data," *The Economic Journal*, December 1973.

_____. "Resources as a Constraint on Growth," *American Economic Review*, May 1974.

Olech, C. "On the Global Stability of an Autonymous System on the Plane," *Contributions to Differential Equations*, vol. 1, 1963.

Olson, Mancur, and H. Landsberg. *The No Growth Society* (New York: W.W. Norton Company, 1973).

Park, C.F., and R.A. MacDiarmid. *Ore Deposits* (San Francisco: W.H. Freeman, 1964).

Pearce, David. *Environmental Economics* (London: Longmans, 1976).

Perry, George. "The United States," in *Higher Oil Prices and the World Economy: The Adjustment Problem*, edited by Edward R. Fried and Charles L. Schultze, Washington, D.C.: The Brookings Institution, 1975.

Pindyck, Robert S. "Gains to Producers from the Cartelization of Exhaustible Resources," World Oil Project Working Paper (MITEL 76-012WP), Department of Economics and Sloan School of Management, Massachusetts Institute of Technology, May 1976.

Radetzki, Marian. "The Potential for Monopolistic Commodity Pricing by Developing Countries," in *A World Divided: The Less Developed Countries in the International Economy*, edited by G.K. Helleiner (Cambridge: Cambridge University Press, 1975).

_____. "Will the Long Run Global Supply of Industrial Materials be Adequate?" Paper presented at the fifth Congress of the International Economic Association, September 1977.

Renton, Anthony. "A Bigger Bonanza," *New Scientist*, September 23, 1976.

Rogers, Paul. "The Role of Less Developed Countries in World Resource Use," in *Future Resources and World Development*, edited by Paul Rogers and Anthony Vann (New York: Plenum Publishing Company, 1976).

Rose, Sanford. "Third World Commodity Power is a Costly Illusion," *Fortune*, November 1976.

Ross, Marc H., and Robert H. Williams. "Energy Efficiency: Our Most Underrated Energy Resource," *Bulletin of the Atomic Scientists*, November 1976.

Russell, Robert W. "Governing the World's Money: Don't Just Do Something, Stand There," *International Organization*, Vol. 31, Winter 1977.

Rustow, D.A., and John Mugno. *OPEC: Success and Prospects* (New York: New York University Press, 1976).

Samuelson, Paul A. *Economics: An Introductory Analysis*, 9th ed. (New York: McGraw-Hill, 1975).

Scarf, Herbert, and T. Hansen. *The Computation of Economic Equilibria* (New Haven: Yale University Press, 1973).

Seaborg, Glenn. "The Recycle Society of Tomorrow," *Futurist*, June 1974.

Shoven, J.B., and J. Whalley. "General Equilibrium with Taxes: A Computational Procedure and Existence Proof," *Review of Economic Studies*, October 1973.

Smith, G., and F. Shink. "International Tin Agreement: A Reassessment," United States Treasury Department OASIA, Research Discussion Paper no. 75/18, 1975.

Solomon, Robert. *The International Monetary System 1945-1976* (New York: Macmillan 1977).

Solow, Robert. "Richard T. Ely Lecture: The Economics of Resources or the Resources of Economics," *American Economic Review*, May 1974.

⸻ , "Intergenerational Equity and Exhaustible Resources," *Review of Economic Studies*, July 1975.

Spengler, Joseph. "Population and World Hunger," *Rivista Internazionale di Scienze Economiche E. Commerciali*, December 1976.

Strotz, R.H. "The Use of Land Rent Changes to Measure the Welfare Benefits of Land Improvements," in *The New Economics of Regulated Industries: Rate Making in a Dynamic Economy*, edited by J.E. Haring (Los Angeles: Economic Research Center, Occidental College, 1968).

Swoboda, Alexander. "Inflation, Oil, and the World Economic Crisis," *Journal of World Trade Law*, April 1976.

Takeuchi, Kenji. "CIPEC and the Copper Export Earnings of Member Countries," *The Developing Countries*, February 1972.

Taylor, Gordon R. *The Doomsday Book* (Greenwich, Conn: Fawcett-Crest, 1971).

Timm, Hans J. "Kurzfristige Internationale Rohstoffpreisentwicklung und Konjunkturschwankungen," HWWA Institut für Wirtschaftsforschung Hamburg, March 1976.

Toffler, Alvin. *The Ecospasm Report* (New York: Benton Books, 1975).

Tolley, G.S. "The Welfare Economics of City Bigness," *Journal of Urban Economics*, July 1974.

Triffin, Robert. "Size, Sources, and Beneficiaries of International Reserve Creation: 1970-1974," Princeton University, 1975. Mimeographed.

Tumlir, Jan. "Oil Payments and Oil Debt in the World Economy," *Lloyds Bank Review*, July 1974.

Uri, Pierre. *Development Without Dependence* (New York: Praeger, 1976).

Valery, Nicholas. "The Future Isn't What it Used to Be," *New Scientist*, January 1977.

Vann, Anthony, and Paul Rogers. *Human Ecology and World Development* (New York: Plenum Publishing Company, 1974).

Varon, B., and Kenji Takeuchi. "Developing Countries and Non-Fuel Minerals," *Foreign Affairs*, April 1974.

Wallis, Kenneth. *Introductory Econometrics* (London: Grey Mills Publishing Ltd., 1972.

Warren, Kenneth. *Mineral Resources* (Harmondsworth, England: Penguin Books, 1973).

Weston, J. Fred and Edward M. Rice. "Do Steel Producers Administer Prices?" *Challenge*, November/December 1976.

Witherell, W. "An Econometric Model of the World Wool Market," Ph.D. dissertation, Princeton University, 1967.

Wonnacott, Paul. *Macroeconomics* (Homewood, Ill.: Richard D. Irwin, 1974).

Wonnacott, R.J., and T.H. Wonnacott. *Econometrics* (New York: John Wiley and Sons, 1970).

Zettermark, Sören. "The Long Term Supply of Aluminum," Ph.D. dissertation, The University of Stockholm, 1976.

Index

197

About the Author

Ferdinand E. Banks attended Illinois Institute of Technology and Roosevelt University (Chicago, Illinois), graduating with a B.A. in Economics. After military service in the Orient and Europe, he worked as an engineer and systems and procedures analyst. He received the M.Sc. and Fil. Lic. from the University of Stockholm. He also has the Fil. Dr. from the University of Uppsala (Sweden). He taught for five years at the University of Stockholm, was senior lecturer in economics and statistics at the United Nations African Institute for Economics and Development Planning, Dakar, Senegal, and has been consultant lecturer in macroeconomics for the OECD in Lisbon, Portugal. From 1968 until 1971 he was an econometrician for the United Nations Commission on Trade and Development in Geneva, Switzerland. At present he is Associate Professor and Research Fellow at the University of Uppsala, Sweden, and occasionally lectures on econometrics and the economics of natural resources at the University of Stockholm. His previous books are *The World Copper Market: An Economic Analysis* (1974), and *The Economics of Natural Resources* (1976).

Date Due

DEC 1 7 1982			
MAY 1 0 1986			